"THE PRESIDENT HAS BEEN SHOT"

"THE PRESIDENT HAS BEEN SHOT"

Confusion, Disability, and
the 25th Amendment
in the Aftermath of the
Attempted Assassination
of Ronald Reagan

HERBERT L. ABRAMS

W·W·NORTON & COMPANY·NEW YORK·LONDON

The text of this book is composed in Galliard,
with the display set in Univers 47.
Composition manufacturing by the Haddon Craftsmen, Inc.
Book design by Jacques Chazaud.

Library of Congress Cataloging-in-Publication Data
Abrams, Herbert L.
    "The president has been shot" : confusion, disability, and the
    25th amendment in the aftermath of the attempted assassination of
    Ronald Reagan / Herbert L. Abrams.
        p. cm.
        Includes index.
        1. Reagan, Ronald—Assassination attempt, 1981. I. Title.
    E877.3.A27 1991
    973.927'092—dc20   91–15846

ISBN 0-393-03042-3

W.W. Norton & Company, Inc., 500 Fifth Avenue, New York, N.Y. 10110
W.W. Norton & Company, Ltd., 10 Coptic Street, London WCIA 1PU

1 2 3 4 5 6 7 8 9 0

Contents

Preface

THE PATH TRAVELED FROM THE ORIGIN TO THE END OF A JOURNEY
rarely follows a straight line: more often it wanders through
strange and wondrous alleys remote from its ultimate destination. So it has been with this project.

It began on a day in 1978 when I suddenly realized that it
was possible that the unthinkable might become a reality. As a
physician and as professor and chairman of the Department of
Radiology at Harvard Medical School, I was fully involved in
the teaching, clinical, and research activities that had attracted
me to academic medicine to begin with. For twenty years,
following the completion of the atmospheric test ban, I had
barely thought about nuclear weapons. When I did, it was to
dismiss their use as something beyond the range of the imagi-
nation.

In the late seventies, however, the rhetoric of Jimmy Carter in talking about the Persian Gulf and the potential need to exploit all weapons in our arsenal, including nuclear weapons, caught my attention. On a voyage of discovery, I began to recognize the size of the stockpiles of the great nations and the level of destructive power inherent in the nuclear arsenals.

In the decade that followed, I became heavily involved with Physicians for Social Responsibility and was one of the founders of International Physicians for the Prevention of Nuclear War. My conviction grew that nuclear weapons would not be used intentionally by the leaders of the super-powers. Instead, accidental or unintentional nuclear war seemed to have become a relatively greater threat than the deliberate use of weapons of mass destruction as a means of achieving national goals.

I then began a systematic study of the factors involved in accidental or unintentional nuclear war. When I moved back to Stanford in 1985, I developed a course for undergraduate students that dealt with this subject. In the process, impressed by the relative void in information regarding human reliability in the handling of nuclear weapons, I undertook a study of the 100,000 American military personnel responsible for nuclear weapons handling in the silos, the Strategic Air Command, and the submarines.

While I was completing that study, it became clear to me that the decision makers required at least as much attention as those involved in day-to-day operational responsibility. In considering the problem of disabled leadership, I began to focus on the presidents of the United States. Presidents, like other persons their age, have frequently been afflicted with major diseases that have well-documented cognitive sequelae, which might profoundly impair their participation in the decision-making process. Although the structural constraints that govern high-level decisions have always modified the effect of any single individual in command, in the nuclear age the time for decision making in crisis may be substantially shortened. Under the pressure of time, a disabled leader of the United States might well be forced to make a catastrophic decision.

This exploration confronted me with the mechanism whereby the United States attempts to handle the problem of a temporarily disabled leader—namely, the Twenty-fifth Amendment to the Constitution. It became evident, too, that the first opportunity for invoking the disability provisions of that amendment since its ratification in 1967 was the assassination attempt on Ronald Reagan in March 1981.

My deep interest in the event and its implications followed just that circuitous route. This book is the result of the linkage of presidents and trauma that is a continuing element in American history.

HERBERT L. ABRAMS

Cast of Characters

DR. BENJAMIN AARON: Chief of Thoracic Surgery at George Washington University Hospital; head of the surgical team that operated on Reagan after the shooting

RICHARD ALLEN: National Security Adviser at the beginning of the Reagan administration

MARTIN ANDERSON: White House Chief of Domestic Policy Planning

JAMES BAKER: White House Chief of Staff

JAMES BRADY: White House Press Secretary

GEORGE BUSH: Vice-President of the United States

WILLIAM CASEY:	Director of the CIA; formerly Reagan's campaign director
RICHARD DARMAN:	Deputy Assistant to the President
MICHAEL DEAVER:	White House Deputy Chief of Staff
THOMAS DELAHANTY:	Washington, D.C., patrolman
DR. SOL EDELSTEIN:	Director of the emergency room at George Washington University Hospital
FRED FIELDING:	White House Counsel
DAVID GERGEN:	White House Communications director
DR. JOSEPH GIORDANO:	Head of the trauma team at George Washington University Hospital
ALEXANDER HAIG:	Secretary of State
JOHN W. HINCKLEY, JR.:	The disturbed young man who shot Reagan
DR. WILLIAM KNAUS:	Internist at George Washington University Hospital
TIM MCCARTHY:	Secret Service agent in the detail guarding the President on March 30
ROBERT MCFARLANE:	National Security Adviser from October 1982 to December 1984

EDWIN MEESE III: Counselor to the President; later Attorney General

FRANKLYN (LYN) NOFZIGER: White House Political Director

DR. DENNIS O'LEARY: Dean for Clinical Affairs at George Washington University Hospital; spokesman for the hospital after the shooting

DR. DALE OLLER: Head of the surgical team from Bethesda Naval Medical Center that operated on Reagan in 1985

DR. WILLIAM O'NEILL: Trauma team intern at George Washington University Hospital

JERRY PARR: Secret Service agent; chief of the Secret Service detail guarding the President on March 30

NANCY REAGAN: Wife of Ronald Reagan

RONALD REAGAN: President of the United States

DONALD REGAN: Secretary of the Treasury; traded jobs with James Baker in 1985 to become White House Chief of Staff

DR. DAVID ROCKOFF: Chief of Chest Radiology at George Washington University Hospital

DR. DANIEL RUGE: Physician to the President

GEORGE SHULTZ: Succeeded Alexander Haig as Secretary of State in 1982

WILLIAM FRENCH SMITH: Attorney General

LARRY SPEAKES: White House Deputy Press Secretary; assumed the duties of official White House spokesman after the shooting.

DAVID STOCKMAN: Director of the Office of Management and Budget

CASPAR WEINBERGER: Secretary of Defense

"THE PRESIDENT HAS BEEN SHOT"

1

The Assassin

AT 2:00 P.M. ON MONDAY, MARCH 30, 1981, PRESIDENT RONALD REA-
gan was introduced to 3,500 members of the Building and
Construction Workers Union of the AFL-CIO at the Hilton
Hotel in Washington, D.C.[1] Smiling, and very much at ease
after seventy days in office, he spoke to an audience that was
not exactly sympathetic to his views. His speech was vintage
Reagan, beginning with a story about a baseball player, extoll-
ing the virtues of the work ethic and independence, attacking
big government, whose duty was "to protect the people, not
run their lives."[2] He quoted Franklin D. Roosevelt, decried
government spending, and called for more military spending.
He concluded, "Together we will make America great
again."[3] He received a subdued reception. The audience was

unenthusiastic, and his punch lines failed to elicit the customary response.[4]

When the president finished, he smiled warmly at the assembled union members.[5] His face conveyed the pleasure of a seasoned performer completing a satisfying act on a stage that he is confident of dominating and on which his skills had been honed over many years. As he walked from the platform, the Secret Service men surrounded him. He waved to the audience, the smile never fading from his face, left the auditorium, and exited the Hilton Hotel through the side door, where a small crowd had gathered.[6] He waved, paused for a moment, and then started toward the waiting limousine, accompanied by Jerry Parr, the chief Secret Service man.

The television cameras focused on him, caught the smile with all of its engaging qualities, until the moment when the shots were fired. Then, suddenly, the smile left his face, and it constricted in what was initially a frown and then a look of genuine discomfiture and "stunned disbelief."[7] No sooner had the first shot rung out than Parr grabbed the president and pulled him bodily towards the open door of the limousine. Without waiting to look in any direction, Parr shoved him inside the car and fell on top of him.[8] Within a moment, the car door was closed, and Parr instructed the driver to take them to the White House. They left behind a scene of consternation, shouting, and confusion, with John Hinckley now pinned to the ground, and handcuffed.[9]

John W. Hinckley, Jr., first saw the movie *Taxi Driver* in the spring of 1976 when he was twenty-one years old.[10] The main character in the film, Travis Bickle, stalks a presidential

candidate to win a young woman's attention, and then violently "rescues" a young prostitute, Iris (played by Jodie
Foster), from her pimp. Hinckley identified with Travis and
began to act like him after he had seen the film fifteen times.
He bought the same clothes, ate the same foods, drank the
same liquors, and invented a girlfriend just as had Bickle. In
August 1979, he bought a .38-caliber pistol. In January
1980, he bought a 6.5-caliber rifle. On July 16, he purchased
a .22-caliber rifle. In September, in Lubbock, Texas, he
bought two .22-caliber pistols, and now, like Bickle, he had
one .38, two .22s, and a rifle.[11]

His behavior during this period was remote from an early
childhood of seeming normality in an atmosphere of privilege
and opportunity. Born in Ardmore, Oklahoma, in 1955, he
was the youngest of three children. When he was four years
old, his father, a petroleum engineer, got a job in Dallas,
Texas, and the family moved to University Park, a wealthy
suburb. Their friends considered them "a fine Christian family," and they were regular churchgoers.[12]

Hinckley did well in sports during elementary school, particularly in football and basketball. Jim Francis, Hinckley's
basketball coach for three years, recalled, "He was a beauti-
ful-looking little boy, a wonderful athlete, really a leader. He
was the best basketball player on the team."[13]

When he was nine years old, the Beatles toured the country, and Hinckley became a loyal fan. In the early sixties, the
family moved to Highland Park, an exclusive neighborhood
of Dallas with affluent families and manicured gardens. The
home in which he spent his adolescence was large and comfortable, with a swimming pool and even a private Coke machine.[14]

In junior high school, Hinckley continued to play basket-ball, and he was elected homeroom president in seventh and ninth grades. By ninth grade, he began to lose interest in sports. As the competition became keener, he became less active in basketball.[15]

His parents began to see signs of another John Hinckley. He made few new friends in Highland Park and was a solitary figure. After school, he retreated to his room, played his guitar privately, and listened to Beatles records for hours on end.[16]

About the time that he began high school, in 1970, his father started an oil exploration business, Hinckley Oil, which later became Vanderbilt Energy Corporation. His sister, Diane, was a campus leader, but John stayed in the background, taking part in just a few activities.[17] He left so small a mark in high school that his principal, when asked, had to look up the records to make sure he was a graduate. Those who knew him speculated that some of his problems stemmed from a sense of failure at being unable to live up to the family's expectations.[18]

Years later, Hinckley remembered high school as a trouble-some period, partly because of the changing times. "The atmosphere affected me," he said. "I was becoming more rebellious and uncommunicative. . . ."[19] Increasingly with-drawn, he had little social involvement and spent his time alone except for two cats which "he adored and loved," according to his mother.[20] He looked upon himself as "a rebel without a cause" as he finished high school.

In 1973, Hinckley graduated from high school, and his condition worsened: he began drifting from place to place as his isolation became chronic. When his parents moved to

Evergreen, Colorado, he enrolled at Texas Technical University in Lubbock, Texas. Away from home, he made little attempt to maintain a social life. He remained at college on and off for seven years without graduating, but never made a friend or had a girlfriend. Wandering in and out of the university, he traveled around the country, living in seedy motels and hotels.[21]

Meanwhile, his appearance deteriorated: he was transformed from a thin, smiling boy to an overweight, sullen man. The manager of his college-town apartment building went to repair a clogged sink in Hinckley's flat and found "junk-food bags and empty ice-cream cartons sitting around all over the cabinets. He just sat there the whole time, staring at the TV."[22]

Hinckley imagined himself becoming a rock star, like his idol, John Lennon. Bored with school, he decided to sell his car and go to Hollywood, where he would break into the recording business. He found that he could not get past the receptionists' desks, and he gradually slid into a deep depression. After a few months in Hollywood, he wrote to his parents about an imaginary girlfriend, Lynn, and asked them to send money.[23]

Because he had lost hope of selling his songs, Hinckley had plenty of time to watch movies like *Taxi Driver* and to fantasize. Interested in assassins and death, he read Lee Harvey Oswald's biography, *Maria and Lee; An Assassin's Diary,* by Arthur Bremer, who shot Governor George Wallace of Alabama in 1972; and *The Boston Strangler.*

After running out of money in Hollywood and remaining depressed and withdrawn, he returned to his parents in Evergreen. In his father's view, "All of a sudden everything had fallen apart. John was having problems with his eyes. A man on the street attempted to rob him. The progress he thought he was making with selling his songs had fallen apart. And worst of all, he had broken up with his girlfriend, Lynn."[24] After a short stay at home, Hinckley got a job at the nearby Taylor Supper Club and lived in a motel across the street. Five months later, he embarked on another trip to Hollywood to sell his music. Although this trip lasted only three weeks, Hinckley's depression deepened and he considered suicide. Again he returned home, but soon left for Texas and then drove to Nashville to try to sell his music.[25]

Enrolling in the summer session at Texas Tech in 1978, Hinckley changed his major from business to literature and journalism. At the end of the fall semester, he dropped out of college.[26]

Living in a Dallas apartment by himself, he gained a great deal of weight. Depressed, he returned to Lubbock and spent most of his time reading Nazi literature. In September 1979, he conceived the American Front, a national organization whose goal was to alert the country to minority groups threatening the rights of white Protestants. Although this association existed only in his mind, Hinckley recorded the group's activities and wrote a newsletter for members, in which he called himself "National Director John Hinckley." His parents, who believed there *was* an American Front, worried that their son had made strange friends.[27]

In the same year, Hinckley began an affiliation with the National Socialist party of America, a fringe group of neo-Nazis. He was a member for more than a year. In March 1978, he marched in a Nazi parade in St. Louis.[28] But in 1979, he was expelled from the group. "When somebody comes to us and starts advocating shooting people," the party head explained, "it's a natural reaction: the guy's either a nut or a federal agent."[29]

In 1979, Hinckley did not return home for Christmas, telling his parents that he was meeting Lynn in New York, where he would show his book manuscript to publishers. In actuality, Hinckley stayed alone in Lubbock, playing Russian roulette during the holidays. Increasingly, he suffered from emotional and physical problems, including stress, weakness, and a feeling of vertigo. At the end of January, he went home to be treated by the family physician. His parents were shocked. "My son looked so bad when he came home. He was very, very overweight. And he was very depressed and very wiped out. He just looked sick. John weighed 225 pounds at that time, and his normal weight should be around 160," Mrs. Hinckley said.[30] Although she took her son to numerous doctors, no one could find a physical basis for his complaints.

After a few weeks at home, he visited his sister in Dallas and then returned to Lubbock for the 1980 spring semester, his final encounter with classes at Texas Tech.[31]

He soon formed a mail order company called Listalot, which sold different kinds of lists to its customers through ads in legitimate magazines. The lists, however, were phony.[32]

In May 1980, Hinckley read in *People* magazine that Jodie Foster would be attending Yale in the fall, and soon he was obsessed with her. During the summer, he wrote poems about Foster and fantasized about rescuing her from Yale as Bickle rescued her character in *Taxi Driver*. Over a period of several months, Foster received numerous letters with his signature or initials.[33]

Hinckley's physical problems persisted, and in Lubbock he saw a physician who prescribed an antidepressant, Serentil, and a tranquilizer, Valium.[34] By the end of the summer semester, he could no longer cope. He told his parents he wanted to attend a writing program at Yale. Although no such program existed, they gave him $3,600 for tuition and living expenses. With this money, Hinckley left for New Haven, Connecticut, thinking he would become romantically involved with Foster. When he got to Yale, he slipped poems under her door and spoke with her twice on the phone. Rather than achieving the relationship that he hoped for, their phone conversations were awkward and embarrassing.[35]

He returned home after spending only one week at Yale. Mrs. Hinckley, whose husband was out of town, was upset by her son's sudden appearance. After he explained that he didn't like Yale and that his clothes were inappropriate, she decided not to let him spend the night at home. Instead, she drove him to a motel and then took him to the airport the next morning. He flew to Lubbock once more.[36]

On September 27, he went to Washington, on the twenty-eighth to Columbus, Ohio, and on the thirtieth to Dayton, where a Carter campaign stop took place on October 2. A cameraman caught him on videotape in Dayton, less than six feet from Carter.[37] His intent to assassinate Carter was based on his belief that the act would attract Jodie Foster's attention.

After he left Dayton, he flew to Lincoln, Nebraska, on October 6, supposedly to meet with a leader of the American Nazi party. The meeting never took place. The next day, he moved on to Nashville, Tennessee, where a Carter campaign stop was planned for the ninth. He was unable to bring himself to shoot the president. He was arrested at the airport, trying to catch a plane to New York, with three guns in his bag, thirty rounds of ammunition, and $800 in his wallet.[38] He was fined, the guns were confiscated, and he was driven back to the airport.

Both the FBI and the Federal Aviation Administration were informed of the arrest. The FBI, according to the airport security officer, "told us they did not have time to question the suspect."[39] No one told the Secret Service, however, until after the attack on President Reagan, when the airport security chief recalled the episode and phoned Washington. Hinckley's name, as a result, was not included in the Secret Service list of potential assassins.[40] The Secret Service indicated that it would have liked to have been informed by the FBI about any individual in illegal possession of three pistols when the president was nearby.[41] The head of the FBI said that Hinckley's arrest was not reported to the Secret Service, because it was too "minor."[42]

Four days after the arrest, Hinckley bought two more .22-caliber handguns, at Rocky's Pawnshop in Dallas. Over the front door of the shop, a sign read, "Guns Don't Cause Crime Any More than Flies Cause Garbage."[43]

At the end of November, Hinckley sent an anonymous note to the FBI: "There is a plot underway to abduct actress Jodie Foster from Yale University dorm in December or January. No ransom. She's being taken for romantic reasons. This is no joke! I don't wish to get further involved. Act as you wish."[44] On November 30, he left home, telling his mother that he was going to Lubbock. Instead, he returned to Washington for a few weeks, possibly to stalk the new president-elect.[45]

Hinckley was in Washington on December 8 when John Lennon was assassinated, and he traveled to New York to attend the vigil in Central Park. He flew back to Colorado in mid-December, and on New Year's Eve made a tape in which he discussed suicide and insanity and claimed that the world was really over now that John Lennon was dead. The day after Reagan's inauguration, he bought a .38-caliber pistol of the kind that Mark David Chapman had used to shoot Lennon.[46]

Long before this time, it had become amply clear to his parents that he was ill and needed help. They arranged for him to see a psychiatrist, who worked out a long-term plan which called for Hinckley to have a job by the end of February 1981 and to be out of the house by the end of March. Early in February, fantasizing that he would kill Jodie Foster or kill people in front of her, he flew to New Haven once more. The next day, he left and went to Washington, where he considered assassinating Senator Edward M. Kennedy and had his picture taken in front of Ford's Theater, where Abraham Lincoln was shot.[47]

He returned home on February 19, but left on March 1, 1981, to go to New Haven and subsequently New York. He delivered some notes to Jodie Foster, which prompted the local police to make an effort to locate him to request that he stop bothering her.[48] A few days later, when he called his parents at 4:30 in the morning, he was incoherent, and subsequently his father picked him up at the Denver airport. "John was almost the last one off the plane," Mr. Hinckley said. "I could well believe he hadn't eaten or slept: he was haggard and his eyes were glazed. We found an unused boarding area and sat down while I explained that he couldn't come home.

'You've broken every promise you've made to your mother and me. Our part of the agreement was to provide you a home and an allowance while you worked at becoming independent. I don't know what you've been doing these past months, but it hasn't been that, and we've reached the end of our rope. You're on your own now.'

"He looked at me as if he couldn't believe his ears. I gave him $200 and suggested the YMCA as an inexpensive place to live. He didn't want to live at the Y. 'Well it's your decision, John, from here on out.' "[49]

Neither of his parents saw him during the two weeks of his stay at a motel in Denver. He left precipitously for California on March 25, and immediately turned around and bought a Greyhound bus ticket for New Haven via Washington.

He reached the Greyhound station in Washington at 12:15 P.M., lunched at the terminal restaurant, and later in the day checked into the Park Central Hotel. The hotel is located at Eighteenth and G streets, N.W., across the intersection from the headquarters of the Secret Service at 1600 G Street, N.W.[50] That night, he slept poorly, and the next morning he took a Valium and went out for breakfast at McDonald's. When he returned to his hotel at 11:30 A.M., he lay down, and then opened a copy of the *Washington Star*. On page A-4, he saw Reagan's schedule for the day. Wondering whether he should go to New Haven to shoot Foster and himself, or stay in Washington to shoot the president,[51] he took a shower while he deliberated. Later he recalled feeling a terrible agony, an internal frenzy, and a sort of paralysis. At noon, he took twenty milligrams of Valium.[52]

At 12:45 P.M., he wrote a letter to Foster, explaining that he planned to kill Reagan to prove his love for her.[53] "I would abandon the idea of getting Reagan in a second if only I could win your heart."[54] Arriving at the Washington Hilton, he saw the president look at him and wave, and he was sure this meant that he should stick to his plan. As Reagan went into the hotel, Hinckley thought everything was happening too quickly.[55]

John M. Dodson, a computer specialist with the Pinkerton Agency, was looking at the street through a window on the seventh floor of Universal North Building, across from the Hilton. He saw Hinckley "walking rapidly up and down outside the back door of the hotel. He looked fidgety, agitated—a little strange. He kept turning his body from side to side. I said to myself, 'What if he takes a shot at the president?' " While he was walking, a police lieutenant stared at him several times.[56]

Walter Rodgers, a reporter for Associated Press Radio, was arranging a microphone to catch some comments from Reagan at the conclusion of his talk. He noticed the hostile young man with blond hair and heard him say, "Who does the press think it is?" Hank Brown, an ABC cameraman, said that Hinckley had "penetrated the press corps" at the side entrance.[57]

When the president emerged from the Hilton, he acknowledged the applause of the small crowd and waved.[58] Dr. David Michael Bear, a psychiatrist who later examined Hinckley and testified for the defense, spoke of Hinckley's reaction: "President Reagan came out of the hotel. John was in the press area. He was perhaps twenty feet from the president. He had this thought: 'By gosh, I'm amazed I got so close. Why isn't the Secret Service here?'

"He remembered: Travis Bickle in *Taxi Driver* had

planned to kill a presidential candidate. At the last moment, the Secret Service identified him. They stopped him.

"Hinckley's thought was this: 'I hope someone will stop me. I hope like Travis there will be something that does stop me. I hope the agent will stop me.'

"He always had two thoughts: 'I'll kill, I won't kill.'

"When President Reagan came out so quickly, he was amazed. He said: 'I wasn't ready, I didn't know yet. It was a surprise he came out so fast.' He took out his gun.

"His next thought was this: 'They saw the gun. People saw the gun. Every eye knows it. Now I have no choice. I have to go forward and shoot.' "[59]

An Associated Press reporter standing behind a rope, Michael Putzel, shouted, "Mr. President ———." Sam Donaldson of ABC News called out a question about a possible Soviet invasion of Poland. At that moment, Reagan turned towards them and may have been about to answer when the first shot was fired. Hinckley had chosen a .22-caliber pistol and exploding bullets for the assassination. At 2:25 P.M., the self-appointed angel of death drew himself up in the police posture he had seen so often in movies, crouched with both hands holding the gun, and fired six shots from a distance of about ten feet.[60] The first bullet hit James Brady, the White House press secretary, in the head; the second, Officer Thomas Delahanty of the Washington police; the third went over Reagan's head and lodged in a building across the street; the fourth hit Secret Service Agent Tim McCarthy; the fifth bounced off the bulletproof glass in the limousine; and the sixth ricocheted off the limousine and hit Ronald Reagan.[61]

Watching from his window at the Social Security Administration, Wilmer Kerns heard the shots and looked down.

"These people were falling down. The people who were shot didn't move . . . pandemonium broke loose." Several members of the local police stationed in the neighborhood said that they had not been informed that the president was nearby.[62]

Samuel Lafta, an iron worker who was attending the union meeting at which Reagan spoke, saw Hinckley empty his gun at the president. He thought that one policeman had been suspicious of Hinckley: "He kept looking toward the guy."

Micky Crowe, a young man visiting from Wisconsin, said Hinckley was standing in back of the line of cameras. In that location, "if he was any kind of a shot at all, he would have hit the president."

Don Coffee of Fairfax, Virginia, was on his way to the Federal Housing Authority and turned to look at the crowd outside of the Hilton entrance. Suddenly, the shots were fired "in a couple of seconds." In no time at all, "there must have been fifteen people on top of the guy."[63]

Hinckley was quickly captured by police officers and Secret Service men. He was arrested, and booked on charges of knowingly and intentionally attempting to kill the president and assaulting a federal officer. A .22-caliber pistol was taken from him, and he was then transported to the Metropolitan Police Department Central Cell Block and held without bail.[64]

Hinckley's mother heard about the attack while watching television. " 'The assailant has not been identified,' the newscaster was reading from a slip of paper, 'but witnesses describe him as a light-haired white male in his twenties.' I thought of our own blond son and my heart went out to that young man's family. Thank God that, whatever worries we had had over John, there'd never been any violence or law-breaking," she said.

His father got the news on the radio after Hinckley was identified. "John . . . the gunman? Impossible! Our son could never hurt anything or anybody. John had his problems, God knew. Jo Ann and I had lost more sleep, had more arguments, and prayed more prayers over our third child than over the other two combined. But his difficulties were just the opposite of aggressiveness. Getting John to assert himself was the problem. He didn't want to meet people his own age in Evergreen, didn't want to play tennis, wouldn't even go for a walk with me. I was convinced it was nothing but laziness; whatever the reason, John just got more listless and inactive all the time. Was this a person who could buy a gun, travel clear across the country, and shoot the President of the United States?"[65]

In a few seconds, the vulnerability of the elected president had been shown as graphically and dramatically as ever before. A disturbed young man; fantasies of love and fame; a hamburger at McDonald's, and then fatigue, a casual look at the newspaper. How was it that his eye was caught by the president's schedule? Why was the timing so perfect, so much in tune with the particular hour and the day? Twenty milligrams of Valium played a special role in preparing him for the event. He even had time to write the letter to Jodie Foster telling her about the most exciting act of the greatest show on earth.

2

Before the Attack

The United States is arguably the most powerful nation in the world. Its president controls the button that can initiate the destruction of hundreds of millions of people and the Northern Hemisphere. His health is of abiding interest not only to the citizens of the United States but also to the people of all countries, especially those of Europe, the Western Hemisphere, and Asia. Even as the threat of nuclear confrontation between the superpowers has waned, with radical change in the USSR and Eastern Europe, the resulting period of instability requires a steady hand and mind in the White House.

When the president is disabled, his capacity to make wise decisions may be jeopardized. If so, it is essential that his responsibilities and authority move smoothly through the proper channels into other hands. If there is uncertainty in the minds of the presidential entourage, or if the public is unaware of "who is in charge," or if outsiders detect confusion in high levels of government, particularly during a crisis, then the country is ill served and miscalculation may occur among external adversaries.

The assassination attempt on President Ronald Reagan in March 1981 served as a powerful reminder of the fragility of the president. Had he been standing a few feet away, in the shoes of James Brady, he might well have suffered permanent brain damage. As it was, his injury was sufficiently serious to require multiple blood transfusions and surgery.

At the time, and in the aftermath of the assault, there was a level of confusion in the White House that warrants careful examination. It reflected a crisis atmosphere, poor preparation, and a lack of familiarity both with the laws governing succession and disability and with the measures required for their implementation.

The attack was unique in its timing: it took place seventy days after his inauguration and only five months after the election.[1]

Following the longest and most expensive presidential campaign in history, Reagan defeated Jimmy Carter in a landslide victory with 51 percent of the vote, compared to Carter's 41 percent. On November 4, 1980, with 489 electoral votes, as compared to Carter's 49, Reagan led the Republican Party to control of the Senate for the first time in a generation.[2] The Republicans also gained 33 seats in the House.

At 5:30 P.M. on election day, Carter telephoned Reagan to

concede, the first time that such an acknowledgment had occurred before all the polls were closed. Reagan's landslide victory, together with his support in the Senate and a conservative majority in the House, enabled him to move the country in a rightward direction. The oldest man ever elected president and by far the most conservative since Herbert Hoover,[3] he began his transition by trying to capitalize on his electoral sweep.

The Transition

During the ten-week period between election in November and inauguration on January 20, the new president must take over one of the world's most complex institutions. He now considers in concrete and specific terms the manner, the means, and the time in which to accomplish the goals expressed on the campaign trail. In this brief transition, time is a precious commodity. The president-elect selects the highest officials of the executive branch and begins to determine domestic and foreign policies. He must use this period to "set a tone, to create an important first impression at home and around the world."[4] He discovers the necessity for making decisions at a rapid pace. While this may lead to haphazard choices, based on less than adequate information, it is also true that many decisions are deferred. It may take six months in office for a president to function at the appropriate level; by that time, the official period of the transition is over.[5]

By law, of course, there is no "transition"—only a point in time: "A new president assumes authority and responsibility totally and abruptly the moment he finishes reciting the oath of office."[6] Eisenhower preferred to use the word "turnover" because it more accurately described the change as occurring in an instant—not as a process.

Nevertheless, participants and observers alike perceive a noticeable and major difference in the government during the months immediately preceding the inauguration. Far from being instantaneous, the transformation may last for weeks, months, and even years.[7] Directions change, and policies may be reversed.

The program must be designed and the team that will support the president assembled. Key personnel must be identified for cabinet and subcabinet positions, as well as for the White House staff.[8]

Shortly after the election, Reagan established a political-strategy team, headed by Richard Wirthlin, his chief pollster. Its job was to plan the first hundred days so that they would lay the foundation for future successes. The strategy was simple, derived from Reagan's convictions: restore the economy by reducing government spending and taxes; and increase defense spending in order to strengthen national security.[9]

The major figure in the transition was Ed Meese, who was also the campaign chief of staff. During the summer before the election, Meese oversaw several people working on post-election plans, including E. Pendleton James, an executive-recruitment consultant who developed the personnel operation. James began the search for appropriate individuals for the cabinet in April. In August, he moved from Los Angeles to Virginia in order to organize the "Reagan-Bush Planning Task Force," which was kept separate from the campaign. The new president would have the opportunity to fill twenty-five hundred political jobs, and James began to screen and

recruit possible candidates. Periodically, he met Meese at 6
A.M. in Arlington's Bob's Big Boy restaurant to report his
findings.[10]

After the election, the need for secrecy about the planning
process vanished. The staff now had to be tightly organized
to prevent internal conflicts. Meese, responsible for preelection planning, was named director of the transition on election day. On November 6, Reagan announced that William
Casey, his campaign director, would be chairman of a transition executive committee, maintaining the chain of command
that had existed during the campaign. But Meese was clearly
the number one man on the team. He had been one of
Reagan's closest advisers for thirteen years. During this confusing, hectic interval, he worked smoothly and effectively,
remaining accessible to politicians, reporters, and the Carter
administration. A self-proclaimed "practical conservative," he
functioned like a deputy president, serving as an administrator, coordinator, and spokesman.[11]

Although Reagan personally designated his three top staff
aides—James Baker, Meese, and Michael Deaver—he leaned
heavily on them in the choice of the remainder of the White
House staff and the cabinet.[12] His conservative supporters
worked hard to influence the personnel process. They pushed
for the appointment of William Clark as deputy to Alexander
Haig, the secretary of state, and succeeded in spite of Haig's
opposition. On the other hand, in the face of intense opposition from the right wing, Caspar Weinberger managed to
appoint Frank Carlucci, who had served in the Carter administration, as assistant secretary of defense.[13]

Longtime Reagan supporters were angered by the choice
of James Baker as chief of staff. They were happier with the

new post designed for Meese, whom they had expected to be chief of staff, because his position as counselor to the president appeared to carry even more influence.[14]

In mid-January, Reagan held his first cabinet meeting, urging his nominees to speak frankly during their confirmation hearings. He told them that he needed free, open discussion during cabinet meetings in order to make effective decisions.[15]

Yet the transition, despite its early planning, huge agenda, thousands of personnel, and millions in expenses, still failed to confront one of the most important problems for any administration. Not one of the hundreds of groups studying issues and policy questions was assigned to examine the subject of presidential succession or crisis management in the event of a disaster.

About to turn seventy shortly after the inauguration, Reagan never met with Vice-President Bush to review temporary succession procedures in case of disability. And it is not at all certain that he was fully aware of the provisions of the Twenty-fifth Amendment.

Reagan announced the two top White House positions on November 14.[16] Yet he never reviewed the disability issue with Meese or Baker. Meese believes that the matter of the Twenty-fifth Amendment had never been raised with the president during the transition.[17]

Countless man-hours went into the choice of people for thousands of positions.[18] An equal amount of time was devoted to the articulation of positions on an infinite number of issues. But when March 30, 1981, hit the nation with a potential tragedy for the president and a real tragedy for his press secretary, no one had bothered to consider the many

assassination attempts of the past and the need for full preparedness to maintain stable and competent leadership in the
White House.

After the Inauguration

The inauguration that took place on January 20, 1981, was
the most lavish and expensive in history. Many of Reagan's
wealthy California friends traveled to Washington, including a
large number of Hollywood stars. Frank Sinatra organized a
preinaugural party which featured performances by talented
and well-known performers.

The Inaugural Committee spent over $8 million on the
event, with nine separate balls and a satellite-television link.
The expense was more than twice as high as Carter's in 1976.
Nancy Reagan's wardrobe for the occasion alone cost $25,-
000. It cost some $2,000 for a guest to participate fully in the
extravagant festivities, but it was easy to spend $5,000 or
more on dance and dinner tickets, memorial license plates,
and other souvenirs.[19]

For the first time, the ceremony took place at the Capitol's
West Front, where Reagan gave his inaugural address to a
crowd of about a quarter million. He devoted himself to the
subject of "national renewal": "Let us renew our determination, our courage and our strength."[20]

When the festivities were over, he was confronted with the
task of governing. His plan was to move quickly in order to
take advantage of the public's attention and the general feeling of goodwill. The hostages in Iran were free, and no major
domestic crises were pending. For the first time in decades,

the Senate was Republican as a result of Reagan's landslide victory. The president declared that government was America's problem—not its solution—and he set out to fix it.[21]

Following the ceremony, he retreated to the rarely used President's Room at the Capitol, where he signed executive orders and created a committee to review a list of federal regulations whose cost to industry was thought to be $25 billion a year. He imposed a 15 percent reduction in federal travel, fired two hundred employees chosen by Carter, and canceled twenty-seven appointments.[22] A strict freeze on civilian hiring and lowered personnel ceilings were declared. Thousands of Civil Service employees lost their jobs. David Stockman, the director of the budget, described the freeze as necessary in order to control the size and cost of government. It was an effort to demonstrate Reagan's commitment to cutbacks in domestic spending and personnel.[23]

In the weeks that followed, the president and his staff did everything in their power to generate support for the projected budget cuts. The cabinet was quickly confirmed with little opposition. The United States suspended payments to Nicaragua from a $75 million dollar economic support fund. The president met with South Korea's president, Chun Doo Hwan, and visited Prime Minister Pierre Trudeau of Canada. Secretary of Defense Weinberger asked Congress for a massive buildup of U.S. military forces; and Reagan and Haig met Foreign Minister Masayoshi Ito of Japan to discuss automobile import limitations. The president's agenda, at first packed with meetings and events, soon reverted to a nine-to-five schedule, and he delegated heavily to Meese, Baker, and Deaver.[24]

Crisis in Poland

During the months before Monday, March 30, 1981, the Polish state was rocked by an independent movement of workers, Solidarity, in a series of events for which no parallel in the Eastern block had been observed since 1945. An aging, sickly general secretary of the Communist party of the USSR listened and watched—together with the Politburo and the military—in an effort to weigh the need for an invasion of Soviet troops "at the request of Polish authorities" to maintain order in the land. Both openly and indirectly, the United States warned the Soviet Union of the potential gravity of such an action and encouraged Solidarity to challenge the Polish authorities.[25]

In early 1981, Solidarity's demand for a five-day work week was met as General Wojciech Jaruzelski became the prime minister.[26] From January to March 1981, Solidarity undertook a number of strikes, with greater responsiveness from the government than in the past. On March 18, however, Warsaw Pact maneuvers in and around Poland were initiated. The day following, a sit-in by rural Solidarity was broken up by violent police action.[27]

The Reagan administration began to issue somber warnings of Soviet intervention. Early in March, Leonid Brezhnev was reported to have reprimanded the leaders of Poland during a Moscow visit, indicating that time was running out for the unrest to be controlled. On March 23, the Warsaw Pact staged a landing operation on Poland's northwestern coast and conducted war games involving Soviet, East German, and Polish troops. This was followed by a four-hour strike on March 27, called by Solidarity, with paralysis of industry from the Baltic Coast to the southern Silesian coal mines.[28]

On March 31, an agreement was signed by Solidarity and the government to refer the cause of the violent police actions to a prosecutor; the general-strike plans of Solidarity were abandoned. Nevertheless, two days later, on April 2, Weinberger said that the possibility of Soviet intervention had increased in the last twenty-four to forty-eight hours, with intensified troop movements near Poland.[29] The crisis atmosphere had been created, and no one could predict the direction in which the events in Poland would lead.

Haig and the President's Men: January 20–March 30, 1981

Alexander Haig has been described as an intelligent man with limitless energy, patience, and unswerving devotion to duty and country. These qualities had won him a tough, thankless job: chief of staff of a White House paralyzed by Watergate.[30]

Haig attended West Point and was graduated in 1947, ranking 214th in a class of 310. As a twenty-three-year-old second lieutenant, he became a junior officer on General Douglas MacArthur's small personal staff. In Japan, he served as administrative assistant and aide-de-camp to MacArthur's chief of staff. Then he left for Korea to participate in five campaigns and the Inchon landings.[31]

After the Korean War, he received a master's degree in international relations at Georgetown University, and in

1962 he became a lieutenant colonel assigned to the Pentagon. Secretary of the Army Cyrus Vance chose Haig as his military assistant. In 1964, Haig was appointed deputy special assistant to Defense Secretary Robert McNamara.[32]

McNamara asked him to remain in the Pentagon as the Vietnam War progressed, but Haig preferred to be in Vietnam. As a field commander in 1966, he commanded battle troops, was seriously injured, and was awarded a Distinguished Service Cross. When Henry Kissinger became national security adviser in 1969, he wanted someone with combat experience as his military adviser, and chose Haig.[33]

Although Kissinger was known for his quick temper, lack of patience, and condescending manner, Haig's military training enabled him to accept such a temperament in a chief. Kissinger often left the office in the early evening to attend social events, leaving Haig with piles of paperwork. Haig became famous for his long work hours—from early in the morning to late at night.[34]

He was known as a hawk in the Nixon administration. Secretly supporting Nixon's decision to bomb Cambodia, he helped plan the raids. In September 1972, Nixon promoted Haig to the Army's second-highest post—vice–chief of staff. At the age of forty-seven, Haig was chosen over 240 senior officers with higher rank.[35]

The Watergate episode brought him out of the Army and into the White House once more. In May 1973, when Nixon realized that H. R. Haldeman and John Ehrlichman had to resign, he asked Haig to be his temporary chief of staff. Haig initially resisted, but his loyalty ultimately determined his decision. Subsequently, Nixon asked him to remain on the job.[36]

The Nixon administration crumbled quickly during Haig's

watch. Within his first six months as chief of staff, the Watergate tapes were uncovered; Vice-President Agnew resigned; and the Yom Kippur War began in the Middle East.[37]

Throughout the period, Haig carried out Nixon's orders even as the evidence piled up.[38] In many respects, both in his own perception and in reality, he was in charge of the White House. On April 16, 1974, he was flying back to Washington when a military aide remarked that Senator Mike Mansfield of Montana had called Nixon a few days earlier. Haig bitterly asked his executive assistant why he hadn't been informed of the call. Glaring at the other passengers, Haig warned, "I run this White House and don't you ever forget it."[39] Seven years later, this refrain would come back to haunt him.

Haig presided over the dismissal of Special Prosecutor Archibald Cox when he refused to relinquish the Watergate tapes. He recruited Leon Jaworski to replace Cox, and then tried to persuade him to be lenient with Nixon. His professed goal was to rescue the presidency, but he ended up trying to save Nixon. Nevertheless, it was probably Haig who finally persuaded Nixon to resign.[40]

After Gerald Ford took the oath of office, Haig remained in the White House at his request. In October 1974, he was appointed commander in chief of the United States European Command and Supreme Commander of NATO.[41]

After four years with NATO, Haig was bored, and in June 1978 he announced his retirement at the age of fifty-five. In April 1980, he underwent triple-bypass open-heart surgery. After a speedy recovery, he fought for the post of secretary of state in Reagan's cabinet. Although both Weinberger and Casey wanted the position, Reagan selected Haig after Nixon recommended him highly.[42]

Testifying before the Senate Foreign Relations Committee

on his nomination on January 9, 1981, Haig emphasized that he would be the administration's paramount spokesman on foreign policy, aside from Reagan. Richard Allen would fill a staff role for the president as the national security adviser.[43]

On January 20, with Reagan still in his formal inaugural attire in the Oval Office, Haig approached him with a twenty-page memo. It included a request that the president sign a directive granting Haig broad policy powers. The initiative was immediately leaked to the press by White House officials. Meese, Allen, and Weinberger discussed the memo with Reagan and decided to "table it."[44]

Bureaucratic infighting between Haig and Weinberger over military policy surfaced early.[45] But Haig continued to pursue control over foreign policy. In a press conference on January 28, he said that Reagan had assured him that he would be "the chief administrator for the formulation, the conduct and the articulation of American foreign policy." He denied that he was trying to usurp power in the administration.[46]

In a major test of Haig's foreign policy leadership, a dispute developed over David Stockman's proposed reduction of $2.6 billion in foreign aid. Western allies sent messages of concern to Haig. He fought off Stockman's attempt and obtained a level of direct economic aid higher than that in Carter's last year.[47]

On February 3, Weinberger stated publicly that he favored production and deployment of the neutron bomb; Haig moved quickly to advise European allies to disregard Weinberger's statements.[48]

In late February, organizational plans granting Haig more authority than his recent predecessors (but less than he had asked for) were approved. The plans called for the creation of interdepartmental groups of foreign, defense, and intelligence staff headed by representatives of State, Defense, and the CIA. Some officials interpreted Haig's original proposals as an attempt to move foreign-crisis management from Reagan—or in his absence, Bush—to State.[49]

Meanwhile, Haig was apparently pressing for a decision in favor of a land-based MX missile system, which Weinberger opposed. Haig took pains to rebut Navy Secretary John Lehman's comments that the United States no longer felt legally bound by the provisions of the SALT I and SALT II accords.[50]

On Monday, March 22, one week before the shooting, it was reported that Vice-President Bush had been assigned to direct crisis control in the White House.[51] Haig called Meese to ask if the story contained any truth. Meese replied, "None whatsoever," according to Haig.[52]

When Haig testified before the House Foreign Affairs Subcommittee the following day, he made known his displeasure at the press reports in no uncertain terms.[53] Later in the day, when Haig and Reagan were about to meet Foreign Minister Ito of Japan, Reagan told him the story was a fabrication: "It doesn't affect your authority in any way."[54] But Meese, Deaver, and Baker considered Haig's testimony before the House subcommittee an open challenge to the president. In response, the president made explicit Bush's appointment as head of crisis control, a function that State officials and Haig considered their responsibility. When the written announcement was released, the State Department was not even mentioned.[55]

Disturbed by the limitations placed on his authority, Haig

dictated a letter of resignation. He met with Reagan the following morning. Reagan then issued a statement indicating that Haig remained his "primary advisor in foreign affairs."[56]

But an uncomfortable atmosphere had already been created in the executive branch. With the administration's economic plan at the top of the agenda, Haig was thought to be diverting attention to issues of lesser importance for the moment. The relations between Haig and the president's men— Meese, Baker, and Deaver—remained profoundly strained, and it seemed likely that his proffered resignation would sooner or later be accepted, if repeated too often.[57]

From November 4, 1980, through March 30, 1981, the new administration experienced the exhausting efforts of the transition, the exhilaration of the inauguration, the problems of staffing a huge bureaucracy and of implementing new policies, the powerful threat of events in and around Poland, and the difficult struggles between White House staff and the developing fiefdoms of the executive branch. The massive push for fiscal reform and budgetary goals confronted a Democratic leadership in the House of Representatives with vastly different priorities. The displacement and replacement of the higher ranks of old Washington hands contributed to the instability of the period, as new and inexperienced figures attempted to define their roles and grapple with unresolved issues in their areas of responsibility.

It was a time that called for strong leadership. It required the full use of the power of the presidency to generate clear messages and rapid movement while the impact of the Reagan sweep dominated the thinking of official Washington.

Equally, it was a moment ripe for turmoil if the nation was leaderless or the center of power immobilized. As March 30 approached, the orchestra was not yet playing together as a coordinated ensemble, and the leader was still feeling his way. Small wonder, then, that the sudden attack on the conductor dismayed and disrupted the players and provoked a level of confusion that might have been avoided at a later point in the president's term.

3

The Shooting
and Its Aftermath

THE WASHINGTON HILTON HOTEL STANDS AT 1919 CONNECTICUT Avenue, with the main entrance on Connecticut Avenue, a side entrance on T Street, and the gymnasium on Nineteenth Street at the northeast corner of the hotel. From 1972 to March 1981, U.S. presidents attended meetings and spoke there on 109 occasions.[1]

On March 25, 1981, four days before President Reagan's scheduled speech at the hotel, preparations by the Secret Service to protect the president moved into high gear. Agent William Green, the lead advance man, was assigned to work with Rick Ahearn of the White House staff to assure the president's safety.[2] Such issues as transportation, communication, and liaison with the district and state police had to be planned and implemented.

On Friday morning, March 27, Secret Service agents, White House staff, and the hotel security director met at the Hilton to review the president's itinerary and conduct a "walk-through." Agent Green asked for the names of union officials who would meet the president before the speech, and for an updated list of hotel employees who might be in the vicinity of the ballroom. He then prepared a list of names to be checked by the intelligence division (and was informed on Monday morning, March 30, that none of those on the list was "of record" with the Secret Service).[3]

Meanwhile, Agent Mary Gordon, in charge of transportation for the visit, called Green to find out the president's arrival and departure times and the Hilton entrance that he would use. On the morning of March 30, Gordon called the U.S. Park Police to ask whether they would run through the motorcade routes ahead of time with her. They were busy. She drove the designated streets with a Metropolitan Police Department sergeant and made certain that no construction would be progressing along the way. At 11 A.M., she met with Paul Mobley, a Washington field officer agent, and they conducted a walk-through of the hotel.

A security briefing was held at noon. Neither the Secret Service Intelligence Division nor the Metropolitan Police Department had discovered any adverse intelligence information. Green went through the itinerary once more, the radio-communication frequencies, the location of the security room, and the identification badges and pins that would be used.[4] The security contingent agents were then stationed at their posts.

The grand ballroom of the Hilton is one level below the T Street lobby area and accommodates a few thousand people. The speaker's platform is on the T Street side of the building. Shortly after noon, the ballroom was cleared and carefully inspected by the technical security division. A canine unit, sniffing for bombs, swept the reception area uneventfully. The Metropolitan Police arrived and were posted around the VIP entrance on T Street. Agent Green then authorized the opening of the ballroom, the crowd entering through two checkpoints covered by agents who inspected briefcases and handbags.[5]

Agent Gordon had supervised the coordination of the presidential motorcade. Three cars—known as the "package"—always drive together: the presidential limousine, the Secret Service car, and the control car, which holds the aide with the "football." (The "football" is the black box that contains the codes required for initiating the launch of the strategic nuclear arsenal.) The control car also carried a senior staff person, in this case Michael Deaver, the White House deputy chief of staff.[6] The White House physician rode in the "spare," an extra limousine in case the president's broke down.

Precisely at 1:45 P.M., the entourage left the White House, traveling from Seventeenth and Pennsylvania Avenue down Connecticut Avenue through the tunnel under Dupont Circle. The president was accompanied in his limousine by Secretary of Labor Raymond Donovan and Special Agent-in-Charge Jerry Parr.[7] The Metropolitan Police had cleared the avenue and controlled the intersections along the route. The motorcade turned right on Florida Avenue and then left on T Street (figure 1A).[8] At the hotel, a rope line had been placed about thirty-five to forty feet from the VIP entrance to handle pedestrian traffic. The spectators at the rope were not screened, however, because it was not a "designated press area"; police were stationed at the rope barricade.

The T Street entrance to the hotel has a circular driveway, with one limb closest to Connecticut Avenue and the other near Florida Avenue and Nineteenth Street. The limousine drove to a point directly adjacent to the VIP entrance, and the president left the car after the Secret Service detail had arranged itself to cover his passage. Accompanied by Agents Parr and Ray Shaddick, he entered the hotel, descended on the elevator to the Grand Ballroom one flight down, and met with some of the ranking members of the union in the holding room.[9] He then delivered his twenty-minute speech.

While the president was speaking, the limousine was repositioned so as to face T Street. He would then have to walk twenty-five to thirty feet from the VIP entrance, bringing him closer to the press and spectators. The follow-up car was located behind the limousine, beneath the canopy that served the terrace entrance to the hotel, and four other cars of the motorcade were parked behind it.[10]

When Reagan finished his talk, he was ushered out of the back of the stage into a small anteroom, then to the elevator, and out through the VIP entrance to T Street. He turned to the left and walked under a canopy with the Secret Service men surrounding him, Press Secretary James Brady behind him, and Mike Deaver on his left. There he confronted the reporters and the spectators who had gathered at the T Street entrance, many of them ten to fifteen feet away. The Secret Service countersnipers were on duty, strategically placed around the area.[11] The president paused in front of a brown

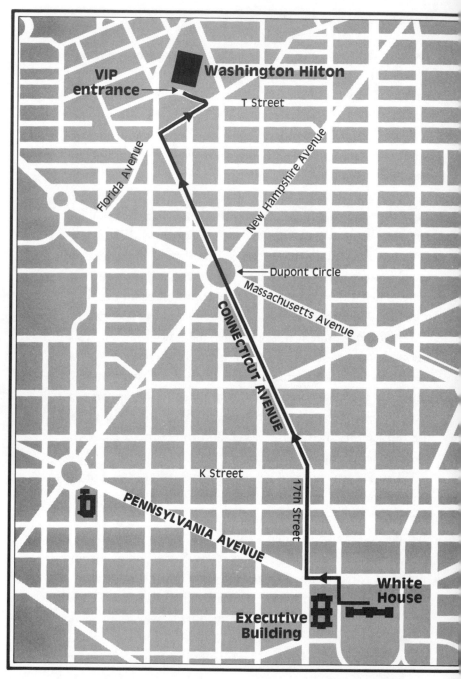

Figure 1A The president's route from the White House to the Washington Hilton.

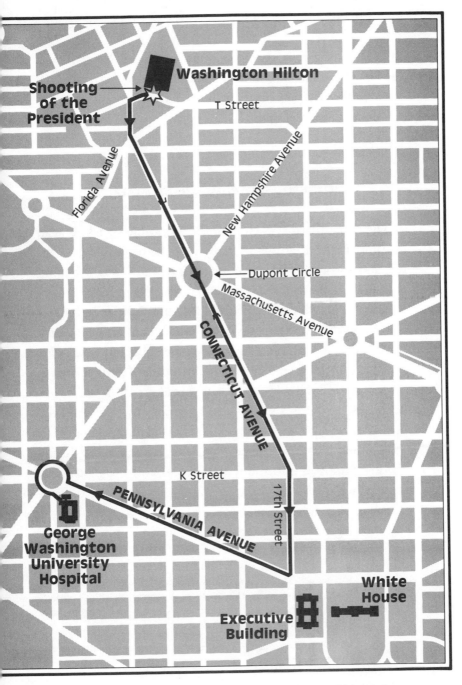

Figure 1B The president's route from the Washington Hilton to the hospital.

concrete block wall. The limousines were ready for transport back to the White House, with the street blocked off to all other traffic. Reagan smiled and waved to the spectators; at this point, Hinckley fired.[12]

From the Hotel to the Hospital*

The bullet that ricocheted off the limousine struck Reagan just under his left armpit.[13] It then hit the top of his seventh rib, and was deflected three inches into the lower left lung, about one inch from the heart and aorta (figure 2).†[14]

Agent Tim McCarthy had opened the right rear door of the limousine for the president, while Parr and Shaddick stayed very close to him. As soon as the shots rang out, Parr shoved the president into the limousine, and Shaddick slammed the door. McCarthy had spread his arms and legs as he turned towards the shots in an effort to safeguard the president, and he was struck in the abdomen by a bullet.[15]

Parr immediately ordered the driver to leave the scene. Shaddick jumped into the follow-up car and the motorcade moved rapidly down T Street, making a left turn on Connecticut Avenue.

When Agent Parr pushed Reagan into the limousine, they

*The precise sequence of events and their timing have been reconstructed from many sources. These included interviews with physicians involved in Reagan's care and with government figures, as well as numerous reports published by the government, newspapers, and journals after the event, and books published at later dates.

†The aorta is the large artery that emerges from the heart carrying oxygenated blood to the body.

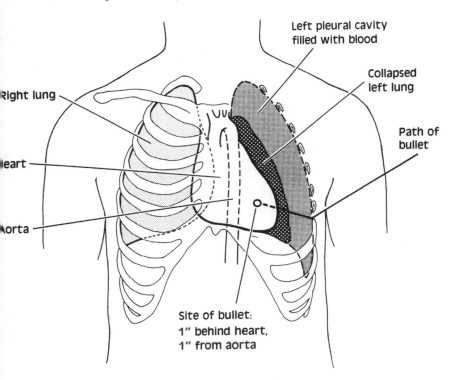

Figure 2 Diagram of the path of the bullet that penetrated Reagan's chest.

landed on the transmission riser between the two seats, with Parr on top of Reagan.[16] Reagan cursed,[17] and told Parr that he had hurt his ribs when the agent landed on top of him (both of them were unaware that Reagan had actually been hit). Subsequently, he would describe it as "the most paralyzing pain . . . as if someone had hit you with a hammer." He added, "[It] came after I was in the car, and so I thought that maybe his [Parr's] gun or something, when he had come down on me, had broken a rib. But when I sat up on the seat and the pain wouldn't go away and suddenly I found that I was coughing up blood, we both decided that maybe I had broken a rib and punctured a lung."[18]

Parr told Agent Drew Unrue to head straight for the White House, considering it the safest place for the president. "The limousine left the T Street exit, went down T Street to Connecticut Avenue, turned left on Connecticut, and proceeded towards the White House." As the car sped along, Reagan and Parr joked about their "flying entrance into the car." "When the president became distressed and started coughing up blood in the tunnel under Dupont Circle, I radioed ahead and told Drew Unrue that we should change and move to George Washington University Hospital," Parr said. He knew that emergency care would be available there, and he informed presidential aide Michael Deaver in the control car of the change in plans.[19] He was aware that Reagan had injured his lung because of the bright red blood coming from his mouth.[20]

"By then," Reagan said, "my handkerchief was sopped with blood and he [Parr] handed me his. Suddenly, I realized I could barely breathe. No matter how hard I tried, I couldn't get enough air. I was frightened and started to panic a little. I just was not able to inhale enough air."[21]

They continued on Connecticut Avenue until it intersected with Seventeenth Street (figure 1B). Three blocks down Seventeenth Street, they turned right onto Pennsylvania Avenue, which had been cleared so that the president could get to the White House. On reaching Washington Circle, the intersection of New Hampshire, Pennsylvania, Twenty-third Street and K Street, the driver went around the circle and pulled up at the emergency room of the George Washington Medical Center. The president was then on the right side of the limousine and could get out easily. The entire ride, unobstructed by traffic, took them less than five minutes.[22]

Dr. Joseph Giordano, the head of the trauma team who directed Reagan's care after his arrival, was asked where the president would have gone if he had not been brought to George Washington University Hospital. He replied that the other place would have been the Washington Hospital Center, because it too had a trauma unit as well as a heliport. The Naval Medical Center at Bethesda, which has a presidential suite, would not have been advisable, because "they don't really have an active emergency service." "I can tell you," he added, "that Jerry Parr deserves the most credit for saving the president's life. The president was very close to crashing while on the way to the White House. When Parr saw the president cough up blood, he took a beeline to the GW, and that saved the day."[23]

The Hospital:
Monday, March 30, 1981 (Day 1)

2:35 P.M. The limousine arrived at the hospital. Although the staff had been called ahead, there was no stretcher for Reagan, and he was helped to the hospital door by Secret Service agents.[24] He walked about forty-five feet, and then his "eyes rolled upward, and his head went back, his knees buckled and he started to collapse," according to a paramedic who helped carry Reagan into the hospital.[25] (The paramedic later said that he "literally froze" when he realized what was happening.)[26]

When the president entered the emergency room, he fell to one knee. "I can't breathe," he said.[27] (The paramedic's description—"he was gasping for air"—was later confirmed by one of the hospital physicians.)[28]

The emergency room nurses, Kathy Paul and Wendy Koenig, had been notified only that three gunshot wound victims were on their way to the hospital. Kathy Paul saw the limousine arrive. The president stepped out, and from his pallor and near collapse, she immediately thought that he was having a heart attack.[29] Together with the Secret Service agents, they carried the president to a stretcher, and began cutting away his clothes. Kathy Paul was the first to note blood on the president. Dr. William O'Neill, the first trauma team intern to see him, thought he was in "acute distress" and in a "life-threatening situation."[30] Dr. Wesley Price, a surgical resident, saw the small hole just below the president's armpit and realized that the bullet had entered the chest.[31] No exit point was visible, so it was assumed the bullet was still inside the chest.

Nurse Wendy Koenig tried to take his blood pressure, but could not hear through the stethoscope because of the noise of Secret Service agents and trauma team members crowding the area. Several resident physicians surrounded the president; altogether about fifteen or twenty people were in the emergency room, besides the president's personal physician, Dr. Daniel Ruge, who was standing next to him. (On the tenth anniversary of the shooting, President Reagan would say, "It was a very close call. Twice they could not find my pulse."[32] Dr. Ruge, however, said that his pulse never disappeared and was palpable throughout.)[33] The nurse put the blood pressure cuff on, blew it up, and as it deflated felt his pulse come through at a blood pressure level of 78.*[34] (His usual pressure was 140/80.) The trauma team members quickly inserted an intravenous tube and began an infusion. To Dr. Giordano, who had been paged without being informed of the patient's identity, Reagan looked pale and clammy; his pulse rate was rapid.[36]

Until his chest was exposed, as Dr. Ruge emphasized, "none of us thought that he was shot. There was no evidence of blood. I walked in behind him, and I saw him fall backward. He was sort of picked up and taken into the emergency room. I had never seen a person have an acute coronary thrombosis in my life, but I presumed that was it because I had been told that he hadn't been shot. . . . The first we knew about his chest wound was when they cut off his thousand-dollar suit and we saw a few drops of blood on his shirt. That was when I became more hopeful, because I had been really afraid that we had a very serious situation on hand. I figured that if he had been shot, that was something that could be taken care of. But if he looked that bad after a coronary thrombosis, I would have feared for his life.

"When his clothes were taken off, I became as unobtrusive as possible; I stood at the foot of the bed and I felt his dorsalis pedis pulse.† Giordano and his gang were absolutely fantastic. They started the IVs; they gave him two units of Rh negative blood. I said, 'Well, he's an O Rh positive—which

---

*A low pressure for the president. Dr. Sol Edelstein, director of the emergency room, said that he had "orthostatic hypotension" (low blood pressure because of positional change) but was never in shock.[35]

†The dorsalis pedis is the small artery at the top of the foot so close to the surface that the pulse, reflecting the strength of the contraction of the heart, is easily felt.

was very easy for me. That's what Nancy is, that's what the president is, that's what Mrs. Bush is, that's what Vice-President Bush is.' "[37]

2:40 P.M. With three intravenous tubes inserted, the president was receiving fluids to keep his blood pressure up. He kept complaining about difficulty in breathing, even while the anesthesiologist administered oxygen by mask. Four units of blood were obtained, and a transfusion was begun. He continued to cough up blood, and his breathing was fast and labored. His blood pressure rose rapidly to normal levels.[38] Meanwhile, the president was unaware that he had been shot. "For quite a while," he later said, "when I was in the emergency room, I still thought I was there because Jerry Parr had broken my rib and it had punctured my lung. Little by little, though, I learned what had happened and what the situation was: I had a bullet in my lungs."[39]

Mrs. Reagan had left the White House for the hospital as soon as she heard of the shooting. Not until she reached the hospital did she learn that the president had been hit. When she saw him in the emergency room, "Ronnie looked pale and gray," she said. "Underneath the oxygen mask, his lips were caked with dried blood. He saw me, and pulled up the mask and whispered, 'Honey, I forgot to duck.' "[40]

2:45–3:00 P.M. Because of the puncture wound, it was thought that the left lung had collapsed. In order to reinflate it, an incision was made just beneath his collar bone and another one between the seventh and eighth ribs. Tubes were inserted into both incisions so as to suction off air and blood that might have gathered because of the bullet wounds. A large volume of blood spurted out of the chest tubes.[41]

2:50 P.M. The president received 900 cc, then 1,200, and subsequently 1,800 cc of blood, essential to keep his blood volume up. Giordano said, "The man had a blood pressure of 70/0; they couldn't get it in the normal ways. He had an enormous amount of blood in his chest, more than I have seen in most injuries of this type. Most of these are handled with a chest tube. The lung expands and that's it. He had initially something like 2,200 or 2,400 cc of blood that came out—a very significant proportion of his blood volume. There is no doubt in my mind that another five or ten minutes and he may have been at the point of no return. He collapsed when he was brought in, so he was very hypotensive; he responded rapidly because we got blood and fluids into him.

"A fifteen minute delay in getting the president to the hospital could have made a big difference and might even have been fatal. . . . If he had lost more blood without receiving some fluid, his pressure would have dropped and he would have gone into shock."[42]

2:58 P.M. A chest film was obtained, which showed blood in the pleural cavity and the bullet behind the heart. The radiologist asked about the caliber of the gun and was initially told by a Secret Service agent that it was a .38. Because the metallic shadow in the chest was too small for a .38, the radiologist requested an X-ray of the abdomen to look for further fragments. None were seen.[43]

3:05 P.M. With the blood loss continuing, Dr. Benjamin Aaron, the chief of thoracic surgery, determined that surgery was required to stop the bleeding. "Not all bullet wounds to the chest go to surgery," as Dr. Daniel O'Leary, the spokesman for the hospital, pointed out. "What pushed them to surgery was that the blood loss kept up, and they didn't want to get into a situation where they'd have a major transfusion problem to deal with."[44]

The first procedure would be a "peritoneal lavage"; fluid would be placed in the abdomen through a small incision and sucked out to make certain that there was no blood in it. If the fluid was clear, it was then unlikely that one of the abdominal organs had been penetrated by a bullet fragment.

3:20 P.M. Reagan was made ready for surgery.

Surgery: 3:24 P.M.–6:45 P.M.

3:24 P.M. Reagan was wheeled into the operating room. He had lost about 2,100 cc of blood, but his bleeding had slowed and he had received 4 ½ replacement units.[45] As he was moved from the stretcher to the operating table, he looked around and said, "Please tell me you're all Republicans." Giordano, a liberal Democrat, said, "We're all Republicans today."[46]

3:40 P.M. He was first anesthetized with a small amount of intravenous Pentothal (a drug commonly used for light anesthesia), together with a skeletal muscle relaxant.[47]

A tube was then inserted into his trachea, and he was

placed on a mechanical respirator.[48] The peritoneal lavage was done, requiring about forty minutes to complete.

4:20 P.M. The peritoneal fluid was clear of blood, and it seemed evident that the bullet had not penetrated abdominal organs. Reagan was now turned on his right side, and draped for the chest exploration. Dr. Aaron made a six-inch incision parallel with the ribs, spread the ribs with retractors, and felt the splintering of the seventh rib where the bullet had grazed it. He removed a large blood clot from the left pleural cavity outside the left lung, and was then able to determine the site where the bullet had entered the lung. The heart and the great vessels nearby appeared undamaged.[49]

"We did not filet the lung to look for the bleeder," Dr. Aaron said. "At the time we looked in, there was a lot of blood in the chest—mostly clotted—maybe a liter or more. The entrance hole in the lung, out of which dark red blood was trickling fairly briskly, was very large. The bullet had traversed the lung and was lying against the pleura on the other side; rather than fish clear through the lung, we made an exit hole for it. The major bleeding was occurring right there locally, at a point not too far from the main pulmonary artery. We were able to take a suture locally and control the bleeding; we didn't have to do anything major. That was it as far as the lung bleeding was concerned."[50]

5:00 P.M. The bullet was not visible, nor could Aaron feel it. He had difficulty removing it, and almost gave up after a few attempts, but felt it was important to get it out.[51] An angled X-ray was then taken on the operating table and showed the metallic fragment in the lower part of the left lung just behind the heart. With the more precise localization, he was finally able to remove it and found that part of the difficulty was that it was flattened into the shape of a dime.[52]

6:00–6:20 P.M. The surgery was now complete, and Dr. Aaron began to close the chest and finally sutured the edges of the incision together. Reagan had lost 3,400 cc of blood, over 50 percent of his total blood volume. Most of this had been in the emergency room, but some as well in the operating room. A total of eight units of packed red cells were transfused; he also received three units of fresh frozen plasma and one unit of platelets, commonly used in efforts to stop bleeding.[53]

6:20–6:45 P.M. He remained in the operating room, on the ventilator, carefully monitored.

The Recovery Room:
6:45 P.M.–6:00 A.M., Tuesday (March 31)

6:46 P.M. Reagan was taken to the recovery room more than three hours after he first entered the operating room.[54] A postoperative chest X-ray showed a collapsed left lower lobe, blood in the pleural cavity, and patches of unexpanded lung.[55] He remained on the respirator, under positive pressure.

7:30 P.M. The anesthetic had partially worn off, and the president was regaining consciousness. He was able to visit briefly with his wife.

8:00 P.M. He was given morphine for chest pain.[56]

8:50 P.M. The anesthetic effect had dissipated, and some fluid was introduced into his windpipe, producing coughing and loosening mucus plugs in the bronchi. Unable to speak, he scribbled an old line from W. C. Fields: "All in all, I'd rather be in Philadelphia."[57]

8:50 P.M.–**2:50** A.M. Reagan had little sleep during the night and required morphine for his chest pain.[58] His blood oxygen had been lower than normal and his carbon dioxide levels high. They improved enough that at 2:15 A.M. he was taken off the respirator and allowed to breathe on his own. At 2:50, the endotracheal tube was removed.[59]

Meanwhile, he had heard one of the medical team say, "This is it," as he was about to remove the tube from the trachea. The president "blanched, clutched a pad of paper and scribbled a note to a nearby nurse: 'What does he mean—this is it?' " He calmed down, after hearing the explanation.[60]

Before the tube was removed, he jotted some notes that reflected his confusion. "Where am I?" he wrote. "You're in the recovery room," he was told. "How long have I been here? How long will I have to stay here?"[61] It was not at all clear that the president actually knew he had undergone surgery until he was specifically told about it hours later.

Tuesday, March 31 (Day 2)

3:00 A.M.–6:00 A.M. He dozed fitfully, and was awake much of the night, talking to doctors and nurses.[62]

The Intensive Care Unit:
6:00 A.M.–9:00 P.M.

6:00 A.M. Taken to the intensive care unit, he was placed on nasal oxygen, deep-breathing exercises, and mild physiotherapy.[63] By 6:45, he was propped up in bed and brushing his teeth.[64]

7:15 A.M. Reagan signed legislation to stop a scheduled increase in farm price supports not long after receiving an injection of morphine for his chest pain.[65]

7:30 A.M.–3:00 P.M. He remained in intensive care, with his family visiting. At 3:00 P.M., chest X-rays showed some expansion of the collapsed lower lobe of the lung, but he was still in distress.[66] Dr. Knaus, the internist caring for him in the intensive care unit, said, "We gave him small doses of narcotics to make him comfortable, because he had a lot of pain from the incision and from the wound itself."[67]

4:40 P.M. Ruge announced, "From time to time he is sitting up in bed. He is converting from non-oral to oral feeding and tolerating it very well. He has had clear liquids such as soup and gelatin. He continues on intravenous fluids and antibiotics."[68]

The Secure Suite:
9:00 P.M., Tuesday, March 31, to Discharge
at 10:44 A.M., Saturday, April 11

Tuesday, 9:00 P.M. The president was moved to a separate suite on the third floor of the hospital, with security carefully arranged.[69] "We pushed to get him out of the ICU," Dr. Knaus said, "because we knew he'd be better some place that was quieter. The environment was getting him a little disoriented."[70]

Wednesday, April 1 (Day 3), 1:00 A.M. Because he had not urinated, he required bladder catheterization. He continued to cough up blood. By morning, his blood oxygen level dropped, and he was again placed on oxygen therapy. But he had a good appetite and ate breakfast and lunch normally.[71] That evening, he fell asleep at 9:00 and was able to sleep until 6:00 the following morning.

Thursday, April 2 (Day 4). The intravenous tubes were withdrawn in the morning, and the surgeons removed the abdominal sutures. Chest tubes were still draining his lungs, and a nasal device was still in place to provide oxygen. He was able to walk for a few minutes. His temperature rose late on Thursday to 102–103°; the white count went up; his color became poor; and he felt tired.[72]

Dr. Aaron, the chest surgeon, was asked how he viewed

this febrile episode. "With great alarm," he said. "For the first couple of days we were living in a dream world. . . . We were talking about getting him out of the hospital in less than a week. I thought to myself, 'That doesn't seem very realistic, but let's hope anyway.' Of course, it didn't turn out to be realistic. When he developed fever on the second and third days after surgery, he had some haziness in the left lower chest area on X-ray. I thought, 'Maybe he's got some infection down there.' That was the first consideration. Then we were concerned when he began to spit up a little blood about that time—maybe within twenty-four hours. I had the thought that he might be bleeding down in the bullet tract and that things mightn't be going so well, especially if it was infected. So I had to consider that he might begin to bleed briskly intrabronchially. We already had declared both to him and his wife that if he did bleed at all aggressively, we were going to take him back and take that lobe out. The entrance hole was so big, and the bullet was flattened, so I surmised that it had tumbled through the lungs because the entrance site in his skin was like a slit, almost like a little button hole. The pleural gap was huge; it was like a ball had gone into the lung—perhaps 2 cm in diameter. And I thought, 'There is going to be a lot of destroyed lung in that lower lobe down there.' I even gave some thought to taking the lobe out during surgery. But it wasn't bleeding that bad; most of the lung looked pretty good; and I decided we'd leave it. It's kind of a calculated risk. When he started showing some anoxia* with the fever, I said, 'First sign of trouble, we're going to take him back; I don't want to have any patient crashing with

*Signs of decreased oxygenation.

blood in his bronchial tree in this setting.' That was Friday—the fourth day after surgery—when we were thinking about that as an option. But he settled down. . . . We never cultured an organism. . . . He had been placed on Cetamandole [an antibiotic] for forty-eight hours, and because he was doing well, we took him off it. Within twenty-four hours, he began to spike this low fever. Then we put him on other antibiotics empirically, without any positive cultures, because we thought the better part of valor would be to cover him for a pulmonary infection."[73]

Friday, April 3 (Day 5). The fever continued at about 102° in the morning, dropped in the afternoon, and rose once more later in the day to 101°.[74] "At about that time," Dr. David Rockoff, the chief of chest radiology, said, "his left lower lobe became relatively opaque.* The portable examinations were not sufficiently revealing. I prevailed upon them to bring the president down to the X-ray department. The Secret Service came, swept the department for security, cleaned it out of unneeded personnel, and early in the morning they brought him down. We got high-quality standard X-rays of his chest, and there was a large area of airlessness in the left lower lobe not too far away from the path that the bullet had traversed. If the fever was coming from the chest, it was from the left lower lobe either as a result of atelectasis [collapse] and pneumonia, or perhaps infection of the pleura related to the bullet's passage, or a combination of the two."[75]

He was scheduled for bronchoscopy, which was then performed.[76] In the evening he began to experience chills. There

*"Opaque": dense, as in pneumonia or collapse.

was concern about the infection in his lungs, and he was placed on a broad-spectrum antibiotic. His breathing exercises were increased. Dr. Aaron described this episode as "a little bit of a setback," adding that the president's schedule was being curtailed to prevent fatigue. Other physicians believed that the pneumonia was more serious.[77]

Saturday, April 4 (Day 6). Even with a good night's sleep behind him, he napped much of the day. He experienced a bout of coughing; the blood that came up was bright red, different from the dark clotted blood previously brought up. The fever persisted, but at lower levels.[78]

Sunday, April 5 (Day 7). New chest X-rays demonstrated patchy densities along the bullet track, presumably areas of pneumonia and hemorrhage. He was now placed on penicillin and tobramycin.[79]

Monday and Tuesday, April 6 and 7 (Days 8 and 9). Fever persisted at a low level, and antibiotics were continued. The chest X-ray showed some clearing of lung densities. By Tuesday, his temperature was close to normal and X-rays showed further clearing.[80]

Wednesday, April 8 (Day 10). With his fever under control, but on continued antibiotic therapy, the president was now able to do about two hours of work daily. Dr. O'Leary said that Reagan would have to limit his workload for ten days to two weeks after his return to the White House. In the hospital, he was not able to read the full text of all of the documents that he signed. While he was febrile, briefings were more condensed than at midweek. A projected television address on April 15 and a planned trip to California and Mexico to begin April 23 were canceled.[81]

Thursday, April 9 (Day 11). The president had a normal temperature and was feeling much better. He had obviously lost weight. One antibiotic was discontinued.[82]

Friday, April 10 (Day 12). There was further improvement, despite the persistence on chest X-ray of a small pocket of air, which might have represented an abscess. It was planned that, unless complications arose, he would leave the hospital the following day.[83]

Saturday, April 11 (Day 13). He felt better, and the chest X-ray showed improvement.[84] He was now in good enough shape to be discharged on continuing antibiotic therapy.

At 10:44 A.M., he left the hospital and was driven to the White House.[85] He walked from the limousine to the White House entrance and then to the elevator, demonstrating his return to strength after the debilitating episode. Nevertheless, he appeared weak and drawn at close quarters, and an aide expressed concern that the country might experience another "Woodrow Wilson" episode—a sick president remaining in office beyond his time.[86]

Sunday, April 12 (Day 14). The president arose at 6:50 A.M. to view the televised launching of the space shuttle *Columbia* on its first voyage. He rested much of the day, planning to work about two hours daily in the study next to his bedroom.[87] A visitor described him as "pale and disoriented

. . . walking with the hesitant steps of an old man." Entering a room, he started to sit down and "fell the rest of the way, collapsing into his chair." He could concentrate for only a few minutes at a time and was able to work and remain attentive for only an hour or so a day.[88] (Haig would later confirm this description of Reagan as "incredibly accurate.")[89]

Monday–Wednesday, April 13–15 (Days 15–17). Fourteen to sixteen days after being shot, Reagan slept late, met with Deaver, Bush, and Allen at 9:00 A.M., and felt better.[90]

Thursday, April 16 (Day 18). He took his first stroll in the Rose Garden and received his first official visitor, Joseph Luns, NATO's secretary general. Two and a half weeks after the attack, he was still delegating official duties to Bush, including presiding over cabinet meetings.[91]

Saturday, April 18 (Day 20). White House officials stated that Reagan had increased his work load to four to five hours a day and was able to do the same amount of paperwork that he had done before the shooting.[92]

Tuesday, April 21 (Day 23). The president was still experiencing pain and discomfort and his pace was slow.[93] Dr. Aaron saw him that day for about thirty minutes. "He seemed pretty much what I would expect a guy to be who was two to three weeks out from major injury. He had a little splinting* of the chest; he said it hurt a little bit. He was not dressed; he was in pajamas and a bathrobe; it was sometime in the morning. I talked to his wife that day, and she was fairly pleased with the way things were going. But others may have been looking at him as the leader of the country, up and charging, and perhaps he wasn't that vibrant person that they expected. He was trying to carry on some work at a time when most people his age could have put it off, and maybe he did reflect a lack of stamina and a lack of concentration."[94]

Friday, April 24 (Day 26). He met in closed session with the cabinet for his first White House appearance in the West Wing since the shooting.[95]

Saturday, April 25 (Day 27). Reagan was told by Dr. Ruge that he would not be well enough to attend his daughter's wedding as scheduled. The president discussed it with Mrs. Reagan, and the two of them made the decision that he should not go, also canceling his proposed trip to meet with the president of Mexico.[96]

May 16, 1981 (Day 48). At seventy years and ninety-nine days of age, Reagan became the oldest president in U.S. history.[97]

May 17, 1981 (Day 49). He went to Notre Dame University, his first trip since the shooting.[98]

*Decreased chest movement during breathing because of the associated pain.

June 3, 1981 (Day 63). His work schedule was now increased and included some ceremonial events.[99]

June 16, 1981 (Day 79). Reagan held his first news conference since March, and announced that he had recovered, nine weeks after the attack.[100]

But Dr. Ruge later said, "So far as I am concerned, he probably wasn't fully recovered until about October. Anybody who has a major operation is not going to be perfectly okay for about six months. We were at the ranch in October, and the president said to me, 'Now I really feel like I am all the way.' He felt better than he did in June."[101]

Thus, the oldest White House occupant in American history had recovered from major trauma and blood loss and demonstrated his physical resilience to a concerned country and a watching world. As we shall see, the severity of his illness had been partially obscured during the week after the attack in an effort to reassure the public. "The president's staff were very anxious to portray the president as being well," Dr. Ruge commented. "But nobody is very well after being shot, and having had an anesthetic, and having lost a lot of blood and having it replaced."[102]

Figure 3 Reagan addressing the AFL-CIO Building Trades Council meeting in the Grand Ballroom of the Washington Hilton Hotel shortly before he was shot. Secretary of Labor Raymond Donovan stands at his left, and he is surrounded by leaders of the council. (White House photo)

Figure 4 Reagan waves to the crowd as he leaves the Hilton. With him are Secret Service Agent Jerry Parr (second from left, in overcoat) and Michael Deaver (on Reagan's left). The other victims are also visible: James Brady (third from left), Washington policeman Thomas K. Delahanty (second from right, facing camera), and Secret Service Agent Timothy J. McCarthy (far right). (White House photo by Michael Evans)

Figure 5 Reagan after the shooting:
A. Approaching the limousine, he grimaces in discomfort as Hinckley begins firing. Secret Service Agent Jerry Parr is behind him, barely visible. (AP/Wide World Photos)

B. Parr places his left hand on the president's arm. (AP/Wide World Photos)

C. Parr attempts to shield the president and shove him into the limousine. The president is in obvious distress. (AP/Wide World Photos)

Figure 6 A Secret Service agent closes the door of Reagan's limousine just before it leaves the scene. Lying wounded are Brady (center) and Delahanty (left of Brady). Officers and agents grapple with Hinckley in the background. (White House photo by Michael Evans)

Figure 7 A Secret Service agent brandishes a machine gun, while two others come to the assistance of Brady. Delahanty is stretched out in the foreground. (White House photo by Michael Evans)

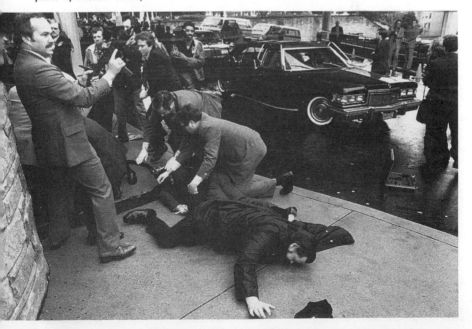

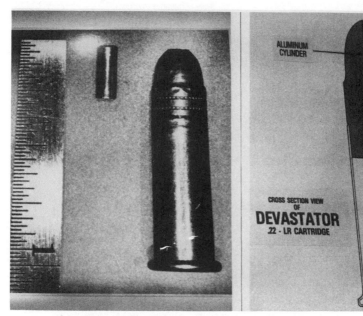

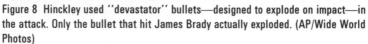

Figure 8 Hinckley used ''devastator'' bullets—designed to explode on impact—in the attack. Only the bullet that hit James Brady actually exploded. (AP/Wide World Photos)

Figure 9 James Baker (left), Ed Meese (center), and Larry Speakes hurry to the emergency room at George Washington University Hospital. (AP/Wide World Photos)

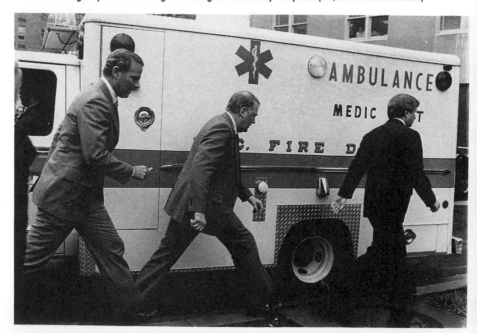

Figure 10 The Situation Room, just before Haig (standing right of center) left to appear before the media. Larry Speakes, in the press room, can be seen faintly on the television monitor in the background. Seated at the table clockwise from Haig are William Casey, William French Smith, Donald Regan, Richard Allen, and Martin Anderson. Standing, from left: White House congressional liaison Max Friedersdorf, Transportation Secretary Drew Lewis, Daniel Murphy (Bush's chief of staff), and Richard Williamson (head of the Office of Intergovernmental Affairs). (White House photo by Karl Schumacher)

Figure 11 Larry Speakes responds to questions in the media briefing room of the White House. His comments irritated Haig because of their vagueness. They conveyed the impression that there was a void in leadership. (White House photo)

Figure 12 Haig left the Situation Room and rushed down a corridor and up a flight of stairs to appear before the press and TV reporters. (White House photo)

Figure 13 The day after the shooting, Vice-President Bush presided over a bipartisan meeting of congressional leaders and White House officials, among them Speaker of the House Thomas P. (Tip) O'Neill (smoking a cigar across from Bush), and Congressman Jack Kemp (two chairs to Bush's right). Sitting two chairs to O'Neill's left is Ed Meese.

4

The President's Men

As THE NEWS OF THE ATTACK ON THE PRESIDENT SPREAD RAPIDLY TO all corners of the country, no reaction was more universally experienced than the recall of the picture of the mortally wounded John Kennedy in 1963. Everywhere, the fear and horror that the nation would once more undergo the agony of a lost president dominated the thinking and consciousness of the people. Work stopped, and groups gathered to listen and support each other, while the tension grew. Was he injured? How badly? And, later, would he come through surgery? If so, would this oldest of presidents survive intact?

The attention of the world was sharply focused on getting the truth, learning every detail of his condition. With Dr. Dennis O'Leary as the spokesman for the George Washington University Hospital, the public was exposed to a professional's description of the president's course and response to surgery.

Behind the scenes, the president's men—sometimes in concert, sometimes in conflict—were acting to keep the government going. The administration, in power barely two and a half months, was as unprepared for the assassin's bullets as the nation itself, and the executive branch reacted in a manner that signified there were lessons to be learned for the future. The actions of the president's advisers must be viewed in the light both of their concerns about the president's condition and of their differing perceptions as to the responses required by the crisis.

The first word of the shooting came in a phone call to Deputy Press Secretary Larry Speakes from David Prosperi, an assistant to Press Secretary James Brady who had accompanied the presidential party to the hotel. After Hinckley emptied his gun at the president, Prosperi ran into the Hilton lobby and called the White House press office from a pay phone at about 2:30. Lacking fifteen cents in change for the call, Prosperi had to have the call charged to his home number.[1] He said that shots had been fired at the president and those with him, and that Brady had been hit. Speakes passed the word on to David Gergen, the White House communications director, who then informed James Baker, chief of the White House staff. Baker went to the Secret Service command post, where a computer that tracks the president's movements showed Reagan to be at the hospital. Meese was then alerted, while the State Department operations center informed Haig, and the Secret Service called Secretary of the Treasury Don Regan.[2]

At 2:38, Baker's phone rang with a call from Deaver, who had been in the president's motorcade to the hospital. He found a telephone bay outside the emergency ward, and told Baker's secretary, Margaret Tutwiler, to keep the line open.[3] "There's been a shooting, and the president's hurt," Deaver said. "We don't think he was hit, but he may have broken a rib."[4] White House aides wrote, "Do not hang up," on a sheet of paper and attached it to Ms. Tutwiler's phone.[5]

Peter Teeley, Bush's press secretary, heard about the shooting from Baker's office. At 2:40, he phoned the vice-president, who had just left the Dallas–Fort Worth airport aboard *Air Force 2* on his way to Austin to address the Texas legislature. He told him that six shots were fired at the president, but that initial reports said Reagan was unhurt.[6]

Regan was the first cabinet officer to reach Baker's office. The Secret Service had informed him that the president was not wounded.[7] Just as Regan finished telling Baker and Meese, Deaver delivered the more accurate message that Reagan had been hit.[8] Baker asked Deaver to put Reagan's physician, Dr. Daniel Ruge, on the line. Ruge had been at the Hilton and followed the president in a limousine to the hospital. He had walked behind him to the emergency room, had seen him fall to his knees, and had then observed the blood stains on his shirt when his suit was cut off. He told Baker that Reagan had a small bullet puncture in his chest and had lost three to four pints of blood, but that his condition was "stable." Ruge added that the president might be headed for the operating room, and recommended that Baker come to the hospital.[9]

Majority Leader Howard Baker interrupted debate in the Senate at 2:43 P.M. to announce the shootings. Half an hour later, the Senate recessed when it was learned that the president had been wounded.[10]

Haig was also initially told that Reagan had escaped injury. He phoned Baker, who called back to tell him that the earlier reports were wrong, and that a bullet had struck the president in the chest: "It looks quite serious." (Haig did not repeat what Baker had just told him about Reagan's condition. In the hours ahead, he would confide this information to no one except the vice-president.) They agreed that the way in which they handled the crisis would have worldwide repercussions. They also decided to set up a command center in the White House Situation Room, where Haig would be the "point of contact" between the aides at the hospital and the Situation Room group. Baker and Meese would leave for the hospital so as to be with the president.[11]

Haig called National Security Adviser Richard Allen at 2:59 P.M. and then left the State Department for the White House. He told his escort not to sound the sirens. He arrived at the White House at 3:02, just before Baker and Meese left for the hospital.[12] He and Allen went to Baker's office, found David Gergen, and then went to the Situation Room, in the basement of the White House. Regan joined them there seconds later.

Haig learned that Bush had not been informed that a bullet had actually hit Reagan. At 3:04, he sent him a telex informing him that Reagan was in serious condition. He then called Bush on *Air Force 2,* but the connection was poor, and he could barely hear Bush say that he would return to Washington.[13]

Others of the cabinet and key administration members were gathering. Allen took notes, and two tape recorders were operating.[14]

Each of the White House principals had learned of the shooting in different ways. Meese's recollections of the afternoon help confirm many of the details:[15]

"I was in my office at the White House sometime after 2:00, and someone came in—I can't remember who it was— saying there had been a shooting that involved the president's party. They said that Jim Brady and others had been shot, but not the president. I went down the hall to Jim Baker's office to see whether he had heard anything. Normally, one of the three of us—Mike Deaver, Jim Baker, myself—would go with the president. On this occasion it was not a major policy speech—I think he was addressing a labor union. For that reason, Mike Deaver went with him.

"I went down to the Secret Service office in the White House basement, and they didn't know much more: there had been a shooting and the president had been taken to George Washington University Hospital. I then visited the living quarters and learned that Nancy Reagan had already gone to the hospital.

"When I returned to Baker's office, a call was coming in from Deaver at the hospital. I picked up one of the two phones (Jim was on the other), and I said, 'Was the president shot?' Mike said, 'No, he wasn't but he was hurt getting into the car.' He was called away from the phone for a few moments and then came back and said, 'He has been shot. We just found that out.' Then he said that they were preparing to take him into surgery.

"Don Regan had come over from Treasury because he had been informed by the Secret Service, and Lyn Nofziger* was

---

*Nofziger was a longtime associate and former press secretary of Reagan's who was on the White House staff.

there. I said to Don Regan, 'Get me a Secret Service car and driver to take me to the hospital.' So he gave me his car, which had a Secret Service driver in it, red light and siren. I headed down to the car, and Jim Baker said he wanted to come along, and I said fine. Then Lyn Nofziger said, 'I think I had better come and handle the press.' That sounded like a good idea, so the three of us got in the car and raced to the hospital.

"When we arrived, there were a great many newsmen outside. Secret Service and city police were at the entrance to the emergency room. Just as we entered, they were taking the president out of a treatment cubicle in the emergency room to the elevator to go to the operating floor. He obviously was in some pain but he seemed alert. Nancy Reagan was with him. We went upstairs, and she joined us later after they had gotten him into the operating room.

"They led us into a chapel, which I guess was the only place available. We stayed there for a while, and they brought in some food. I suggested to Baker that he should work with Lyn on taking care of the press, while I would contact the cabinet members who were important. I talked with Cap Weinberger, who by that time had come over to the Situation Room. I got hold of him to see if he had any additional information on what was happening and to let him know what I knew. He had increased the defense condition one notch in case there were any international ramifications—just a minor alerting of the units around the world, which doesn't do an awful lot except keep people more alert without getting anybody panicky. Then I talked with Bill Smith, the attorney general, to see if there were any reports from the law enforcement agencies about other incidents that might be related;

there were none at that time. He said he would keep me posted. I also talked with Dick Allen in the Situation Room, who was kind of the guy that we had there on the spot in the White House. Eventually we moved from the chapel—Nancy Reagan joined us—to an office complex where we had phones available.

"We kept getting reports from Dr. O'Leary and from others in the course of the afternoon, and kept in touch with the White House. At one time we received a call from the White House—or perhaps a report from the press—that Jim Brady had died. [Brady was in surgery at George Washington University Hospital, while McCarthy had been taken to Washington Hospital Center.] We had talked to the doctors, and they said that was not true. But we were hesitant to say very much about it because he was on such a tight, narrow line between life and death that we didn't think giving any information out was appropriate at that stage. That lasted until around five. The president had now come out of the operating room, I think somewhere between four and five. Nancy Reagan went up to his room. At that time, Jim went back to the White House, and I went to pick up the vice-president, who had been flying in from Texas. Rather than helicopter directly onto the White House grounds, which only the president does, he chose to helicopter to his home at the Naval Observatory, where I met him and then briefed him on the way to the White House."

Martin Anderson, chief of domestic policy planning, recalled, "I was in my office on the second floor of the West Wing, when my secretary walked in without warning, an unusual circumstance. She told me that he was shot, and for a few minutes I tried to verify that. I then walked down to the

Situation Room because that seemed to be the place where the cabinet would gather. For me, it meant going down two flights of steps and opening the door and walking in. The chief of staff, the White House counsel, and the assistant chief of staff [Baker, Meese, and Deaver] were out of the White House, and my sense was that the cabinet would be gathering there."[16]

David Gergen learned of the attack from Speakes. "We immediately gathered in Baker's office and started making phone calls. Baker was there at that time. Deaver, of course, was with the president. Baker called Haig, and then began calling others. He called the hospital as quickly as possible to find out what happened, and what was needed. But we started to ask people to come over. We asked Weinberger to come to the White House, which was really the center of operations. Richard Darman [a staff assistant to Baker] was in the room; I was there, Craig Fuller, the cabinet secretary, maybe one or two others. It was agreed that Baker should go to the hospital and direct events from there, and we then all repaired to the Situation Room. Haig came, and subsequently Weinberger. It was a group of about eight to twelve people, and varied in size. We operated from there until the time that Bush arrived, and I remained throughout except for a few moments when I left for various things.

"We had gathered in the Situation Room because it seemed the natural place. It is the communications center of the White House. It is the most secure place. We didn't know what we were dealing with, after all; we didn't know whether we had a lunatic on our hands, or some sort of conspiracy or some major threat to security. There may be some larger national security plan that calls for people to go to that room, but I'm not aware of one. It was just a better place to operate."[17]

Weinberger was working in his office at the Pentagon at about 2:30 when he was notified of a "shooting outside the hotel where President Reagan had been speaking." He asked if the president had been involved and was told by Captain Bovey, his naval aide, that "the radio reports did not indicate so." "I continued work on the briefing papers for my next meeting, which was to be a talk with Admiral Bobby Inman, who was introducing his successor at the National Security Agency, General Lincoln Faurer. . . . Captain Bovey again appeared and said that the radio had now reported that the shooting had taken place in the presence of the President, but that it appeared the President had not been hit and was in his car, apparently going to the hospital to see how some of the people who had been hit . . . were faring. . . . Admiral Inman and General Faurer came in, but almost immediately my secretary told me that the White House had called, and I was wanted at the Situation Room immediately."

Efforts were made to locate Weinberger's driver, but he could not be found. Inman then offered to drive to the White House, and Weinberger rode with him, getting more detailed radio reports indicating that the president had been hit and was under treatment at the hospital.[18] Weinberger was delayed in arriving because of the period while he reviewed his briefing papers, waited for his driver, and at length joined Inman in his car. The midafternoon traffic on the drive from the Pentagon to the White House was another delaying factor.

As word of the attack spread, other members of the cabinet continued to converge on the White House. It was possible that they might have to vote on the invocation of the Twenty-fifth Amendment to the Constitution, which provided for temporary replacement of a disabled president by the vice-president. If a crisis developed as an outgrowth of the turbulence in Poland, decisions would have to be made that required a full and accurate information base. Hence, the cabinet assembled in order to simplify communications and allow for the rapid implementation of succession provisions, if necessary. Regan claimed that the Situation Room was Allen's idea, while Haig maintained that he had suggested it to Allen. Others believed that Baker and Meese had decided on it before any cabinet members showed up.[19]

Located in an area that had once been a bowling alley for the White House staff, the Situation Room is about twenty-five feet long and fifteen feet wide with a phone-equipped table running down the center.[20] Kissinger claimed that it derived its name "from the illusion of an earlier president [than Nixon] that the international situation could be represented currently by maps on the wall."[21] It was christened the Situation Room rather than the Operations Center "to make clear that it was a facility—not a command post except in most unusual circumstances."[22] Small adjoining offices contain communications equipment for secure linking of the White House to embassies and security agencies around the world. A staff of twenty-five, under the direction of the National Security Council and the national security adviser, is responsible for handling the communications equipment and sorting out incoming data. Presidents have used the room for other than emergency purposes, such as special discussions requiring maximum security. Many other meetings on national security matters are held there, usually under the chairmanship of the national security affairs adviser or his deputy.[23]

The facility was established by Kennedy and McGeorge Bundy after the Bay of Pigs incident demonstrated the inadequacy of White House crisis management capabilities. At that time, unsecured phones had to be used to communicate decisions from the Cabinet Room to the Pentagon on the movement of U.S. ships and planes.[24] Now considered the "supersecure headquarters . . . from which the nation's most sensitive commands are issued in times of crisis,"[25] it has acquired a certain mystique as "the symbol of a president-in-action."[26] But on March 30, 1981, the Situation Room was more aptly a symbol of an administration striving to handle the crisis of a president out of action.

Haig, as secretary of state, was the senior cabinet officer and the only one with significant previous experience in the Situation Room.[27] The primary task of the group, according to Haig, was "to remain at the nerve center of the government and maintain its authority and its communications with the wounded President and with the rest of the world until the Vice President returned."[28]

The White House aides at the hospital held a different view. Baker considered the aides at the hospital the key actors, with those in the White House playing a supporting role restricted to monitoring outside information while tracking events at the hospital. Important news announcements were to come from the hospital. Speakes shared this view.[29]

The Situation Room, "tiny, uncomfortable, low ceilinged, oppressive,"[30] was seldom occupied by more than twelve people. By the time Haig entered, twenty were already packed in. Most had no function to perform. There were no windows. The air conditioners were overburdened, and the atmosphere became oppressive. So many staff members were moving in and out that Allen tried to shut the door to restrict traffic. Some left, some came back, and in a continuing chain moved out once more.[31]

More serious shortcomings began to emerge. Secure communication with the vice-president's plane was difficult. The phone link to the hospital proved difficult to keep open. Although the conference table was equipped with phones, only one was secure, to which Haig quickly laid claim. Much of the information came from the single television set on the wall. Those at the nerve center of the government had little better idea of what was happening than did the average citizen. Most of them were in the dark about the medical facts of Reagan's condition. The president's physician, Dr. Ruge, did not fully brief the cabinet on Reagan's state of health until 7:30 the next morning.[32]

Beyond these inadequacies, lack of contingency planning was the greatest source of confusion. The group in the Situation Room possessed no guidelines, formal procedures, or plans for managing crises. Bush, recently designated as the head of crisis control, was a few thousand miles away. No one was officially in charge. While the cabinet and the staff agreed informally that Bush would assume presidential power if a major crisis arose,[33] the president's condition and Bush's absence left a command vacuum in Washington.

A first priority for the government was to determine if a conspiracy was at hand, and if the United States was endangered militarily. Soon after 3 P.M., military intelligence reported detecting no unusual signs around the globe, and the FBI found no evidence of domestic disturbances. They had located Hinckley's hotel room and ascertained that he had acted alone.[34]

The White House informed the press of Reagan's injury at 3:10 P.M., shortly after the decision for surgery had been made. Bush, meanwhile, had learned that Reagan was shot,[35] and received the teletype from Haig, spelling out the known facts of the shooting. (Bush's reaction, according to House Majority Leader Jim Wright, was "one of shock and disbelief . . . that anyone could work up sufficient hatred" of Reagan to want him dead.[36] The thought occurred to Bush that he might have to assume the presidency. "I can't say it never crossed my mind. . . . But I never dwelt on it. . . . The question was more, what do you do to be helpful in a situation like this, than one of these lonely, awesome-burden seances you hear about.")[37] Haig kept the phone conversation that followed deliberately vague because of the absence of a secure phone line to the vice-president's plane.

Conventional ground-to-air phone transmissions can be monitored by a third party. Planes that have military applications generally also have encrypted communications, or at least the capability to use them. Nevertheless, the vice-president's plane was apparently lacking in voice encryption devices.

Bush's plane landed in Austin at 3:25 to refuel for the trip back to the capital.[38] Bush remained on board, where he was visited by a group of Texas officials, including Governor William Clements. Clements described Bush as "calm, and anxious to get back to Washington."[39]

At 3:30, Haig asked Gergen to prepare a brief summary of what was known at that time. Together with Regan and Allen, Haig reviewed and cleared the draft. He then called Baker, who told him that Reagan's condition was stable, but who once again "gave the impression that the President's wound was serious. Omitting any reference to the gravity of the injury, [Haig] passed this information on to Regan and Allen and Gergen and Darman.''[40]

Haig then sent a cable to foreign ambassadors saying that Reagan's condition was stable and that Bush would return to Washington soon. He spoke to House Speaker Tip O'Neill, Majority and Minority Senate leaders Robert Byrd and Howard Baker, and House Minority Leader Robert Michel. He also called former Presidents Nixon, Ford, and Carter.

The Secret Service gave Regan a preliminary report on Hinckley: his name, some background, height and weight, and the fact that he had the cards of two psychiatrists in his wallet. On one of the cards, "Call me if you need me" had been written.[41]

There had been a brief discussion of the Twenty-fifth Amendment before Baker and Meese left, with Haig participating.[42] When Baker and Meese joined Deaver at the hospital, and heard that Reagan was in stable condition, they looked at each other and "nodded agreement" that there would be no need to employ this option.[43] Some time later, after the president had gone into surgery, Baker, Meese, and Lyn Nofziger briefly discussed and again dismissed the notion of invoking the Twenty-fifth Amendment.[44]

Gergen appeared in the press briefing room at 3:37 and declared that Reagan had been shot once in the left side of his chest, adding that his condition was stable, and a decision was being made on surgery. He said that the White House was in communication with the vice-president, who was on his way to Washington. At about the same time, Weinberger and Casey arrived at the White House to join Haig, Regan, Allen, Attorney General William French Smith, Transportation Secretary Drew Lewis, domestic adviser Martin Anderson, and

White House Counsel Fred Fielding. Each member of the crisis team reported on relevant activities in his own area of responsibility. Fielding and Smith briefed Secretary Lewis and the other cabinet members on the Twenty-fifth Amendment. Meanwhile, the Air Force notified those in the Situation Room that Bush would land at Andrews Air Force Base in about two and a half hours.[45]

Fielding had brought to the Situation Room the documents required if Section 3 or 4 of the Twenty-fifth Amendment were to be invoked. These included the letters informing the Speaker of the House and the president pro tem of the Senate that the president had temporarily been relieved of the powers of office, and that the vice-president was now the acting president. While he was reviewing them in detail with Haig and Admiral Daniel Murphy (Bush's chief of staff), Darman approached and told them that neither the subject nor the documents belonged on the table. Darman was responsible to James Baker as chief of staff. He took possession of the papers and locked them in his own safe after obtaining authorization from Baker.[46] It was the kind of action that was totally outside Darman's prerogative and more properly resided in the province of the vice-president and the cabinet. Nevertheless, Haig later said, "Certainly the preparation of papers on the subject was ill-advised."[47]

Speakes, now acting as official press secretary, was sent to the White House from the hospital in order to deal with the reporters in the West Wing briefing room. Speakes was unaware of the gathering in the Situation Room and, in any case, believed that the command center was wherever Baker and Meese were located. Hence, when the reporters approached him, he went directly to the briefing room, bypassing the Situation Room, where his image soon appeared on one of the television monitors. He would not confirm whether Reagan was in surgery, and had not been instructed on how to reply to queries on the functioning of the government. When asked, "Who's running the government right now?" he was unable to answer.[48]

Haig watched the broadcast for a few minutes, got to his feet, thrust his forefinger at his own chest, and pointed toward the ceiling. He then stormed upstairs, together with Allen. He sent a note to Speakes telling him to go to the Situation Room. Delivery of the note alarmed some reporters, particularly when Speakes refused to divulge its contents and left the rostrum.[49]

Haig arrived at 4:14, just as Speakes was stepping down. He was out of breath and sweating from the climb.[50] He stepped to the podium before the reporters and cameras and said, "As of now, I am in control here in the White House, pending return of the vice-president, and in close touch with him."[51]

Asked who was making the decisions, he replied, "Constitutionally, gentlemen, you have the President, the Vice-president, and the Secretary of State, in that order."[52] His voice cracked. If his presence and statements were meant to reassure the public and the media, they may have had precisely the opposite effect. Baker and Meese, watching from the hospital, were "flabbergasted." The Situation Room group were equally astonished because Haig had neglected to consult with them before embarking on his briefing. Weinberger, returning from a phone consultation with General David Jones (chairman of the Joint Chiefs of Staff), could not believe that Haig, who had just been sitting with him, was upstairs.[53] Don Regan said to Weinberger, "What's all this about?"*⁵⁴ Haig informed the media that no alert measures were being contemplated, but Weinberger had just directed an incremental heightening of the alert level in response to some ambiguous signals concerning Soviet force readiness.⁵⁷

When Haig returned to the Situation Room, he and Weinberger had a difficult discussion. Haig questioned Weinberger's wisdom in altering the level of alert.⁵⁸ In turn, Weinberger reproved Haig for his "misstatements" on television of the alert status and of the constitutional line of succession.⁵⁹ Haig retorted to Weinberger, "You should read the Constitution," and asked Fielding whether his own version was not correct. Fielding was forced to reply, "No, Al, it isn't."⁶⁰ (Despite Haig's claim, the succession actually runs from the president, to vice-president, speaker of the house, president pro tempore of the Senate, and only then to the secretary of state and other members of the cabinet.)

At 4:55 P.M., the Secret Service informed Regan incorrectly that Brady had died.⁶¹

Baker called at 5:20 to tell the group that the Twenty-fifth

---

*Memories—and even diaries—are repositories of the true, the half true, and the false. David Gergen, eight years later, described in an interview how "Larry [Speakes] was getting into deep water. . . . Dick Allen and Haig were both concerned. . . . Al said, 'I had better go up and say something.' Dick went up, and I went with them. Al was really running. . . . He was out of breath when he got to the press briefing room. . . . He very quickly began perspiring. . . . I was there."⁵⁵ Don Regan's recollection in his memoirs was that Gergen remained in the Situation Room while Haig was appearing on television. Regan said, "Gergen looked shocked. He asked me how it had happened."⁵⁶

Here then was Regan, supposedly talking to Gergen in the Situation Room, when Gergen, by his own account, was hundreds of feet away with Al Haig and Richard Allen in the briefing room. Which story should we believe? When credible primary sources of information disagree on such specific matters, how much faith can we place in the "high government official who did not wish to be identified?"

Amendment was no longer an issue, because the bullet had been removed from the president's lung and the medical reports were encouraging. Meese informed Bush, whose plane was still an hour from Washington, that the surgery on the president had gone well. The White House staff decided to leave further briefings to the doctors. At 5:35, they learned that the reports of Brady's death were erroneous. Deaver and Nofziger remained at the hospital, while Meese went to meet Bush on his arrival.[62] Meanwhile, Baker returned to the Situation Room at 6:15 to tell the gathering that the doctors were confident that Reagan would recover fully.[63]

Bush's plane landed at Andrews Air Force Base at 6:30. A helicopter took him to the city, where he landed on the grounds of the Naval Observatory, the vice-president's official quarters, at 6:49. He arrived at the Situation Room at 7:00, and presided over a "crisis management meeting" that lasted half an hour. He asked for a report on Reagan and the other casualties, and information on Hinckley and the international situation. He also raised the question as to who in the room held "codeword" clearance.[64]

Allen reviewed the essential items: the president's health, the world intelligence situation, the status of U.S. military forces, what the press and public had been told, the information given privately to members of Congress, the outline of the statement drafted for Bush, the question of whether Bush should visit Reagan at the hospital, information about the first family, the cancellation of Bush's planned trip to Geneva, and an update on the next day's schedule. He brought up the possibility of a transfer of power, but Bush said it was not necessary, because Reagan's condition was good.[65] Bush told the group that he would hold cabinet and congressional leadership meetings the next day, and that "we want to make the government function as normally as possible." At 8:20, he went with Speakes to give a briefing to the press upstairs.[66] He announced that the president had come through surgery "with flying colors"[67] and that he could "assure the nation and a watching world the American government is functioning fully and effectively."[68]

After Bush spoke, Speakes attempted to clear up some of the confusion about the command structure. Crisis management had not been in effect, Speakes said, and the secretary of defense, not the secretary of state, was third in command after the president and vice-president.[69] He added that Bush had automatically inherited "national command authorities."[70]

The next morning, at 6:45, Baker, Deaver and Meese found Reagan propped up in bed, and they held their customary morning meeting in the hospital room rather than in the Oval Office. Reagan signed a bill restricting federal price supports for dairy products.[71]

Bush arrived at the White House at 7:45 A.M. and later presided over a cabinet meeting. He met with a bipartisan group of congressional leaders and then visited the hospital. It was decided that Bush would substitute for the president at the Tuskegee Institute, in Alabama, the following week. He spoke to reporters in a hallway of the Capitol shortly after 11:00 and told them that during his brief visit to the hospital he had found Reagan awake but in need of rest. Throughout the day, the president's men were occupied with the problem of creating an illusion of "normality." Bush was carrying out a larger role than usual in filling in for the president. He had a working lunch with the prime minister of the Netherlands. But it was emphasized that Reagan was in control and would be involved in important decisions, such as might be required if the situation in Poland worsened. Bush also insisted that there was no rift between Haig and Weinberger.[72]

The events in Poland now seemed less explosive after Solidarity voted to abandon plans for a general strike.[73]

On Wednesday, the National Security Council met and approved in principle the sale of AWACS and F-15s to the Saudis.[74]

The following day, April 2, Weinberger stated that the possibility of Soviet intervention in Poland had heightened in the last twenty-four to forty-eight hours. Stepped-up troop movements were observed near Poland, and *Pravda* attacked the Polish Communists with increased intensity.[75]

By Friday, it was reported that the Soviets had begun airlifting helicopters into their military district headquarters in Legnica, in southwest Poland, and that they had established an autonomous communications network allowing them to bypass the Polish military command. Russian and East German troops were organizing fuel and munitions depots just inside the Polish border. An increase in coded radio transmissions and in military transport flights to Soviet airfields in Poland was observed. A disproportionate amount of the exercise was devoted to landing operations on the Polish coast. Meanwhile, *Pravda* attacked the Polish government again, criticizing the party leader Stanislaw Kania for making concessions to Solidarity. A State Department spokesman asserted that Soviet readiness for a possible intervention was at a higher level than at the time when Carter had been told of an imminent incursion.[76]

With the president now febrile and battling an infection in his lungs, Baker, Deaver, Meese, and Darman once again considered invoking the Twenty-fifth Amendment. Reagan was scheduled to undergo bronchoscopy, a procedure in which a tube passed through the mouth into the lungs allowed a look at the bronchial tubes to localize sources of bleeding. Anesthesia was sometimes required. Members of the White House staff had requested that heavy sedation be avoided so that the president would be capable of making a decision on the response to the Polish crisis if necessary. Bush was never told that he might have to be acting president.[77]

In spite of the president's condition, Weinberger left for Europe to meet with the NATO leaders and to preserve the appearance of "business as usual," while Haig departed for a ten-day mission to the Middle East. He delayed his departure time in order to confer once more on the situation in Poland.[78]

During the weekend of April 4 and 5, the cabinet remained concerned about the Polish situation, and Weinberger commented in London that the Soviet force buildup in and around Poland was continuing. On Monday, the eighth day after the attack, Brezhnev flew to Prague for meetings with other Warsaw Pact leaders at the Czech Communist party meeting. He had not attended such a meeting for several years. The commander in chief of the Warsaw Pact forces, Marshal Viktor G. Kulikov, supported by other military leaders, had apparently been leading a campaign to persuade Brezhnev to intervene in Poland.[79] Bush briefed Reagan on the events abroad and then told reporters that the president was "fully on top of the situation." Reagan sent a strongly worded message to Brezhnev on Soviet military moves in and around Poland.[80]

While Reagan ran a slight fever on Tuesday, he was now said to be handling paperwork for about an hour each day.[81]

Weinberger, in Europe, said that Poland was threatened by invasion by "osmosis," a gradual filtering in of Soviet forces and supplies.[82]

In Prague, Brezhnev listened as the Czech leader Gustav Husak warned that the Warsaw Pact members would not passively watch the undermining of the Communist system in Poland.[83]

By Wednesday, Reagan's fever had subsided, but his aides decided that he was "too feverish to tackle a complicated one-page 'decision memo' on leasing of the outer continental shelf for oil and gas exploration." Letters that Haig carried to Middle Eastern heads of state were not reviewed by Reagan as they normally would have been.[84]

Brezhnev said that he thought the Polish Communists would be able to end the crisis themselves. Eight hours later, the military exercises in and around Poland ended.[85]

Although Reagan's work load was increased to two hours per day on Thursday, visitors reported that he had lost weight and looked drawn.[86]

NATO defense ministers warned the Soviet Union that military intervention in Poland "would have profound implications for all aspects of East-West relations."[87]

The next day, Weinberger contended that Soviet intervention was still a "real possibility" despite the appearance of a more conciliatory Soviet attitude. Haig, on the other hand, said the United States was "somewhat relieved" by developments in Poland. Both the House and Senate budget committees rejected Reagan's tax proposals.[88]

On Saturday, April 11, the day the president left the hospital, the Polish parliament approved a resolution calling for a two-month suspension of strikes, citing extreme economic conditions.[89]

During the next week, Reagan increased his work load to four or five hours per day.[90]

A few days later, the Polish Communist party, in its first detailed commentary on the military exercises conducted earlier in the month, said that they were "exceptionally modest" and that the West had exaggerated their size to make them seem a threat to Polish sovereignty.[91]

On Saturday, April 24, Reagan met in closed session with the cabinet for his first White House appearance since the shooting.[92]

5

Confusion: In the White House and the Hospital

THE ADMINISTRATION THAT HAD COME TO POWER ON JANUARY 20, 1981, was clearly unprepared for a wounded president seventy days later, on March 30. The White House legal staff's "emergency book" had not yet been put together, as Counsel Fred Fielding would acknowledge some years later.[1] On the morning of the attack, Larry Speakes had completed planning a meeting with the Secret Service for 4:00 P.M. to determine how they should handle an assassination attempt against the president. The meeting never took place.*[2]

---

*Speakes had been working on President Ford's staff on the two occasions when attempts were made on his life. On September 22, 1975, when Sara Jane Moore's bullet barely missed Ford in San Francisco, Speakes was unable to obtain any information from the Secret Service or

Speakes was the assistant to the wounded James Brady, who had served as a shrewd, effective, and popular press secretary.[4] When Speakes returned to the White House from the hospital, he was now under the gun, substituting for a boss who was used to the pressure of the media and the moment. His information was sparse. On reaching an office crowded with people at 4 P.M., he was asked whether U.S. forces were on increased alert. "Not that I am aware of," he said.[5] Other questions followed:

Q: Would [the Vice President] assume emergency powers? . . .
SPEAKES: Not that I am aware of. . . .
Q: If the President goes into surgery and goes under anesthesia, would Vice President Bush become the acting president . . . ?
SPEAKES: I cannot answer that question. . . .
Q: Larry, who'll be determining the status of the President and whether the Vice President, should, in fact become the acting President?
SPEAKES: I don't know the details on that.[6]

---

the San Francisco police. The motorcade traveling with Ford to the San Francisco airport had been placed on radio silence. Not until Ford's limousine reached *Air Force 1* on the tarmac at the airport could Speakes determine what had happened and inform the press. It was in the light of that experience that Speakes planned the meeting with the Secret Service for March 30.[3]

Al Haig, the Man "in Control"

Speakes was unaware that those in the Situation Room were viewing his exchange with the media on television. Don Regan apparently spoke for the group when he said, "We were amazed. There were cries of 'Get that guy off!' and 'Why is he saying that?' and 'Who authorized that?' "[7]

"What's he doing there?" Haig asked.

"Haig was visibly restless during this performance, and said Speakes should not be answering questions," according to Weinberger.[8] Haig jumped up, turned to Allen, and said, "We've got to straighten this out."

Haig believed that Speakes's comments raised more questions than they answered and implied uncertainty in the White House. He took it upon himself to fix what he saw as a critical problem: the perception that with Reagan out of commission, no one was in command of the government.[9] He stepped to the podium in the press room to clarify the situation.

QUESTION: Who is making the decisions for the government right now?

HAIG: Constitutionally, gentlemen, you have the president, the vice-president, the secretary of state, in that order. . . . As of now, I am in control here, in the White House. . . .[10]

There was an eruption in the Situation Room once more. Weinberger, who had been on the phone outside, returned, saw Haig on a monitor, and commented, "I wonder why they're running an old tape of Al Haig's."[11] When he realized that Haig was actually appearing before the media in the briefing room and heard some of his responses, he said, "I can't believe this. He's wrong; he doesn't have any such authority."[12]

Haig's assertions provoked a flood of criticism. Designed to restore the confidence of the public in the solidity of the leadership, they had the opposite effect. One reporter commented, "I had never seen Haig look so shaken or sound so unsteady. It made me wonder just how serious the president's condition was."[13] Haig was characterized as the only top White House official to "choke up" in the crisis.[14] Richard Allen said, "I thought he was going to collapse. His legs were shaking as if they were gelatinous. It was extraordinary, absolutely extraordinary."[15] Don Regan said, "Is he mad?"[16]

Larry Speakes, who had occasioned Haig's dash to reassure the nation, later said that Haig "lost control." "Haig seemed to panic under pressure; the beads of perspiration on his forehead and his out-of-breath declaration gave a concerned public reason to worry. From then on, other members of the Reagan team would be viewing him with suspicion, and within fifteen months their hazing would drive him out of the White House. . . . In doing my best to answer a difficult question . . . I set in motion the events that would bring an early end to the political career of someone as formidable as Al Haig."[17]

Martin Anderson was viewing Speakes on the television monitor, when suddenly Haig disappeared from the Situation Room. "Haig was upset because Speakes was giving the impression that he didn't know what was going on, but Speakes couldn't know, because *none of us in the Situation Room actually knew what was going on* [italics added]. Haig took it upon himself, knowing the enormous audience he would have, to assert a stronger role than he could possibly have had. If it is true that Jim Baker told him that he should be the 'contact point,' that surely did not mean that he was in charge. It meant that he was a messenger. Allen actually was chairing the meeting. If anyone was in charge of the Situation Room, it probably should have been Allen because that was an extension of the national security adviser's domain. Casey, because of the strength of his personality, might have taken over, but certainly no one would have listened to Haig."[18]

Furthermore, his remarks "set off an explosion of concern. . . . For millions of Americans watching for news of whether President Reagan was alive or dead, Haig's words sounded ominously like a veiled grasp for power," according to Anderson. "What he saw, and seized, was an opportunity to talk to millions and millions of Americans and to give them the impression that he was in charge. It was literally a once in a lifetime opportunity to show his stuff to the country. Haig had toyed with the idea of running for president before he became Secretary of State. . . ."[19]

David Gergen had a different perception. "What triggered Haig entering the press briefing room," he said, "was that Speakes came back [from the hospital] and was not yet plugged in to the Situation Room. He went directly into the press room, and probably didn't realize what he was going to run into, because there was an army of cameras there and an enormous amount of pressure. We were watching in the Situation Room on live television, and Larry was getting into what we thought was deep water on this question of state of alert, readiness, what was going on. Haig was extremely upset, as were others in the room, about the message that was being delivered. Dick Allen and Haig both were concerned, and others agreed that we had to correct the record; we had to set things straight. It was at that point that Al said, 'I had better go up and say something.' So he left the room on the double because he wanted to get Larry off the podium and just take over, in effect. Dick Allen went up, and I went with him. Al was really running because he thought there was damage being done.

"If you look at the geography of that place, he had to run through a couple of hallways, not that far, but then up a set of stairs, and then bang, right into the press briefing room—well, this was a man who was out of breath when he got to the press briefing room. And suddenly, you walk in and an incredible number of cameras are staring at you with all of this light and everything like that, and he very quickly began perspiring. I was there. I think what happened was that he had not had time to think about it, and he arrived breathless. When he got up on the podium and started getting questions . . . it came out in a very unfortunate way. He's lived with that politically ever since. But it conveyed an extremely misleading impression of the actual control that he exhibited throughout the afternoon in the room. I will just tell you that there are those who have reason in their memoirs to hurt him, and I think they have treated him unfairly.

"I had worked with Al Haig when he was chief of staff in the Nixon years. He was an extraordinarily steady player under much more difficult circumstances than what we faced on this day. There were various suggestions that his heart problems had changed him when he came over as secretary of state. Indeed, I thought he was more volatile than I had remembered him. But I was with him there for three or four hours in the Situation Room—he was calm, very steady, very much in control of the meeting. He ran things well; he ran them crisply."[20]

Haig had his own version of the episode: "I was wholly intent on correcting any impression of confusion and indecision that Speakes's words may have inadvertently created. Certainly I was guilty of a poor choice of words, and optimistic if I imagined that I would be forgiven the imprecision out of respect for the tragedy of the occasion. My remark that I was 'in control . . . pending the return of the Vice President' was a statement of the fact that I was the senior Cabinet officer present. I was talking about the arrangements we had made in the situation room for the three- or four-hour period in which we awaited the return of the Vice President from Texas. Less precise, though in the same context, was my statement that *'constitutionally* . . . you have the President, the Vice President, and the Secretary of State, in that order.' I ought to have said 'traditionally' or 'administratively' instead of 'constitutionally.' If, at the time, anyone had suggested to me that I believed that the Secretary of State was third in order of succession to the President, the press would have had the pleasure of even more vivid quotes. For many months, in this same house, I had lived hourly with the question of succession in case of the removal first of a Vice President and then of a President; I knew the Constitution by heart on this subject."[21]

Meese viewed Haig's appearance as an effort "to reassure our allies and other people." And Baker corroborated Haig's account: "I personally had discussions with Haig in which we agreed that he would be our point of contact here in the situation room at the White House, as he quite properly should have been as the senior Cabinet officer. . . ."[22] Deaver noted that "it was understood that Haig, as the senior Cabinet officer, should run the Situation Room."[23]

But the damage had been done, and the picture of Haig—drawn, sweating, anxious—would remain in the public mind as a symbol of instability, as would his apparent confusion over the succession.

Haig versus Weinberger: Who Was in Charge?

Because the State Department was the first cabinet department created by an act of Congress in 1789, the secretary of state is the senior cabinet officer. Next in line is the secretary of the treasury, and third is the secretary of defense. Quite apart from the laws of succession, what Haig meant—in his response to the question as to who was making the decisions—was that after the president and vice-president, the secretary of state was the most senior person in the executive branch in the general line of authority.

When Haig returned to the Situation Room, Weinberger claimed that Ed Meese had told him that the secretary of defense was third in line of command after the president and the vice-president. Haig correctly stated, "On defense matters, this was quite true. . . ."[24] But the nation was in the midst of a civil crisis, not a military confrontation, so Weinberger's comment on the "third in line of command" depended on what he meant by "command."

Weinberger was referring to the National Command Authority (NCA), designed to govern the authority to order the use of nuclear weapons. Meese had told Weinberger, "Under these circumstances, it is my understanding the National Command Authority devolves on you."[25] Weinberger, however, stated that the chain included the vice-president, rather than just the president and secretary of defense, as stipulated in the National Security Act and the Defense Department directive of 1972.[26] The vice-president's role in the National Command Authority was and still is a somewhat ambiguous matter. In the Carter administration, Walter Mondale was included and received briefings on the details of emergency nuclear command. The arrangement was then apparently continued in the Reagan administration.[27] But the presumption had been that the vice-president, if he was in the National Command Authority, would play a role only if the president was disabled, an event that should have been signaled by the invocation of the Twenty-fifth Amendment.

The argument that took place in the Situation Room, however, had less to do with the National Command Authority than with Haig's apparent misstatement of the constitutional guidelines for succession.[28] The Constitution refers only to the vice-president as successor to the president. From 1792 to 1886, the Succession Act named the president of the Senate pro tem and the Speaker of the House as successors if both the president and the vice-president should be dead or incapacitated. In 1886, that was changed to make the secretary of state, treasury, war, and so on, successors in the order of the creation of their departments. Not until 1947 was the present succession established by the Congress—the vice-president, Speaker of the House, president pro tem of the Senate, and members of the cabinet in the order in which their departments had been established.[29] With the Twenty-fifth Amendment, in 1967, the problem of "temporary" disability was finally dealt with.

Haig had misstated the "succession" but not the sequence of executive authority in peacetime. Weinberger said, "Haig seemed to be referring to the old statute, under the now superseded constitutional provisions, that established the Secretary of State as the next to take over in the event of the death or disability of the President and the Vice President. That statute has long since been changed by the Congress, by Acts of September 9, 1965, and October 15, 1966, under the Twenty-fifth Amendment to the Constitution, to provide that after the President and Vice President, the succession devolves, not upon the Secretary of State, but on the Speaker of the House and then the President Pro Tem of the Senate. I [Weinberger] repressed an impulse to tell him [Haig] that if he had read the current version of the Constitution he would find that some of his statements on television were not correct."[30]

Weinberger was mistaken, however, in his belief that the succession to the Speaker of the House and beyond originated in the Twenty-fifth Amendment, which dealt more with the mechanism for temporary replacement of a temporarily disabled president. The current Law of Succession was actually passed on July 18, 1947, rather than on September 9, 1965, and October 15, 1966, as Weinberger stated.*

---

*Weinberger was in fact referring to the recapitulation of the Law of Succession included in the amendment of September 9, 1965, that simply added the secretary of health, education, and welfare and the secretary of housing and urban development to the chain of succession. His second reference, to October 15, 1966, was to the amendment that incorporated

The uproar occasioned by Haig's statements in the briefing room forced the administration to attempt to clarify the matter.

One effort that further befogged the issue was made by Speakes. At a 9 P.M. press conference on Monday, March 30, he spoke of the National Command Authority as though it had been brought into play. He said that Bush had "automatically" assumed "national command authorities" (usually the province of the president) to respond to emergencies during Reagan's surgery. He failed to make clear that he was describing a chain of command governing nuclear weapons use and applied only in certain military crises. There was no evidence that such a military crisis actually existed, nor was it clear what powers were now delegated to Bush with the president still "in command." One former national security official suggested that such an interposition in the chain of command, without invocation of the Twenty-fifth Amendment, might well represent a violation of the National Security Act.[32]

Speakes also said that Weinberger, the secretary of defense, not Haig, would be third in command, after the vice-president.[33] This further compounded the confusion because he did not make clear that he was referring only to a military crisis. Speakes subsequently reported that Haig had been "completely wrong when he thought he was in command" while Weinberger was in the White House.[34]

Speakes's characterization of command authority succession was viewed, whether rightly or wrongly, as an inadver-

---

the secretary of transportation in the chain of succession.[31] Neither of these amendments to the Sucession Act of 1947 was "under the Twenty-fifth Amendment to the Constitution," as Weinberger had said. Whereas Haig misstated the succession, Weinberger confused the Twenty-fifth Amendment with the Law of Succession.

tent revelation of a secret arrangement within the administration. If the president had been dead or declared incapacitated under the Twenty-fifth Amendment, his successor (the vice-president) would have assumed command authority.[35] But the president was alive and said to be "in command at all times," so a transfer of his powers to the vice-president was not legal, nor was there any way in which the vice-president could preempt the authority of the secretary of defense except for explicit delegation of authority by the president. Beyond the legal aspects, Bush was in flight to Washington at precisely the time he was supposed to have assumed command authority,[36] and there is no evidence that he was informed of his new and broadened responsibilities.

"As the afternoon wore on, the Reagan White House left the distinct impression it didn't know who was in control," according to an experienced White House correspondent.[37] Not long after Speakes's conference, Gergen conceded that officials were hazy on the succession statutes and suggested that the arrangements Speakes had referred to were "informal."[38] Don Regan bluntly declared, "We Cabinet members had never been instructed on the chain of command under various circumstances," which explained our "ignorance."[39]

On the following day, the matter was again "clarified" by the White House staff: Situation Room protocol normally invested the defense secretary with responsibility second only to the president's because it is technically a military command post. It contains the communication lines to the Pentagon and other military centers. (After Lyndon Johnson's decision to bomb targets in Vietnam, operational authority was vested in the secretary of defense, even in the presence of the secretary of state.)[40]

But the nation was at peace, and under normal circumstances, Richard Allen, the national security adviser, was responsible for much of the day-to-day activity in the Situation Room.

The disagreement was convoluted because four issues were involved: (1) the succession, as defined in the Constitution and congressional acts; (2) seniority in the cabinet; (3) the National Command Authority; and (4) authority in the Situation Room. Since no military crisis existed, Haig, in Bush's absence, should have been considered the highest official. Furthermore, Baker and Meese, with or without proper authority, had told Haig to be the contact man in the White House.[41] (Does the White House chief of staff give directions to the senior cabinet officer in a presidential emergency? Are there legal grounds for such an assumption of power, or does it establish a far-reaching precedent which degrades the authority of duly appointed officials? Although the president has broad rights to delegate authority, did he actually do so?)

In yet another attempt to clear up the muddle, James Baker told reporters on Tuesday, March 31, that the cabinet had gathered in the Situation Room to invoke the Twenty-fifth Amendment, or the National Command Authority (NCA), if necessary. Both steps were rejected, he said, specifying that the NCA applied only in "a narrow set of circumstances," which were classified.[42]

Further clarification (or confusion) was furnished by Defense Department lawyers, who released a statement saying that the chain of command ran at all times from the president to the secretary of defense, directly contradicting Speakes's Monday night assertion that had Bush ahead of Weinberger.[43]

Speakes has explained his vague answers at the first press

briefing on Monday: "In the hectic events that had followed the gunshots, no one had considered passing the reins of power. . . ."[44] Even his later, second briefing, with details about command authority succession, was disavowed by Baker.

Confusion on the Twenty-fifth Amendment

The uncertainty of administration spokesmen on the various succession stipulations existed in parallel with discussions among government lawyers. When Reagan was in the operating room, the Justice Department's Office of Legal Counsel was involved in an analysis of the implications of the Twenty-fifth Amendment. For days afterward, White House, State and Defense Department lawyers held intensive discussions on the succession provisions. Although Fielding was "confident that the command authority procedures that we have established cover every contingency,"[45] an extraordinary lack of coherence and clarity dominated the White House comments that followed the shooting. The cabinet agreed informally to treat Bush as the person who would assume presidential power if a crisis occurred while Reagan was anesthetized; they were thus in effect ignoring the need to invoke the Twenty-fifth Amendment before such a transfer of power could occur.

One cabinet member summed up his experience in the Situation Room: "The men at the heart of the government did not possess much more information than the ordinary citizen. . . . Even less did the men gathered in the Situation

Room know what action they were authorized to take or expected to take."[46]

This confusion, as we shall see in chapter 9, was at the heart of the rejection of invocation of the Twenty-fifth Amendment after Reagan was injured.

Haig versus Weinberger: Alerting the Armed Forces

Weinberger arrived at the White House at 3:37 P.M., according to Haig, who sensed that "Weinberger seemed somewhat self-conscious. Perhaps he was embarrassed by his late arrival. The attack on the President had taken place slightly more than an hour before."[47]

In Weinberger's version, he reached the Situation Room "a few minutes before 3:00."[48] This was the first of several discrepancies in their records of the events. By Haig's account, Weinberger, shortly after his arrival, abruptly said, "I have raised the alert status of our forces." Haig was shocked by his words.

"Depending on the nature of the instructions issued by Weinberger, any such change would be detected promptly by the Soviet Union. In response, the Russians might raise their own alert status, and that could cause a further escalation on our side. The fact that this was happening would be reported on television and radio, and the news would let loose more emotion, exacerbating the existing climate of anxiety and anger and fear. Moreover, the Soviet leaders might very well conclude that the United States, in a flight of paranoia, believed that the U.S.S.R. was involved in the attempt to assassinate the President. Why would we alert our military forces if a lone psychotic had been responsible? The consequences were incalculable.

" 'Cap,' I said, 'what do you mean? Have you changed the Defcon* [defense condition] of our forces?' "

"I cannot recall Weinberger's exact words, but his reply did not answer my question. He appeared, instead, to be quibbling over my choice of words.

" 'This is important, Cap,' I said. 'Will you please tell us exactly what you've done?' "

"Here I again used the term 'Defcon' and other shorthand terminology to describe different states of strategic military readiness. This jargon is commonplace to all who have been involved in the Presidential management of strategic, that is to say nuclear, forces. *Weinberger did not respond in a way that suggested he was fully familiar with these terms* [italics added]. This was natural enough: he had not dealt with such matters in the past, and he had been Secretary of Defense for barely ninety days, hardly long enough to absorb the complete vocabulary of the job. I kept pressing him for a clear description of his actions. At length, he said that he had ordered pilots of the Strategic Air Command to their bases. 'Then you've raised the Defcon,' I said.

"He disagreed. This raised the temperature of the conver-

---

*"Defense Condition 5," Weinberger later wrote, "essentially means that our forces are in their normal peacetime condition: some in training, some on leave, etc. There are four Defense Conditions requiring higher degrees of readiness and alertness. In DEFCON 4, there are always some Air Force crews ready to take off in 12 to 15 minutes. DEFCON 1, the highest degree of readiness, would be declared if hostilities were imminent or actually under way."[49]

sation. I began to suspect that Weinberger did not know whether he had raised the Defcon or, if he had raised it, to what level. Once again, in the plainest possible language, I asked Weinberger to describe the action he had taken.

" 'I'll go find out,' he said. He left the room in order to telephone in private. He was absent for perhaps ten minutes. When he returned, he told us, unequivocally, that he had not formally raised the alert status of our forces. He had merely sent a message to field commanders informing them officially of the situation in Washington. Most important, U.S. strategic forces remained in their normal defense condition."[50]

Meanwhile, Haig had rushed to the briefing room to counteract Speakes's vague responses, and in his first comment to the media stated, "There are absolutely no alert measures that are necessary at this time. . . ."[51]

"On my return to the Situation Room," Haig recalled, "Weinberger expressed displeasure at my statement on the alert status of American forces. I was surprised and asked if I had not been correct in my understanding of what he had told the crisis team earlier on this subject. Weinberger gave no clear answer. I said, 'Cap, are we or are we not on an increased alert status?' Instead of answering my question in direct fashion, he referred to the status of Soviet submarines off our coasts."[52]

Weinberger's account is quite different. He left the room during Speakes's exchange with the press so as to talk with General David Jones, chairman of the Joint Chiefs of Staff. It was during this discussion with Jones that he requested an increase in the alert for the Strategic Air Command forces, and his confrontation with Haig *followed* Haig's televised performance, rather than both *preceding and following* it, as Haig suggested.

"I then asked about the alert condition of our forces. General Jones said there had been no change in the alert and that the major part of the forces were in the condition called DEFCON 5 (Defense Condition 5), except that, as was normal, some Strategic Air Command bomber crews and other forces were on the next higher degree of alert, called DEFCON 4.

". . . I asked about the position of the Soviet forces, and he said they were more or less normal except that there were two Soviet submarines 'outside the box'. . . . USSR submarines within the normal area are called 'inside the box.' The two that General Jones referred to that were 'outside the box' were somewhat closer to the United States than was normal. . . . General Jones said that having two Soviet subs outside the box was not considered extremely unusual. . . .

"We discussed the general differences between DEFCON 5 and DEFCON 4. I still had in mind the possibility that more than the assassination of the President was intended, so I then told General Jones that we should increase the alert for the Strategic Air Command forces, not raising it to DEFCON 3, but that instead of having the alert bomber crews on regular alert and restricted to their *bases* . . . , they should now be restricted to the *alert area* within the base, which would save anywhere from three to six or seven minutes in getting the bombers aloft if need be."[53]

Weinberger returned to the Situation Room and noticed everyone watching Haig on the television screen. He heard him say that no alert had been given to our forces or was contemplated, and that none was necessary.

When Haig reentered the Situation Room, he told those gathered that they should all act in accordance with the statements he had just made.

Weinberger said, " 'Al, one problem with that is that you should know I have already ordered an increase, although a very small one, in the alert conditions of the Strategic Air crews,' and I then told him of my call to General Jones."

"Haig said, 'Did you do this simply because of the Soviet subs, or because of the incident?' " I said that I did it because of the incident, and because I did not know whether it was simply an isolated incident or the opening episode of some coordinated plan, and that the location of the two Soviet subs mentioned above had indeed also been part of the reason.

"He pressed again, stating in effect that the only reason I had changed the alert was because of the subs.

"I said that, no, it was because I did not know enough about the whole matter, and that it seemed to me a prudent and necessary thing to do. He argued that the fact that I had taken that step might get out, and would tend to discredit his previous statement on television. . . .

"I told him that it was only a small increase in the alert posture, that I had not raised the regular SAC alert condition to DEFCON 3 . . . but that in any event it seemed more important to me to make that increase in the alert than to worry about whether any statements he had just made on television were contradicted or not. He pressed again on the matter, saying something to the effect that it wouldn't be a good thing for the fact that I had changed that alert to get out.

"I responded that it was my understanding that I had to make decisions in the field, and that the decision I had made represented my best judgment. He said that I should read the Constitution."[54]

Weinberger claimed that the disagreement was not a serious one, but others described it as "a dramatic moment of confrontation. Their differences were clear and sharp."[55] Haig was manifestly irritated.[56] In Deaver's words, "The two of them squared off and angry words were exchanged."[57] According to Speakes, "An angry discussion over who was in charge erupted, with Haig and Weinberger glaring at each other across the table."[58]

The issue is not a trivial one. Haig was concerned that an increase in the alert level of our forces might be misinterpreted by Soviet leaders, and that some kind of "ratcheting" effect might occur, particularly with the possibility of a Soviet invasion of Poland. Weinberger was new on the job, and probably unfamiliar with the details of the "DEFCON" ladder, certainly in Haig's eyes. The concept that a domestic crisis might have important international ramifications— caused by precipitate and uninformed actions on Weinberger's part—was a central consideration underlying Haig's peppery response to the change in alert.

Communications Problems

Many of the miscues that plagued the White House at the time of the shooting stemmed directly from inadequacies of the communications system. The problem with secure lines to Bush on *Air Force 2* has already been described.[59] Even the seemingly prosaic task of establishing and maintaining contact between the White House and George Washington University Hospital proved complicated. After the initial call from Deaver, the line was kept open with difficulty, and reports dribbled into the White House "from time to time."[60] Forty minutes passed before secure voice channels were set up from the hospital to the White House.[61] Speakes's ineptness before the media (and Haig's explosive response) stemmed from a lack of information to support the effort to inform the public.

Baker and the other top aides believed that the presidency and the U.S. government followed the president wherever he went. Baker adopted the approach that news announcements should be made at the hospital; officials at the White House "would merely echo them."[62] But there were more reporters at the White House than at the hospital.

Weinberger had to leave the conference room to make secure calls to the Pentagon, using equipment located in a small office outside the Situation Room.[63]

To a great extent, the cabinet members and staff in the Situation Room, with access to the world's most sophisticated communications gear, were dependent on sources outside the government for their information. They learned of Speakes's ambiguous press briefing at the same time as the rest of the world.[64]

The report of the "death" of James Brady demonstrated how rapidly misinformation could be spread. Once Brady reached the George Washington University Hospital emergency room, it was quickly determined that the wound might be fatal and that his only hope was surgery. A CAT scan of his brain was discouraging, but the neurosurgeon, Dr. Arthur Kobrine, moved quickly to take him to surgery, open the skull, and clean out the blood, bullet fragments, and dead tissue. Six hours later the surgery was complete, and still no one was able to predict what the final outcome would be.[65]

Meanwhile, at 4:55 P.M., Secretary Regan was informed by the Secret Service that Brady had died. Regan announced the news to the group, and Allen asked for a moment of silent prayer. The Secret Service agents had gotten the news from an FBI agent. Regan informed Senate Majority Leader Howard Baker, and the news quickly moved to the networks.[66] It was reported to the nation a few minutes later, after two sources, one in the White House, the other on Capitol Hill, "confirmed" it.[67] Apparently, a reporter had asked David Prosperi, a White House press aide, if Brady had died, and Prosperi, responding to a question from a different reporter on a different subject, answered, "Yes." At 5:41, almost an hour after the first report of Brady's death, Speakes received a denial from the hospital and reported in the press briefing room that Brady was still alive.[68]

The extraordinary aspect of the confusion over Brady was that the Situation Room had an open line to the hospital; Baker, Meese, and Deaver were all at the hospital; and Dr. Ruge was also available to confirm or deny the report. But Baker, Meese, Deaver, and Nancy Reagan saw and heard the news of Brady's death as they were watching television in one of the doctor's offices,[69] and apparently nobody thought to ask Dr. Ruge until fifty minutes after the report had gone out to the country.

When the news of Brady's death was broadcast, Dr. Kobrine, operating on Brady, was informed of it by one of the physicians. "No one has told Mr. Brady or me," he replied.[70]

The President's Nuclear Code Card

When Reagan left the Hilton Hotel, he was accompanied by a military aide carrying a briefcase. There are three aides, one from each service branch, one always on duty. The aide rides, along with the president's physician, in the "control car," third in line in the motorcade.[71] He is responsible for the football (or "black box" or "black bag"), a briefcase containing the codes and targeting information the president would require to order or authorize a nuclear attack. His job is to remain close to the president at all times in case a nuclear military emergency arises.[72]

When Hinckley fired, the aide, Lieutenant Colonel José Muratti, dropped to the ground. He rose immediately after the shots, ran for the motorcade, and was picked up by the "control" car. Muratti arrived at the hospital shortly after Reagan, and stayed into the evening.[73]

The aides who carry the football know the lock combination and allegedly are "never more than a few steps away" from the president.* "Not one president could open the football—only the warrant officers, the military aides, and the Director of the Military Office have the combination."[76]

The football was instituted in response to the development of ICBMs, which reduced the delivery time to minutes. It was designed to enable the president to order a nuclear attack within thirty minutes no matter where he was located. During the Eisenhower administration, both Eisenhower and Nixon had footballs. When Kennedy and Johnson entered the White House, a football was sent to Johnson's office. A Johnson aide returned it, saying that the vice-president did not want it. Vice-President Bush apparently had his own version of the

---

*When President Carter visited his home in Plains, Georgia, the football and the aide stayed at a hotel in Americus, Georgia, ten miles from Plains.[75]

football, which was close by at the time of the shooting of Reagan.[77]

At the time of Kennedy's assassination, the football was "a thirty-pound metal suitcase with an intricate combination lock. Within were various Strangelove packets, each bearing wax seals and the signatures of the Joint Chiefs. Inside one were cryptic numbers which would permit the President to set up a crude hot line to the Prime Minister of the United Kingdom and the President of France on four minutes' notice. A second provided the codes that would launch a nuclear attack. The rest contained pages of close text . . . carefully designed so that any one of Kennedy's three military aides could quickly tell him how many million casualties would result [from the various targeting options available]."[78]

By Ford's tenure, it had evolved into "a very slim and elegant [briefcase]: supple black pebble-grained leather with a flap of soft leather fastened by four silver snaps."[79] A more recent description listed the contents as a seventy-five-page "black book" of targeting options (the set of choices presented is reportedly "virtually incomprehensible"); a book, about the same size as the "black book," listing secret presidential evacuation sites; an eight- to ten-page manila folder describing procedures for the Emergency Broadcast System; and a three-by-five-inch card of authentication codes.[80]

It was this "football," then, that Jose Muratti carried as he dropped to the ground when he heard the shots from Hinckley's gun. If Muratti had been wounded, what would have happened to the football? Would the D.C. police have taken it as "evidence" to the city jail? Would the FBI have held it in its headquarters?

Each person with a role in the emergency procedures, including potential presidential successors, receives an authentication card. Each card is numbered: the president's is number 1, the vice-president's number 2, and so on. Other than the identification numbers, the cards are imprinted with identical arrangements of numbers and letters which, when read back, "provide an easy way of verifying that the person you're talking to has a card and therefore is on the list of players involved in the decision-making process."[81]

While Reagan was in surgery, the FBI took possession of his voice authorization code card, the only authentication device personally carried by the president. The card is designed specifically to cover situations in which secure voice communications are unavailable.[82]

Reagan usually kept the card in his wallet, which at the time was in his jacket pocket. His jacket had been stripped off in the emergency room and scooped up later during evidence gathering by local police, Secret Service technicians, and FBI agents. FBI agents discovered the code card as they catalogued the items recovered. While the president was in surgery, Muratti and Edward V. Hickey, Jr., a White House security assistant, interrupted the FBI agents to ask for the code card back. The FBI refused to return it. Attorney General William French Smith, in communication from the Situation Room with the FBI command center, backed the refusal. The card was not returned until two days later.[83]

Administration officials contended that the nuclear command system had in no way been affected by the removal of Reagan's card. They said that it was just a part of the system and that its importance was "academic" because Bush had been in contact with the White House and Weinberger. In a military situation, presidential orders would be fed to the defense secretary. Under Reagan administration rules, the vice-president, if the president was disabled, would issue military orders to the defense secretary.[84]

While it is true that the president was in no condition to deal with a crisis, at no time was his disability legally declared, which could have been done only by invoking the Twenty-fifth Amendment.

The attorney general's actions during the incident were particularly perplexing. The authentication card had no possible value as evidence.[85] Its role was to facilitate communication between command principals over unsecured lines, such as those that linked the aides at the hospital to the cabinet members in the White House. Smith's rationale for instructing the FBI to retain possession remains unexplained.

But the confusion over the location of the president's authorization code card raised questions about the fail-safe character of the command of nuclear weapons.[86] In particular, it brought into focus the problem of whether the mandated protocol of temporary succession means anything when an incapacitated president is declared competent, and whether it will hold sway over predelegated authority or the definition of the chain of command in the National Command Authority. Does predelegated authority survive an incapacitated or deceased president? Since no executive can be bound by his predecessor's administrative rules,[87] it seems equally unlikely that a disabled president's arrangements can be construed as binding his temporary successor.

The Caliber of the Bullet

About twenty minutes after the president reached the emergency room, a portable chest X-ray was obtained. It showed blood in the pleural cavity and the bullet projecting through the shadow of the heart. The radiologist, Dr. David Rockoff, immediately inquired of the Secret Service agent standing nearby, "What caliber bullet was it?"[88] The agent was uncertain but indicated that he would find out.[89] Rockoff's attention had been attracted by the small size of the bullet; if the pistol was a .38 caliber, the metallic shadow might represent only a fragment of a bullet, rather than the whole. Other fragments might have scattered elsewhere and possibly perforated organs in the abdomen.[90] If the spleen, liver, or kidneys had been injured, the president could be suffering hemorrhage below the diaphragm as well as in the chest.

As Rockoff described the moments that followed in an interview, "[He] listened as the Secret Serviceman turned to a superior and said, 'They've got to know the caliber.'

"The agent's superior said, 'Then call the FBI. They've got the gun.'

"The Secret Service agent went to a nearby phone and called the FBI [which refused to furnish the information].

" 'What do you mean you 'can't' tell me?' the Secret Serviceman said. 'The doctors here have to know.'

"He turned to his superior and shouted: 'They won't tell me.'

" 'You tell them they've got to tell you! It's the *President.*'

"His voice rising, the Secret Serviceman told the FBI: 'We've got to know, and we've got to know now!'

"There was a moment's silence before the Secret Serviceman turned to Rockoff and said: 'It's a .38.'

"Rockoff, stunned by this information, relayed it to colleagues. 'It's a .38,' he said. 'We need a belly film to look for the rest of the bullet.' "[91]

Dr. Aaron recalled, "The piece of metal in his chest was relatively small, at least as we were viewing it on a PA of the chest. But somebody said, 'We think that was a .38-caliber plug.' Dave Rockoff, the radiologist, said, 'That's really a little small for a .38 slug. I wonder if there is more bullet someplace else.' That statement kind of set things off because there was a chance he might have some in his belly. It raised the issue of whether what we saw on the initial chest X-ray was all the metal he was carrying."[92]

An X-ray of the abdomen was then obtained. No bullet fragments were visible. If the bullet had splintered before hitting the president, the pieces might well have dispersed prior to entry. Nevertheless, the decision was made that it was too important to know about bleeding in the abdomen to disregard the disparity in size between the fragment in the chest and a .38-caliber bullet.

It was then that the fluid was placed in his abdomen and found to be negative for blood when withdrawn. This meant that none of the organs below the diaphragm had been injured, so that chest surgery could now go ahead.[93]

Although the lavage took about thirty to forty minutes, the total time elapsed between the president's arrival at the hospital (2:35 P.M.) and the onset of chest surgery (4:20 P.M.) was almost two hours. Meanwhile, the surgery on Secret Service

Agent McCarthy had revealed that the bullet was indeed a .22, not the .38 that the FBI had claimed.[94] But Dr. Aaron thought it was a .38 until he actually got the bullet out. "I couldn't identify it as a .22," he said, "but I've seen .38s and they are a lot bigger than this slug."[95]

When Aaron was asked about the need for the abdominal procedure, he said, "Hindsight is a good thing. The peritoneal lavage was unnecessary, but the rationale at that time was that there might be some metal in the abdomen. In retrospect, I'd have to say, 'Gee whiz, if we'd known, then clearly he would not have needed the peritoneal lavage.' But the problem was it was pretty near the diaphragm, so we might have gone ahead anyway. It was at least possible that this thing traversed the top of his diaphragm; we didn't know whether it went through it or above it or whether the spleen or some other organ was injured."[96]

The erroneous information provided by the FBI to the Secret Service fortunately did not affect the outcome of surgery. The abdominal procedure might have been done anyway, and the forty-minute delay did not hinder the chest surgeon from doing his job. But if the bleeding in the pleural cavity had been more massive, the size of the bullet might well have been a critical factor in delaying essential surgery on the lung.

Why was the mistake made? No explanation has ever been given. In fact, the Secret Service issued a denial that the episode had ever occurred, through John Warner, assistant to the director:

"The Secret Service would like to set the record straight concerning the March presidential assassination attempt.

"Dr. David Rockoff apparently described a Secret Service

agent's telephone conversation that day in the hospital emergency room. From what Dr. Rockoff overheard, he concluded that the FBI had at first refused to divulge, and had subsequently given incorrect information concerning the caliber of the gun used by John Hinckley.

"The Secret Service has just completed a full investigation into all events surrounding the attempt on the President's life. According to this investigation, Secret Service agents at the hospital made no such call to the FBI."[97]

This official disclaimer simply did not square with the facts. Rockoff not only heard the conversation between the agent and the FBI, but "it was in the company of that Secret Service agent that Dr. Rockoff told the other physicians attending the president that it was a .38 caliber bullet."[98] Rockoff had no good explanation of the FBI's confusion on this matter.[99]

Quite independently, however, the confusion about the caliber of the bullet was confirmed by Haig: "The Attorney General," he said, "received information that the assailant's weapon had been identified as a .38 caliber revolver. . . . It was not until 4:10 that we learned that the bullets that wounded the President and the other three men were actually much less powerful .22 caliber long rifle cartridges."[100]

The attorney general could have received his information on the caliber of the bullet only from the FBI, since the weapon was in their custody. There is no evidence that the FBI tried to correct this error by communicating with the hospital when it was discovered. Instead, it was the removal of the bullet from McCarthy that first established the caliber unequivocally.

A possible explanation lies in the actions of one of the U.S. Park Police officers. After the shots, he ran over to help subdue Hinckley. He dropped his .38-caliber revolver when he reached the crowd of special agents, and it hit the ground near the spot where the injured Brady was lying. For at least some time, it was thought to be the weapon used by Hinckley, until the officer subsequently reclaimed the revolver.[101]

The Lost Black Book

On the evening of Friday, April 3, 1981, an aide to a Republican congressman was making a telephone call in a page booth outside a bar on Route 1, south of Alexandria. He saw a black notebook on the shelf beneath the phone. On inspection, it turned out to contain confidential telephone numbers of the command post outside Reagan's hospital room. There were also notes about telephone calls to the president recorded on the day of the shooting, including one at 3:38 by a man who claimed, "There's going to be another threat on the president's life."

The notebook was left in the phone booth by one of the Secret Service agents who was guarding the president during his hospitalization. Richard Hartwig, the spokesman for the Secret Service, said that none of the information was classified or confidential.[102]

Mistakes and differing perceptions of events occurred both at the White House and at the hospital. Even during the transport of the injured president from the hotel, there was confusion in some of the motorcade vehicles as to the destination, and the Secret Service failed to inform the hospital emergency room that the president had been injured.[103] Because of this, there was no stretcher waiting for him when he arrived. The more serious issues were largely related to a new administration in power for a short time without adequate preparations for such an emergency. The question of who was "in charge"; the public character of the incorrect statement of the succession; the gaps in knowledge of the constitutional mechanism for handling a disabled president; the allusions to the National Command Authority, as though the United States were a country at war; the argument over alerting the forces; the removal of the president's nuclear authorization code card; and the misinformation on the caliber of the bullet—all reflected different levels of confusion during a crisis. Actions meant to reassure the public resulted instead in uncertainty about leadership and direction that was avoidable.

6

How Well Was the President's Condition Reported to the Nation?

A PARAMEDIC WHO HELPED CARRY REAGAN INTO THE EMERGENCY room said, "He looked like he was in shock. . . . He was gasping for air . . . he turned in my direction and said, 'I can't breathe.' "[1]

But the public was largely unaware of the gravity of the president's injury following Hinckley's attack.[2] Were Americans misinformed? Did the president's men insist on painting a rosier picture than the reality? Or was it the physicians? Did Dr. Dennis O'Leary, the hospital spokesman, obscure the seriousness because of White House pressure? What about the reporters? Were they involved in a modified "conspiracy of silence"?

The White House staff and physicians to the president have

a powerful history of deceiving the public on the nature and seriousness of presidential illness. Drs. Cary Grayson (for Wilson), Ross McIntire (for Franklin D. Roosevelt), Janet Travell (for Kennedy), and George G. Burkley (for Johnson)[3] gave profoundly misleading information in an effort to prevent disclosure of their patients' medical conditions.

Following the attack on Ronald Reagan, the public reports were clearly designed to minimize the impact of the bullet wound. Dr. Dennis O'Leary, dean of clinical affairs at George Washington University Medical School, had been chosen as the hospital spokesman. He claimed that Reagan "was never in any serious danger." The bullet was "never close to any vital structure," he said,[4] and not less than several inches from his heart.[5] "He is alert and should be able to make decisions by tomorrow."[6] He "does not require an intensive level of medical care. He's doing extremely well."[7] According to O'Leary, he required no transfusions in surgery. (In fact, while 3 ½ units of blood were administered in the emergency room, Reagan received 4 ½ units during surgery.)[8]

Secretary Haig, in his press conference while Reagan was undergoing surgery, said, "The President's condition . . . is stable."[9]

These official comments were at odds with other observations. When a bullet enters the chest, it lacerates the lung over the course of the bullet track. By violently disrupting the tissue traversed, it produces a cavity that may be considerably larger than the size of the track. The degree of injury depends on the size and velocity of the bullet and the amount of energy transmitted to the adjacent tissues. The closer the gun is to the chest, the greater the degree of tissue destruction associated with burning gases at the end of the gun barrel.

The effect of the injury is magnified by the penetration of blood vessels (or the spinal cord).[10]

Unlike the direct wound suffered by James Brady, the president's resulted from a richocheted bullet, so that much of the energy was dissipated as the bullet hit first the car and then his chest. Nevertheless, it tore not only lung tissue but also blood vessels, with consequent massive hemorrhage in his pleural cavity. While the entry site of the bullet appeared diminutive, the tear in the pleura and the lungs was far larger, so that the surgeon, Dr. Aaron, speculated that it must have had a rotary movement until it reached its final deposition point. By the time Reagan entered the operating room he had lost roughly one third of his circulating blood volume.[11] As air entered the pleural cavity through the wound, the lung collapsed and produced the profound respiratory distress that he had experienced first in the limousine a few minutes after the incident.

When Dr. Giordano first saw the president in the emergency room, "he was just at that point where, if he had lost more blood without receiving some fluid, his pressure would have dropped and he would have gone into shock." After Giordano inserted a tube into Reagan's chest, a large volume of blood spilled out immediately, but instead of a steady decrease in blood flow, "he kept putting it out."[12] It was the continued loss that prompted the decision for immediate chest surgery.

Once the bleeding was controlled, the removal of the bullet extended the length of the operation. The surgeon who operated on Reagan, Dr. Aaron, observed, "I had a hard time finding the bullet. Twice I almost gave up. But I had a strong feeling in my brain I shouldn't leave that bullet in the president, an inch from his heart. . . ." If it had not been removed, said Aaron, "I think there's no question but that we would have had to go back into his chest again and take it out, because it might have ruptured and started leaking."[13] The bullet was a "devastator" type, designed to explode on impact. Aaron could not have known that, however, because the Secret Service agents at the hospital were first informed of it at about 7 P.M. The FBI was apparently not aware of it until three days later, on Thursday, April 2.[14] In fact, it should have been known even earlier, when the bullet was recovered from McCarthy at surgery on Monday afternoon.

John Pekkanen, a writer who studied the case in detail, was uncertain about the cause of the delay. "It may have been lost in the shuffle because it seemed so secondary to the fact that the president was alive and they got the guy that shot him. But there was some controversy over whether it could do any more damage than a normal bullet after it lodged in somebody. I heard that Mike Dennis, the neurosurgeon who operated on Delahanty [the Washington, D.C., police officer who was injured] should have worn armor plating when he did the second surgery, and he had a bulletproof vest to guard against an explosion. I guessed he was really worried. I called him up, and he said, 'Oh, no, that's nonsense; I wasn't worried about a bullet going off.' Somebody finally said to me, 'Well, it is a devastator bullet, but it detonates on impact; if it's inside somebody, it's not going to suddenly explode someday.' "

Pekkanen asked Aaron why he wanted to get the bullet out, assuming that he would get a technical medical explanation. "It was one of those interesting surprise answers, because he said, 'I felt I had to; the world was watching; I mean I wasn't about to be the surgeon who left a bullet in the president of the United States.' So in essence it was almost a political decision to take the bullet out. He said, 'You know, we routinely leave bullets in chests—you close up a chest and leave it there, and it heals.' But it was that matter of 'this is the president.' Another undercurrent may have been that this was an assassination attempt and we want to get that bullet out for evidence. Those were the two reasons, the former one stronger. As you know, Aaron used a wire to track the bullet. He said that was kind of the 'Eureka' moment, when he found the bullet and got it out."[15]

Aaron directly contradicted O'Leary's statement about the position of the bullet, which was actually one inch from the heart and the aorta. O'Leary later acknowledged some errors. While O'Leary thought that the president "probably still would have been okay" if he had had to travel another twenty or thirty minutes, Aaron said that "he wouldn't have tolerated much more traveling anywhere. I mean, the man collapsed in our emergency room, which was only about ten minutes after the fact."[16] "Another 20 minutes and he might have been in trouble" and could have died. This was because his internal bleeding was vigorous and he was "approaching a shock state."[17] Dr. Knaus agreed with Aaron. "Dennis [O'-Leary] is a good guy, but Dennis hasn't been at the bedside in a number of years. Ben's [Ben Aaron's] interpretation is correct."[18]

A few hours after surgery, Reagan was still on a mechanical respirator attached to a tube inserted through his nose into his trachea. His brother-in-law, Dr. Richard Davis, a Philadelphia neurosurgeon, indicated that he needed assisted breathing longer than anticipated. It was Davis's understanding that the tube had been "removed for a brief period or the respirator was shut off" so that Reagan might try to breathe on his own. But the blood oxygen levels proved to be too low. "Then he was put right back on the ventilator. . . ."

Dr. Sol Edelstein, the director of the emergency room, noted, "As he came out of anesthesia, the President was very agitated, trying to get up. The situation was never life-threatening, but it could have been had it gone unrecognized."

Dr. Jack Zimmerman, director of the intensive care unit, heard around 7:30 that evening that the president was having lung problems. "I had no idea of the severity of his wound or anything that was going on until I got down there," he said.[19]

Dr. Ruge, the president's physician, subsequently said, "Of course we could have lost him . . . things could have gone wrong to put his life in danger . . . but the way things unfolded, there was never any danger. . . ."[20]

In the light of the opinions expressed by the physicians who cared for the president, it seems apparent that the injury was serious enough to be a matter of deep concern. With less expeditious care, it might, in fact, have been fatal. One prominent surgeon said, "Why would you give that amount of blood if he was not in a life-threatening situation and the patient's life was not in serious danger?"[21]

Secretary Haig had heard from the attorney general that Hinckley had used a .38-caliber revolver, and noted that "this news, coupled to the anxiety generated by Jim Baker's continued description of the President's condition as 'serious,' was unsettling." He later commented that "President Reagan was gravely ill after the attempt on his life . . . and he and the White House misrepresented his condition to the public." "If you knew the true story, it would make your hair stand on end," Haig said. (When asked if Haig's statement was accurate, Dr. O'Leary replied, "No. I know the former secretary and believe that is a self-serving comment, if I may say so.")[22]

Speakes wrote in his personal notes, " 'Doctors believe bleeding to death. . . . Think we are going to lose him [one doctor said]. Rapid loss of blood pressure. Touch and go.' . . . It was a crisis we would deal with for a long time." To the public he announced, "The president will make all of the decisions. . . ."[23]

Baker at 6:15 P.M. also stated that the president was in good condition.[24] O'Leary declared, "He is alert and should be able to make decisions by tomorrow" (that is, by the day after surgery).[25] "His vital signs were rock stable."[26]

On Tuesday, March 31, the day after surgery, O'Leary said, "He can attend to the important matters of government today."[27] Meese was talking of his "remarkable recovery" at a time when he was developing pneumonia, and soon to have his temperature flare up.[28] "Recovery Amazing," read the *New York Times* headline of April 1, quoting Vice-President Bush.[29] The White House staff claimed, "If a really grave crisis occurs, Mr. Reagan would be on top of it."[30]

Baker said, "We have had to cancel very few activities."[31] (What did he mean? The president's personal calendar was obviously suspended. Bush was standing in for him at cabinet meetings, and was greeting visiting dignitaries.[32] The "activities" of the president were largely confined to lying in bed.)

Speakes declared, "By the day after the assassination attempt, my main task was . . . to make sure that everyone knew the President was recovering and was in charge of the government. . . ."[33]

Donald Regan pointed out, "Some of that information was flawed. After the fact, we understood that the threat to the President's survival had been far greater than we realized. . . ."[34]

By Wednesday, April 1, it was said that "there were signs of uneasiness now at the White House . . . concerning the president's condition." Coughing, essential to keep his bronchi clear, was painful.[35] Dr. O'Neill, who had said that Reagan was in a life-threatening situation, was no longer permitted to discuss the case.[36] Meanwhile, Speakes said, "There has been no attempt to paint an unduly rosy picture." But photographs of the president were delayed because the chest tubes and intravenous catheters were still in place.[37] (When the first photograph of Reagan since the shooting was released that week, it showed the president smiling with Mrs. Reagan at his right side. To the left, Reagan's nurse held a container connected to the chest tube which came out from under his robe, but she was cropped out of the picture. Mrs. Reagan insisted that her husband not appear as an invalid.)[38]

On April 2, the third day, the president required bronchoscopy to clear away some plugs and blood from the left lung. He still had a nasal catheter in place to provide a continuous oxygen supply.[39] Tip O'Neill, who visited briefly that day, was struck by his state of exhaustion: "In the first day or two after the shooting he was probably closer to death than most of us realized."[40] This was the day when Reagan developed fever because of his pneumonia and had "a little bit of a setback," according to Dr. Aaron.[41]

Reagan remained feverish on April 3, the fourth day. That day, Dr. Aaron said, "Blood loss . . . is one of the more severe forms of trauma. He probably, for a period of two or three weeks, will be tired very easily . . . and will have to have periodic rest periods."[42] Aaron curtailed Reagan's schedule because his lung "is not functioning as well as it might be."[43] For the next few days, he had fever and evidence of pneumonia and hemorrhage on chest films.[44]

Weeks later, the question was raised as to how the president, "physically and mentally grazed by death," would conduct the presidency with his scars to remind him that he would always be a target of sorts.[45]

The evidence is compelling that the public was given a picture painted in rosier hues than the reality of Reagan's condition warranted. Was this an effect of White House staff control over medical information given to the media?

Certainly not directly. Dr. O'Leary said, "I wrote all of the press releases. Those were based upon my discussions with the physicians involved in his care, Aaron and Giordano in surgery, [Carmelita] Tuazon in infectious disease, Rockoff in radiology, and the others. Based on that information I constructed a report, and I would share it with Dan Ruge, not with the White House aides. Dan might have changed two words out of twenty-seven press releases; he wasn't a tough editor. I would then call it over to Larry Speakes, and he would give it to the media. Meese, Deaver, and Baker were not involved in the nature or the amount of information released at all."

O'Leary used such terms as "good," "stable," "positive," and "excellent" to describe Reagan's condition. "I understood the need of his staff to convey a positive picture," he said. "Basically, he was doing well. If the question of a pneumonitis had not arisen, he probably would have gone back to the White House around day 6. It was planned that he would be released that weekend, but then he spiked a temperature and all bets were off. This complication was discussed in detail in the press so that readers could make their own judgment as to what kind of shape he was in. Tactically, we provided as much information as we could because that curtailed speculation."

It was O'Leary who claimed that the bullet was never close to any vital structure and not less than several inches from his heart, a demonstrably incorrect statement. In his defense, he commented, "I went in to the press conference with whatever information I could glean from the people who operated on him. I gambled that it was close enough to be accurate, but there is always a risk that you may not have all the information or you may even have misinformation. I did not have a clear picture of the pathway of the bullet and where it had lodged at the time of the press conference. Victor Cohen subsequently wrote a sensational story for the front page of the *Washington Post*, stating that the bullet was only an inch from his heart. My reaction was, so what? Close is close but that's about it."[46]

Dr. Aaron thought that the portrayal in the media was reasonably accurate. "We were really quite open. We made the decision early on not to withhold information or try to make things look good." The blackout that was imposed on all information except through O'Leary "was done for a purpose. We didn't want medical students, interns, and nurses talking about a lot of things they didn't know about or misrepresented. Every day, the doctors involved sat down with O'Leary, and we discussed the events of the day. We got a clear story together that best represented the facts, and then he went out to the press."

Dr. O'Neill, the surgical intern who gave a press interview the day after the shooting, was forbidden to discuss the event with reporters. Aaron thought that was "exactly right; he had no business opening his mouth about anything."[47]

Dr. Knaus agreed that the "information blackout," except through Dennis O'Leary, was voluntary. "My recollection is that Joe Giordano and a bunch of medical staff got together with Dennis. Everybody at that point had pink slips two inches deep on their desks from reporters who knew us and were trying to get some information. We said, 'Look, this is nonsense. Even if everybody says the same thing, it will never come out the same.' I think we all agreed that Dennis would give information to the press. It wasn't a 'blackout' so much as an effort to cut down confusion. Everybody was getting calls, including the cleaning ladies. By way of coordinating the public response, no one talked to reporters while Dennis was making his formal statements. With a reporter whom I knew well, I would call and say, 'Listen, I really can't tell you anything for publication now, because you know Dennis is the spokesman; after this is all over, if we want to talk about it, that's fine.' "

Whatever pressure there was to minimize the seriousness of the situation was accomplished "in an interesting fashion," Knaus thought. "To those of us who were taking care of Reagan, it was obvious that the rosy appearance that some people interpreted from what Dennis said was not exactly what was going on. He was reporting the facts as accurately as he could. In his attempt to reassure the nation that everything was okay, I think it came out a little more positive than it really was. It wasn't *untrue;* but the tone was a little more upbeat than it might have been."[48]

"We had decided as an institution to have one spokes-man," Dr. Giordano said. "The decision was made and discussed with us. We were asked not to speak to the press, to let the spokesman do all of the talking. It was made clear that this was a voluntary thing, and I think everybody agreed to it."[49]

Dr. Ruge believed that a "little pressure" might have been applied to portray the president as healthier than he actually was. "I might have even been guilty of some of that," he said. "I was probably euphoric once I saw a situation that could be corrected. First of all, it was a shooting. I was with him during that whole first night except for about an hour. My God, here is the president of the United States. He's my friend; he's my patient; and we're winning this one. That's the way it was. I don't believe that good physicians have to scare the hell out of their patients or their family or have to exaggerate. In other words, if things are going well, why make a big deal out of it. I happen to have been a neurosurgeon, and I didn't make a habit of telling the family how difficult things were, even though they might have been difficult.

"I understand that in Tip O'Neill's book he talks about how ill the president was, and I think he was absolutely correct. He is not a doctor, and he was no judge, but I am sure what he said was absolutely correct in his eyes. Vernon Jordan came in; Howard Baker was there. There were other people who were around a great deal because that was the 'in place' to be. Even in George Washington University Hospital, they knew it was like being in Buckingham Palace.

"I thought Dennis O'Leary did a good job. The first time I met O'Leary was when he and Nofziger were in Dennis' office at GW—I think that was around 5:30 or 6:00 P.M., after

the operation was finished. Nofziger asked me, 'Who do you
want to be the spokesman?' I didn't know who Dennis was,
so I said, 'I want the hospital to take care of that.' Nofziger
asked me, 'Are you serious about that?' and I said, 'Sure.'
'Well,' he said, 'you made the right decision.' He said there
might be some questions about my credibility as the physician
to the president."

"There *was* the possibility that people wouldn't believe
me, because I was a part of the team. To some, that might
mean I was part of the conspiracy to clean up the story for the
public. People might think that I couldn't be objective about
his condition without feeling I might be violating his pri-
vacy."

In reflecting on Haig's comment that "the White House
misrepresented his [Reagan's] condition to the public,"
Ruge said, "Bob Woodward, in his book about the president,
says the same thing. They're both wrong. Woodward even
talks about him having oxygen at the White House, and that's
not true. Do you know what the trouble is? We have leakers.
There are big leakers and little leakers. The big leakers are,
say, the men in the inner circle who curry favor with the press
because they like to be written up. Then there are little leakers
who are pretty far down the totem pole but they like a moment of glory, so they often tell things they don't know. This
is exactly what happened. Woodward claims that he talked to
250 people. Well, he should have talked to 251 or 249 because somebody misled him. What we had at the White
House was a thing called a respirex—one of those little things
that has a Ping-Pong ball—and the president was blowing
into that to expand his lungs. It was the idea of people at GW;
they gave it to me, and I took it to the White House and

taught the president how to use it. I had never seen one before. Some maid at the White House saw the president blowing into that respirex; then somebody said it was a respirator. It was just the opposite."[50]

John Pekkanen agreed that "many of the hospital statements were designed to allay public apprehension more than to give a fully accurate medical description. There were probably two reasons for that. One was that no one wanted people thinking the president was dead or dying when the doctors thought he was going to pull through. Why alarm them unnecessarily? The other was a physician attitude that people are better off without knowing all the details. I don't think that's peculiar to President Reagan's shooting. It is in evidence when doctors confer with families and people on a whole range of issues. There is the feeling that patients and family may not understand all of this if I tell them and spell it all out in black and white, so I will just paint with a broad brush and make the glass half full instead of half empty. These two factors converged. There is no question in my mind after exhaustive interviews (probably in excess of fifty people who were involved) that the president was 'shocky' and probably headed towards shock; I think he was right on the edge of it."[51]

In regard to Dennis O'Leary's statement that the president would still have been okay if he'd had to travel twenty or thirty minutes to another hospital, Pekkanen said, "Every bit of medical evidence I was able to gather indicated that was simply not true. There is a possibility that Dennis was not as aware of those early moments, of his blood pressure, for instance. I don't know. He might have gotten there when they were putting fluids into him and he began to stabilize and his blood pressure began to go up and he assumed that it was never a problem. It is reasonable to believe that if the president had not gotten to a hospital for another twenty minutes or half hour, he would have died. It could have even been shorter than that. He had a very low blood pressure. If it stayed low enough long enough, he could have reached a point at which shock was irreversible. His organ systems could have been compromised beyond repair. Particularly in a fellow at an advanced age."

The reason the information to the public was channeled through O'Leary, whether correct or not, was that "the hospital made an important decision at the urging of Ben Aaron. The first decision was that they were going to treat the president like any other patient, as a seventy-year-old man with a gunshot wound. There was a tremendous fear of getting all of the consultants involved and practicing what they call 'celebrity' medicine—everybody with an opinion, things slipping through the cracks, a kind of paralysis of decision making. Then there was also the belief that there should be one voice speaking for what happened, rather than many contradictory comments. I think they shut off everybody and told them, 'Don't talk to the press. There will be one announcement coming.' Dennis O'Leary usually made it.

"But that was basically it, not to give mixed messages, not to care for the president in a committee kind of way, not to have comments from different doctors with one saying the president is doing well and another doctor saying, 'Gee . . .' You don't want three or four people saying his temperature was this, and his blood pressure that, without anyone really evaluating it and trying to present a consensus. It was a reasonable approach.

"In those early hours, Dennis wanted to placate any public perception that the president was dying or was going to be terribly damaged. When he was walking across the street to the press conference with Lyn Nofziger, Nofziger said, 'Just because they ask a question, Doctor, it doesn't mean you have to answer it.' Dennis took that in a couple of ways; one, a literal way, and one 'I will put a bright face on this.' 'Sailed through surgery' wasn't quite accurate. The president, while he may have 'sailed' through in the sense that there was no crisis, did not sail through the postsurgical period at all."

Pekkanen was asked whether cropping the photograph of President and Mrs. Reagan in order to omit the nurse holding the chest drainage tube was not deliberate altering of information for the public. He replied that "it was a political decision, not a medical one. That was a decision from the White House. Probably Mrs. Reagan had a powerful voice in it."

Reagan was bronchoscoped on April 3 because of his continued coughing up of blood. This was kept from the media at the time because they had painted a rosy picture of the president's health. "They thought that somebody would see them bringing in a bronchoscope to the president, assume the worst, and alert the press. The *Washington Post* got a couple of leaks from somebody, and the hospital got very out of joint about that. The press was very persistent; they were following nurses and doctors. One nurse was approached by a reporter, who met her as she came out of the hospital at night. He followed her to the parking lot, while she kept saying, 'No comment.' Clearly, this was *the* story, and the fear was that it might be exaggerated.

"When you get into a crisis situation, it's difficult to decide what the public should know about the hour-by-hour condition of the president. Will this information, distilled and interpreted by the press, really cause a lot more harm than good?"[52]

As we sort out the facts and opinions about the injured president, it becomes clear that there was a sustained effort to obscure the seriousness of his illness. ("The president will make all the decisions."[53] "It's really business as usual.")[54] There was an attempt to represent the president as unimpaired, unaffected by the bullet wound and surgery, fully capable of holding the reins of government. Years later, Mrs. Reagan would say, "There was kind of an unspoken agreement that none of us would let the public know how serious it was and how close we came to losing him. . . . I was so afraid that I would leave the hospital alone. And I remember when we did leave, a doctor said to me, 'You know, we could be leaving here under different circumstances.' And I said, 'Yes, I know.' "[55]

The White House staff organized a pattern of response to the press and public inquiry that minimized the trauma to the seventy-year-old man. As for O'Leary, he admitted to having "less than complete information." "I tried to be as upbeat as possible without damaging my credibility," he said.[56] He collaborated with the demand for optimism so as to reassure the public. While he did a fine job of assuaging national concern, we may wonder why he was not a little more insistent on precision and accuracy in presenting all the facts. The statement that the president "was never in serious danger" was false, whether or not it was meant to be reassuring. The attack could have turned out to be a disaster. Did not the public have a right to know at the time, rather than weeks or months later?

7

Was His Capacity for Decision Making Unimpaired?

THE OPTIMISM ABOUT THE PRESIDENT'S INJURY AND HIS "AMAZING" recovery was neither uniformly shared nor fully in accord with the facts. Even if Reagan's postoperative course had been as benign and uncomplicated as that of a younger man, was it correct to assume that he could have participated optimally in the complex decision making of a potential crisis?

Within a brief period, he experienced a dangerous bullet wound, a collapsed lung, severe blood loss, anesthesia, surgery, and the administration of drugs that have profound effects on the brain and on behavior. Throughout this period, he was said to remain "in command"—even when unconscious—and fully capable of executing the duties of the presidency, according to the president's men. By their affirmations of his stability and alertness, they implied that his judgment, memory, capacity for abstract thinking and problem solving, concentration, learning skills, and control of his emotions were unimpaired. This was hardly consistent with the description by a physician of a man "in acute distress" and in a "life threatening situation."[1]

Trauma is known to produce major cognitive changes associated with anxiety.[2] The stress on trauma victims may result in "difficulty in concentrating, memory impairment . . . , and sleep difficulties." There are feelings of "intense fear, helplessness, loss of control" that usually reflect the severity of injury.[3] Physicians and nurses are accustomed to seeing disturbances in the organization of thought; they accept it as a common consequence of the event. Depression, perplexity, flightiness, and excessive dependence are frequently observed in trauma patients.[4]

Was it appropriate to burden an injured president with the weight of the responsibilities of office? The debilitating effect of even minor trauma may be extreme. Victims of crime such as burglary or robbery may experience emotional distress for sustained periods. Violent assaults are sometimes followed by fear, suspicion, and confusion in the victim for as long as a year or more afterward. The recovery process is generally characterized by confusion and depression.[5]

Reagan's wound required *surgery*. One of the common aftermaths of major surgery is confusion severe enough to interfere with clarity of thought. Patients may lose the ability "to grasp concepts, to use deductive and inductive logic." They may experience disorientation as to time, space, and people, and impaired memory.[6] In Reagan's case, on the second day after surgery, Mrs. Reagan noted that he was disoriented as to time and expressed her concern about it.[7] No one who knew the president as well as she and was staying as close to him could have been mistaken about such an observation.

The elderly are especially susceptible to confusion and tend to remain bewildered longer than younger patients with comparable illness, even after the physiological causes are corrected. Postoperative mental impairment is a well-documented effect of surgery.[8]

Depression, anger, and anxiety occur in many patients. Among those over sixty-five, a 50 percent incidence of disabling postoperative depression has been reported.[16] Such individuals commonly withdraw, focus inward on their own turmoil, and have little interest in anything else. They resist activities involving responsibility, believe that no possible outcomes of an event will turn out well,[9] and have difficulty making decisions. Indecisiveness characterizes one-half of the mildly depressed and three-quarters of the severely depressed patients. They wish to avoid decisions, and they lose the will to act. Lyndon Johnson demonstrated this reaction after his gallbladder surgery in 1965. He resisted the efforts of his staff to impose the burdens of the presidency on him. Asked for a response to a complex memorandum, he wrote on it in inch-high letters, "I'M SICK."[10]

There is also difficulty with even mundane, daily decisions, such as which clothes to wear. The sense of helplessness may be profound, and the patient tends to surrender to his dependency needs. When anxiety becomes intense, patients can neither reason clearly nor make decisions without difficulty.[11]

Blood loss can be life threatening to anyone and is even more hazardous in a man of Reagan's age.[12] A major loss of blood volume may produce a state of shock; Reagan lost over one-half of his. Although fluid replacement and transfusions were started promptly, his initial blood pressure was low. With blood loss and low blood pressure, oxygen deprivation occurs; a collapsed lung aggravates this condition. Even on the third day, his blood oxygen level dropped, and oxygen therapy was again required.[13] Headache, fatigue, and inability to concentrate characterize decreased oxygen availability. The performance of complex tasks is impaired in a lowered oxygen environment. Agitation and confusion are prominent features in those with significant blood loss.[14]

The *drugs* received by the president before, during, and after anesthesia have complex effects. The anesthetic administered was Pentothal, a drug that induces anesthesia promptly. It is rapidly absorbed and then released slowly and metabolized. It may take as long as six to seven days to be eliminated. A sustained hangover effect is sometimes experienced. The drug is also known to affect memory, reduce self-restraint and inhibitions, and encourage overconfidence. More than eight hours after a dose of Pentothal, physiological effects (slow reaction time, and increased errors in motor activities) are still detectable in young, healthy subjects.[15]

Reagan received the opiates morphine and codeine, and the synthetic drug meperidine (Demerol) during his hospital stay. Their primary effect is relief from pain, frequently accompanied by drowsiness. Morphine may cause mental clouding and a sense of detachment from the environment in the user. Elderly patients tend to be particularly sensitive. Demerol is a weaker analgesic than morphine, but its effects are longer lasting.[16]

Diazepam (Valium) was also administered to the president. It functions as both a muscle relaxant and an anti-anxiety drug and has been found to impair learning. The effects may last from eight to fifty hours.[17]

The impact of trauma, blood loss, anesthesia, surgery, and drugs—with their major effects on the brain—could be enough to ensure that a young man would have difficulty in making important decisions rationally. Is it credible that an older man, like Reagan, was fully prepared to handle any and all decisions that might be required of him?

We know that in the four hours following the shooting he was short of breath, in great pain, losing blood from his chest wound. He had a collapsed lung and blood in the pleural cavity. He remained on a respirator for twelve hours after the shooting, and required morphine for his pain during the night and early morning hours.

Hours after the surgery was finished, while Reagan was still in the recovery room, he was bewildered by the setting. Apparently he did not even know that the operation had been performed.[18] This was the patient who was described by the hospital spokesman, Dr. Dennis O'Leary, on the morning after surgery, as "obviously able to function . . . in terms of the capacity to make decisions and so forth, he can probably put in a full time day today as long as he gets a nap this afternoon," although "he did not get a lot of sleep last night."[19] This judgment of his "capacity to make decisions" was remote from the kind of thoughtful assessment of an impaired president that would have best served the nation. It was entirely consistent with the general effort to obscure the potential seriousness of the president's condition. In a way, it constituted a deliberate blurring of two separate issues: the president's physical ability to handle the episode and recover, and the degree to which his mind and energies could focus on the responsibilities of office.

By way of demonstrating that Reagan had no problems, some of his quips were released through different sources. When he first saw Nancy Reagan in the emergency room—looking terribly worried—he calmed her by saying, "Honey, I forgot to duck," a line made famous by Jack Dempsey after his 1926 boxing loss to Gene Tunney.

"If I had this much attention in Hollywood, I'd have stayed there," he wrote in a note while surrounded by medical staff.[20]

This banter reflected both the gallantry of the man and the instincts of the seasoned trouper. It said nothing about his ability to participate in the decision-making process.

An outside surgical expert asserted, "The fact that the president is 70 years old is not a problem."[21] What he meant was that other seventy-year-olds had undergone chest surgery and survived; what he did not mean was that in the postoperative period, *all* seventy-year-olds—or all patients, for that matter—would be fully capable of marshaling their intellectual and cognitive resources to arrive at the best possible decision. Reagan had received morphine not long before he signed an important farm bill early in the morning after surgery. Speakes, when presenting the signed bill to reporters, was asked, "That's not the president's normal signature, is it?" He answered, "Yes." Reporter: "Have you looked at it?" Speakes: "Yes." Reporter: "It's a little wobbly." Speakes: "I can assure you that is a very able signature."[22] Deaver later commented, "The signature was weak and wobbly and if I had seen it under other circumstances, I might have called it a forgery."[23]

Dr. Knaus, the internist who was caring for the president in the ICU the day after surgery, was asked whether he had perceived the "disorientation" that concerned Nancy Reagan.[24] He responded that Reagan "was an elderly man who had gone through a lot and who looked actually better than he was at times. Once you start getting narcotics for pain relief, your sensorium is not normal. He was more disoriented the next day than he was the first. He was also exhausted.

"There was a Secret Service agent in the bloody room the whole time; the room was too hot; they had these damn blankets over the windows to keep a kook from shooting in. We had fans going all the time. It was crazy. So he didn't get much rest, and by the next day he was beginning to develop ICU psychosis to a minor degree. Yes, he was getting a little spacy because of all of this stuff going on. And it was really creating problems for us.

"At times, he seemed extraordinarily detached. He was the president of the United States and he had almost been killed, and what was the world doing without him? He didn't have the least bit of concern about that. . . . They brought him a paper to sign. . . . He really didn't ask any questions about it; he just signed it.

"Reagan was very focused on himself. . . . He was thinking about his own mortality in a way that he had never thought about before. I mean, he almost died. He was talking about death and how close he had come to it, and it was very much in the center of his mind and thought."[25]

Tip O'Neill, visiting Reagan three days after the shooting, "was shocked by his condition. He was clearly exhausted and in pain."[26] Reagan aides worried for twenty-four, even forty-eight, hours that the president might not survive. The infection that he developed, the fever of 102°, the bronchoscopy that was required because of his bleeding—all contributed to his continuing discomfort and distress.[27]

A week after the attack, on April 6, Baker said the president was receiving paperwork that took sixty to seventy-five minutes to read, but not "items that can appropriately be deferred."[28] The public was informed that his condition was such that he would not "rush" his return to work. A one-page "decision memo" on off-shore oil drilling was considered too complicated for him to review. He was able to read some summaries but not the "full texts" of all of the documents he had signed.[29]

We have no solid handle on the degree of cognitive impairment that he experienced following the attack. No truly critical evaluation of memory, concentration, integrative ability, perceptual acuity, retentiveness, and all of the other factors essential for rational analysis and balanced decision making was undertaken. When this problem was raised with the doctors who were responsible for his care, the response was that at various points he appeared alert, or was "telling jokes," or was able to converse. When they were asked specifically whether they would have trusted him to make life-and-death decisions for the nation in the first forty-eight hours and, indeed, during the first ten days, there was a mixed response. Attention was then more sharply focused on his capacity to absorb the large volume of information that would have followed a Soviet invasion of Poland. Most of the physicians who saw him would have been reluctant to place the fate of the nation in his hands during the immediate postoperative period.[30]

On April 9, ten days after the attack, Reagan's temperature was still not normal, but he was said to be working two hours a day in his hospital room. Two days later, he left the hospital, with the understanding that he would pursue a limited schedule during the period of convalescence.[31] While his staff publicly stressed his remarkable recovery, those in close contact knew he had been "horribly drained."[32] In the days that followed, Reagan was able to work or remain attentive about an hour a day.[33]

Not until nine weeks after the attack did he declare himself "recovered." He worked his first full day on June 3, more than two months after the shooting.[34]

At no time did any member of the White House staff publicly question the ability of the injured president to function "as usual." Their posture was that he continued to operate and held all of the powers of the office throughout. Speakes was explicit: "The president remains the president."[35]

Even weeks later, when Reagan was discussing issues with his staff or advisers, his interest waned and he became fatigued after half an hour.[36] Years later, when the Iran-Contra controversy was in full swing, Attorney General Meese suggested that Reagan's failure to recall his approval of the decision to send arms to the Iranians might be related to his recovery "from a serious illness" (the July 1985 operation to remove his colon cancer). "His memory could have been impaired as a result of post-operative medication."[37] By that time, Meese fully understood that drugs—before, during, or after surgery—might well affect memory, concentration, and decision making. He apparently considered it a useful explanation of Reagan's memory lapse when confronted with his agreement to give arms to Iran and thus to deal with terrorists.

During the week after the attack, Bush, who should have taken the place of the disabled president, reassured the public that the president was "all right."[38] The next morning, Ed

Meese said, "It's really business as usual."[39] Baker claimed, "The President is fully capable of taking actions."[40] Speakes said, "The president will make all the decisions, as he always has."[41] Meese repeated the refrain: "The decisions are being made by the president,"[42] a reassuring but manifest inaccuracy, as though Ronald Reagan could possibly have made the critical decisions at the time.

8

A Response to Presidential Disability: The Twenty-fifth Amendment

For two and a half months, from March 30 to June 16, 1981, the president of the United States was unable or unwilling to hold a press conference. For decades, the press conference had been used as a central vehicle to explore presidential thoughts and actions on the important issues of the day. The format was more than just a series of handouts. Subjected to the searching questions of many of the best reporters in the country, the president was exposed to the public at large through the sharp eye of the television camera—answering, elaborating, justifying, hedging, denying, affirming.

During the seventy days from January 20 to March 30, Reagan had held two full-fledged press conferences, three "briefings" of reporters, five informal exchanges, and an in-

terview with Walter Cronkite. The absence of press conferences during the eighty days after the attack was surely a
considered reaction to injury. In later years, when his contacts
with the press were few and far between, it became apparent
that his success with the "canned" speech was so great that
the risk of fumbling in a free exchange with reporters was too
high. Even when he held his sporadic meetings with the
media, his three-by-five cards acted as a crutch to bar the
press from catching his mind at work.

But in the early months of his administration, he should
have been eager to communicate with the public, to clarify
and push his program during the honeymoon. His failure to
do so was a direct consequence of his need for a prolonged
convalescence to recover from trauma and surgery.

For two hundred years, the Constitution had been lacking
in provisions for handling the problem of temporary presidential disability. In 1967, the Congress and the states had
finally created a mechanism, and it might have been thought
that March 30, 1981, was the ideal time to invoke it.

How did the Twenty-fifth Amendment come into existence?

On September 24, 1955 (the year in which John Hinckley
was born), President Dwight D. Eisenhower awoke at 2:30
A.M. with a severe pain in his chest ("It hurt like hell," he later
said). The pain worsened, and his physician arrived and administered morphine. When the diagnosis of a heart attack
was confirmed, Eisenhower was hospitalized and spent the
next two weeks in an oxygen tent.[1] One month after the
attack, he took his first walk since entering the hospital, and a

month later he held his first cabinet meeting. It was not until three months after the attack that he returned to the White House, feeling recovered.[2]

Eight months later, on June 8, 1956, he experienced unremitting, cramping abdominal pain and began to vomit. He had developed intestinal obstruction due to regional ileitis (Crohn's disease), and required emergency surgery in order to short-circuit the area of intestinal narrowing. He remained in the hospital for twenty-two days. During his six-week period of convalescence, he became depressed, as he had after his heart attack.[3]

The following year, on November 25, Eisenhower suffered a stroke, which impaired his speech. Thereafter he had occasional difficulty in enunciation and word choice.[4]

Eisenhower was disabled, for all practical purposes, for many months during these three bouts of illness. He became concerned that he might end up as the impaired and incompetent president that Woodrow Wilson had become in his last year and a half in office. He urged Congress to seek a remedy, especially for the difficult problem of a president who was unable to declare his own inability: "When you are as closely confined to your bed as I was for some time, you think about lots of things, and this was one of the foremost in my mind. I do believe that there should be some agreement on the exact meaning of the Constitution, who has the authority to act. . . . You can well imagine a case where the president would be unable to determine his own disability. I think it is a subject that, in its broadest aspects, every phase of it should be studied by the Congress. . . ."[5]

Under the Constitution, the president is charged with executive power and responsibilities. As commander in chief of the Army and Navy, he is responsible for the supreme command and direction of the military forces once war is declared (but not for declaring war or raising and regulating fleets and armies, a role reserved to the Congress).[6] If the president dies, if he is unable to discharge the powers and duties of his office, if he is removed, or if he resigns, the vice-president assumes presidential authority.[7]

Under the Presidential Succession Act of 1947 (PL-80-199), the Speaker of the House is next in line after the vice-president; thereafter the president pro tem of the Senate. The succession then moves to the cabinet in the order in which the departments were created: State, Treasury, War (later Defense), Justice, Interior, Agriculture, Commerce, Labor, and so on.[8]

At the time Eisenhower was urging the Congress to act, neither the Constitution nor the Succession Act provided for a temporarily disabled president to relinquish the powers of his office and then reclaim them if and when his condition improved. Eleven years later, the Twenty-fifth Amendment became law. The legislators, political leaders, and scholars who shaped it in the fifties and sixties were responding not only to Eisenhower's illnesses but also to Kennedy's assassination and their knowledge of the crippled presidencies of Garfield and Wilson. They believed that a clear definition of the respective roles of the president, vice-president, cabinet, and Congress in the event of presidential inability was essential in the modern era. It was no longer safe or prudent for a bed-ridden president to defer vital decisions, or for executive authority to fall into the hands of a doctor, a first lady, or a handful of White House aides. Continuity of presidential leadership was more urgent than ever before, as a prominent jurist emphasized: "When President Eisenhower underwent surgery at the Walter Reed Hospital for ilcitis, he was under anesthesia . . . for four hours. . . . If during this period the United States had suffered an atomic or missile attack, there would have been no Commander in Chief to coordinate defense, counterattack, and civilian evacuation. . . . At all times [we must have] a Commander in Chief ready to respond to any emergency."[9]

The danger arose from the ambiguities and shortcomings of Article 2, Section 1, Clause 6, of the Constitution: "In Case of the Removal of the President from Office, or of his Death, Resignation, or Inability to discharge the Powers and Duties of the said Office, the Same shall devolve on the Vice President, and the Congress may by Law provide for the Case of Removal, Death, Resignation or Inability, both of the President and Vice President, declaring what Officer shall then act as President. . . ."

In 1787, John Dickinson asked his fellow framers at the Constitutional Convention, "What is the extent of the term 'disability' and who is to be the judge of it?"[10] One hundred and sixty-eight years later, when Congress began a formal consideration of the problem, nobody had yet answered Dickinson's question or clarified the array of related issues that his query implied.

In September 1955, shortly after Eisenhower's first illness, Emanuel Celler, chairman of the House Judiciary Committee, launched the congressional effort by distributing a questionnaire to legal and political scholars: What was intended by the term "inability"? Should a definition be enacted into law? Who should initiate the question of the president's inability? Who should make the determination? In the event of temporary presidential inability, does the vice-president succeed to the powers and duties of the office or to the office itself? Does Congress have the authority to enact legislation to resolve any of these questions, or is a constitutional amendment required?

Twenty-six experts responded to Celler's questionnaire or testified on its principal questions during the initial hearings. Their answers and the early testimony set the tone for the years of discussion that would follow. From the beginning, there was almost universal accord that the need for continuity of leadership required the vice-president to assume the powers and duties of a disabled president. In both the Garfield and the Wilson cases, the president retained the power of office while unable to act, so that others were functioning for him. This violation of the constitutionally defined presidential role, it was agreed, should not be allowed to recur.[11]

Moreover, the "Tyler precedent" had to be clarified. Vice-President Tyler had insisted on assuming the *office* of the presidency upon the death of President Harrison, instead of merely taking over the powers and duties of the office, as the Constitution seemed to require. With Garfield and Wilson, Vice-Presidents Chester A. Arthur and Thomas Marshall had lacked clear authority to declare the president disabled, and the Tyler precedent made such a move potentially explosive. As long as there was uncertainty over whether a vice-president acting in place of a disabled president had ousted him from office, the historical trend of neglecting or concealing presidential inability was bound to continue. What was needed was a law that confirmed the Tyler precedent in cases of the death or resignation of the president, but allowed for the interim assumption of presidential power in the event of temporary presidential inability.[12]

Although there were areas of early consensus, it was also

apparent that the issue would be subject to prolonged, frustrating debate. Clearly, it was best that the president declare his own inability and temporarily hand over the powers and duties of office.[13] The procedures and safeguards required when a disabled president was unable or unwilling to declare his own incapacity, however, were at the core of the controversy. The scholars and the legislators were divided on the mechanism whereby he should be deprived of his authority by others. They suggested nine different methods for determining the presence of inability, and eight for deciding when inability had terminated.

All desired a process that would afford a rapid and informed decision on inability. All were concerned to preserve the doctrine of the separation of powers, to protect the presidency, to disentangle the question from partisan politics. Depending on the goals that were emphasized, the solutions offered were distinctly different.

Those who stressed the separation of powers wished to retain within the executive branch the decision on inability: the vice-president should initiate the process.[14] Others argued that the vice-president was perhaps the *worst* choice to raise or determine the issue; his interest in the outcome might tempt him to usurpation, on the one hand, or inhibit him by making his motives suspect, on the other.[15]

A variety of permanent or ad hoc councils or committees were proposed to assess the president's fitness. They were usually composed of members drawn from Congress, the cabinet, the Supreme Court, and the medical profession, either separately or in combination. Former President Hoover suggested the cabinet, while Truman proposed a board of medical experts selected by a "Committee of Seven" representatives from the three branches of government.[16] But there was little agreement as to how such a body should be constituted and how it should function: Congress might be too partisan or cumbersome,[17] cabinet members too loyal,[18] the issue too political for the Supreme Court,[19] and civilians too lacking in the necessary political sophistication to be involved.[20]

Disputes also arose over whether a constitutional amendment was required, or if a statutory solution was feasible. Celler later said that the divergence of opinions led to the failure of the House hearings.[21] Nevertheless, the embryo of the Twenty-fifth Amendment emerged from the hearings, in the form of the Eisenhower administration's first proposal. At a meeting of the cabinet in February 1957, Eisenhower suggested the formation of a special committee, including the chief justice of the Supreme Court and medical experts, to decide on cases in which the president was unable or unwilling to declare his own inability.[22] But by the time Attorney General Herbert Brownell presented the administration's proposed constitutional amendment to the Senate in April 1957, the administration had dropped the idea of such a committee. The Eisenhower-Brownell proposal foreshadowed the Twenty-fifth Amendment in important respects: it provided for the president to state the beginning and end of his own inability, and allowed the vice-president with the concurrence of a majority of the cabinet to declare inability when the president could not or would not do so himself.[23] Giving the vice-president and the cabinet this shared power, Brownell argued, would preserve the integrity of the executive branch while avoiding the pitfalls of a decision solely by the vice-president: "The Cabinet, after all, is an executive body. It is the President's official family. A decision of this body along with the Vice President is likely to receive public acceptance—at least certainly on the point of making it clear that if this group acted, there would be no question of the Vice President usurping power on the pretext of inability—and, moreover, the Cabinet is right there on the job and in a position to know at once whether the President is able to act."[24]

Celler initially greeted the proposal with skepticism, suggesting that cabinet members' "loyalty and personal feelings to the Chief" or fear of losing their jobs might prevent them from acting. "I think we had that made clearly manifest in the case of the Wilson Cabinet," he said.[25] The arrangement was also criticized because it contained no provision for overriding the president's decision on the termination of inability short of impeachment. Representative Kenneth Keating said that it could result in a "chaotic condition by having the Vice President say the President was unable, and the next day the President saying 'I am able,' and then the Vice President the next day saying he is unable, so that you would have a day-by-day President."[26]

Shortly after the debate subsided in the House, it began in 1958 in the Senate Judiciary Subcommittee on Constitutional Amendments, under Chairman Estes Kefauver. Matters were simplified somewhat when Chief Justice Earl Warren told Congress in a letter that, in the opinion of the justices, an inability commission should not include members of the Court, "because of the separation of powers in our Government, [and] the nature of the judicial process."[27]

On February 18, 1958, Attorney General William P. Rogers, who had replaced Brownell in 1957, again presented the

Eisenhower proposal, modified to meet Keating's objection by allowing the vice-president and a majority of the cabinet to disagree with a president and put the issue of the termination of his inability before Congress. This change brought the proposal a step closer to the form that the amendment would finally take.[28]

Meanwhile, Eisenhower, worried about his health, felt he could not wait for Congress to solve the problem of inability. He later recalled, "This was the thing that frightened me: suppose something happens to you in the turn of a stroke that might incapacitate you mentally and you wouldn't know it, and the people around you, wanting to protect you, would probably keep this away from the public. So I decided that what we must do is make the Vice President decide when the President can no longer carry on, and then he should take over the duties, and when the President became convinced that he could take back his duties, he would be the one to decide."[29]

On March 3, 1958, the administration announced a memorandum of agreement between Eisenhower and Vice-President Nixon which provided for the president to declare and terminate his own inability, and allowed the vice-president, "after such consultation as seems to him appropriate," to proclaim the president disabled when the president could not.[30] But such an arrangement was only a temporary solution at best. As Nixon later said, the letter "had no force in law . . . if an argument developed . . . a letter that the President may have written to the next in line of succession wouldn't mean anything at all, in my opinion."[31]

The next day a bipartisan majority of the Senate Judiciary Committee introduced an amendment similar to the revised

Eisenhower proposal, but it failed to reach the whole Senate. Reintroduced in both the Eighty-sixth and Eighty-seventh Congresses (1959 and 1960), it again lost momentum in the Senate Judiciary Committee.[32]

Although the Kennedy administration announced on August 10, 1961, a "tentative informal agreement" based on the Eisenhower-Nixon memo, the new administration did not take a position on the constitutional amendment until June 18, 1963.[33] Deputy Attorney General Nicholas Katzenbach endorsed Senate Joint Resolution 35, which, unlike the Eisenhower proposals, would not specify procedures in the Constitution for determining inability, but would instead merely authorize Congress to establish such procedures.[34] This simpler form was proposed by Senators Kefauver and Keating as a way of postponing the disputes over methods, and was preferred by those who favored keeping the Constitution as spare as possible. With the support of the American Bar Association, Senate Joint Resolution 35 was reported to the full Judiciary Committee on June 25, 1963. Further favorable action seemed likely, until Kefauver's death, in August 1963, brought the matter to a standstill.[35]

Kennedy's assassination in November 1963 rekindled interest in Congress and the general public. Legislators and commentators again began pushing for reform. Senator Edward Long of Missouri expressed the mood of the moment: "For any who might doubt the necessity for constitutional reform, only two of many most grave possibilities need be pointed out: suppose the bullet which killed President Kennedy had strayed an inch or two and left him alive but disabled either for a long period of time or permanently; or suppose that Vice President Johnson had been killed or wounded at the same time."[36]

Such hypothetical situations were alarming, but the reality was disturbing, too. Lyndon Johnson, a man with a history of heart disease, became president, leaving the vice-presidency vacant. Two old and ailing congressional leaders, House Speaker John McCormack, seventy-five, and Senate President Pro Tem Carl Hayden, in his eighties, were next in line for the office.[37]

On January 20, 1964, the American Bar Association convened a special two-day conference in an attempt to forge a compromise between the conflicting approaches represented by the Kennedy and Eisenhower proposals. Their recommendations were similar to the revised Eisenhower plan. A clause was added allowing Congress to replace the cabinet with some "other body" to consider and specify inability.[38]

With the loss of Kefauver's leadership, the Senate Subcommittee on Constitutional Amendments had virtually disintegrated and was about to be closed down when Senator Birch Bayh of Indiana stepped in and resurrected the effort.[39] He initiated hearings and then helped introduce Senate Joint Resolution 139, similar to the modified Eisenhower proposal. It also contained provisions for filling a vacancy in the vice-presidency and for presidential succession beyond the vice-president.[40] Its sections on succession were dropped, and the bill was amended to contain the ABA provision allowing Congress to substitute some "other body" in place of the cabinet. The "other body" clause provided a safeguard against cabinet inaction or presidential reprisals against disloyal cabinet members. The joint resolution was passed by a unanimous vote of the Senate on September 29, 1964.[41]

The House took no action in 1964, a presidential election year, but on January 6, 1965, an identical amendment was introduced in both the Senate and the House. Three weeks later, President Johnson lent his endorsement. With Vice-President Hubert Humphrey now in office, House members who might have been reluctant to approve new succession procedures for fear of offending the aging Speaker McCormack could support the amendment.[42]

Each house approved its own version, but when the two reached the conference committee stage in May, an impasse developed which nearly derailed the entire process. The House version proposed that congressional debate to resolve a challenge to the president's resumption of powers be limited to ten days, so that filibustering and other delaying tactics would not keep a president out of office. The Senate favored greater flexibility to deal with unforeseen circumstances, and resisted altering the hallowed Senate tradition of unlimited debate. The bill seemed on the verge of collapse until Senator Bayh pushed through a compromise time limit of twenty-one days.[43]

The final version was approved in July 1965 and ratified by the necessary thirty-eight states on February 10, 1967. It was formally proclaimed the Twenty-fifth Amendment to the Constitution on February 23, 1967.[44]

Bayh later expressed his conviction that the question that John Dickinson had asked at the Constitutional Convention in 1787—"Who is to be the judge" of disability in a president?—was finally answered 180 years later.[45]

The provisions of the final bill represented a compromise engineered through the great skill and pragmatism of Senator Bayh and his colleagues. Section 1 clarified the "Tyler precedent" by providing that the vice-president shall become president (not merely assume the powers and duties of the office) if the president dies, resigns, or is removed from office.

Section 2 enabled the president to fill vacancies in the vice-presidency. Section 3 empowered a president who recognized that he was disabled to remove himself from office temporarily by informing the Speaker of the House and president pro tem of the Senate in writing. The vice-president then became acting president.

In the event that a president could not or failed to recognize his incapacity to govern, the vice-president and a majority of the cabinet under Section 4 could declare presidential inability in writing to the Speaker of the House and the president pro tem of the Senate. The vice-president then assumed the position of acting president.

An incapacitated president could reclaim office by written declaration that no inability existed, unless the vice-president and a cabinet majority transmitted their disagreement within four days. At that point, if the president still insisted on reclaiming office, Congress would have to decide whether to support the majority decision of the vice-president and cabinet. During the interval of congressional review, the vice-president would continue to serve as acting president. But if a two-thirds vote affirming presidential inability was not secured in both the Senate and the House, the president would regain his authority once more.[46]

Sections 3 and 4, then, were the provisions that were operative and pertinent when Reagan was injured and the decision for surgery was made. Unfortunately, prior to the attack, they had received little or no attention from the president, the vice-president, or the White House staff. As a consequence, there was an extraordinary gap in their understanding that the Twenty-fifth Amendment had been fashioned precisely for the kind of episode in which a wounded president was about to undergo major surgery.

9

The Failure to Invoke the Twenty-fifth Amendment

THE TWENTY-FIFTH AMENDMENT WAS FIRST INVOKED IN 1973, AT A time when the Watergate drama was unfolding. Vice-President Agnew was separately enmeshed in charges of bribery and corruption stemming from his tenure as governor of Maryland. He was forced to resign in October 1973, enabling President Nixon to choose a successor under Section 2 of the amendment. Gerald Ford was appointed on October 12, 1973, and sworn in on December 6. Ten months later, when Nixon was forced to resign, Ford became president. He then appointed Nelson Rockefeller to the vice-presidency. For the first time in its history, the United States had both an unelected president and an unelected vice-president.

The attack on Reagan provided the first opportunity to

apply the provisions of Section 3 or 4 of the Twenty-fifth Amendment to a disabled president. Why did the members of the executive branch fail to activate this carefully crafted mechanism?

Dr. Daniel Ruge, the White House physician, claimed that Reagan was capable of signing a letter until he went under anesthesia.[1] In such a letter, under Section 3 of the amendment, the president would have informed the Speaker of the House and the president pro tem of the Senate that he was going into surgery and under anesthesia. Vice-President Bush would then become acting president until such time as Reagan felt well enough to assume the responsibilities of office once more.

If it had been felt that the president was *physically* capable but that his mental state associated with massive bleeding and a collapsed lung was not conducive to a full understanding of the situation, Section 4 could have been invoked. The vice-president, while en route from Texas to Washington, could have been informed that the president was going under anesthesia and would be incapacitated for a period of time. With many of the cabinet in the White House Situation Room,[2] he could then have proposed the invocation of Section 4, and a vote could have been taken immediately, followed by a brief formal letter delivered to the Speaker of the House and the president pro tem of the Senate. Fred Fielding, counsel to the White House, had already prepared such papers.[3] As the president began his convalescence, he could then have felt secure in the knowledge that an acting president whom he had selected as his running mate was in place.

Indeed, under quite different circumstances four years later, with no bullet in his chest, no massive blood loss, no collapsed lung, the president transferred power to Bush on July 13, 1985, when he was about to undergo surgery for cancer of the colon.[4]

No such action was taken in March 1981.

When Reagan's men first gathered at the White House Situation Room, they were unsure of the president's condition. Fielding had brought the documents on succession to the Situation Room, where he and Attorney General William French Smith explained briefly how the Twenty-fifth Amendment was designed to work.[5] He had the papers to be signed if Section 4 were invoked to make Bush acting president. While reviewing them with Haig and Bush's chief of staff, Admiral Daniel Murphy, he was told by Richard Darman, a young and brash assistant to the president, that the subject was inappropriate. Darman, whom Larry Speakes described as "the ultimate second-guesser," was afraid that a more general discussion might provoke doubts about Reagan's condition, and he therefore quite literally acted to prevent the cabinet members from pursuing their constitutional obligation to consider invocation. He accomplished this by taking the documents from Fielding and removing them from the Situation Room. With Baker's approval, he placed them in a safe in his office.[6] "The concern was that the press not get wind of any actions that would raise questions as to whether the president was capable of acting," Meese later explained.[7] Haig, Weinberger, Regan, and Smith agreed that the subject should be avoided.[8]

Meanwhile, at the hospital, Baker, Meese, and Deaver rejected use of the amendment.[9] Dr. Ruge told Baker prior to the surgery that Reagan's condition was stable. According to Deaver, the three "looked at each other and nodded. The decision was made right there: not to invoke the Twenty-fifth Amendment. . . ."[10] This was precisely the time when the president was receiving blood transfusions because of continued bleeding in his chest.

While the decision for surgery was being made, David Gergen issued a report for the White House on the shooting of the president. He had just spoken with Baker. He was "asked whether the vice-president would be acting as the president *under any conditions.* Mr. Gergen replied, 'No.' "[11]

How could Gergen know that Bush would not become acting president "under any conditions"? In fact, he expressed a consensus so readily reached that it hardly needed discussion. Later, Gergen commented, "There is a very great reluctance to move on the Twenty-fifth. Everyone is hesitant because in effect you are expressing less than full confidence in your chief executive. There is an overwhelming urge to convey a serene view to the world, and I think everybody in the room wanted to say, 'Hey, unless we are forced, we don't deal with that.' "[12]

After the president went under anesthesia and into surgery, Baker, Meese, and Nofziger reviewed the possibility of a temporary designation of Bush as acting president.[13] With the operation still under way, Baker and Meese consulted one of the surgeons, Dr. Joseph Giordano.

"Jim Baker and Ed Meese came up to me," Giordano said, "and there was a discussion as to how the president would be able to function in the immediate postoperative period. I said that I thought initially he was not going to be able to make major decisions, because he was under an anesthetic, and would be coming out of anesthesia. All anesthetic drugs have some effect on the mind and brain, and he would also be getting heavy-duty pain medication. They asked me how long it would be, and I think I remember saying a couple of days. . . . A major operation, major blood loss, a certain degree of pain and discomfort, just the pain and discomfort would affect the way an individual could think. . . ."[14]

This was the only time Reagan's aides consulted a physician regarding the effects of the attack on the president's ability to function in office, although Secret Service agents and the first lady did so on other occasions. Despite Giordano's evaluation, Baker, Meese, and Nofziger decided against invoking the amendment.[15] They believed that if a military crisis arose while Reagan was under anesthesia, the National Command Authority would be able to cope.[16]

Fielding and Smith went over the contents and the meaning of the amendment with Bush on his return to Washington, while he officiated at a crisis management meeting attended by Haig, Weinberger, and other cabinet members. According to Baker, both the Twenty-fifth and the National Command Authority were discussed and their use rejected, although it is not clear whether he meant by the cabinet or just by the White House staff.[17] Allen apparently brought up the question of a "shift in authority," but Bush said there was no need to discuss the matter.[18]

The failure to invoke was related in part to ignorance of the provisions and the meaning of the Twenty-fifth Amendment. Bush's absence might have been construed as a reason for setting the wheels in motion, so that the cabinet members would be fully prepared and would understand their role together with Bush in the process of invocation. The president's men were also on soft ground in their belief that a major military decision necessitated by a crisis while Reagan was under anesthesia—if Russia invaded Poland, for example—could readily be based on the National Command Authority stipulations.[19] The National Command Authority might have kept the most important elected official—Bush—"outside the loop," unless the president was declared disabled.

Meese cited what he called the *"derivative power"* of the aides closest to the president as the authority on which the decision was made.[20] There is no mention of "derivative power" in the Constitution, and only Congress has the authority to grant invocation powers to a body other than the vice-president and the cabinet. The concept that White House aides had the authority to reject invocation was never even discussed in the original Senate and House hearings.

Many of the key figures in the Situation Room were only vaguely aware of the role of the Twenty-fifth Amendment.[21] Even the legal experts seemed unprepared to deal with a succession crisis. The administration had not yet developed a coherent set of contingency actions to be taken in the event of an emergency. (After the shooting, Fred Fielding, the White House counsel, together with his staff, completed a book defining the appropriate responses.)[22]

While the president was undergoing surgery, the language of the amendment and its legislative history were under study at the Justice Department in an effort to clarify congressional objectives at the time of its drafting.[23]

The profound feelings of relief over Reagan's prospects for survival and recovery overshadowed the question of whether his faculties might be impaired. "Particularly once he got out of surgery, there was never a concern about survival. All of the rest—the discomfort and pain and shortness of breath—

were there. But he had obviously come through the operation well," Meese noted. The fact that he could sign a bill in a shaky hand the morning after surgery satisfied his aides. "I doubt if we directly addressed his cognitive powers at the time. . . . But we could see from our own observation that the president was capable of understanding what was going on. He was not in a daze or anything like that," Meese observed.[24] Relieved that Reagan appeared to be pulling through and impressed by his stamina and courage, they made no effort to determine whether he was impaired.

The administration was fearful of being the first to invoke the inability provisions. Use of the Twenty-fifth Amendment might "diminish or put limitations on the power of the presidency and set a precedent for future presidents," in Meese's words.[25] Reagan's age was also a factor: serious questions had been raised about his ability to govern for four years, let alone eight. Such doubts would arise recurrently during Reagan's presidency as he fumbled with certain questions in his press conferences, bungled others, and was unable to recall important details of recent events.

Quite aside from the confusion and uncertainty surrounding the Twenty-fifth Amendment, the conclusion is inescapable that one of the principal reasons for the failure to invoke was the belief that "it would have alarmed the American people and our allies."[26] As Meese explained it, "there was a real concern not to provide any appearance of a president unable to continue to run the country."[27] "We wanted to convey a sense of security to the country. We did not want people to think it was suddenly falling apart," Gergen said.[28] Hence, from the moment Reagan was shot until he left the hospital thirteen days later, the fiction was maintained that he was governing the United States "as usual." Even in the operating room, even under anesthesia, he was the man in charge.[29]

With all of our knowledge of his injury and the medical-surgical aftermath, we must ask ourselves two questions: Who was legally in charge? Who was actually making executive decisions?

To the first question the answer is clear: Reagan maintained formal presidential power throughout the entire period. The thinking of the president's men on temporary replacement was emphatically and repeatedly stated.

On the afternoon of the attack, Lyn Nofziger was asked, "What is Bush's status, technically?"

"He is the vice-president."

Question: "Is he the stand-in president?"

"No, he is not."[30]

And later: "The president is the president."[31]

Speakes insisted that control of presidential power was always in Reagan's hands. "The president remains the president."[32] "[He] will make all of the decisions, as he always has."[33]

Meese said that "it's really business as usual,"[34] and that "the decisions are being made by the president."[35] Baker commented that "the president is fully capable of taking actions,"[36] as though that meant he was actually making decisions on the major issues that confronted the country. What Baker really meant was that the president could eat, talk, and sleep, all of which he was, in fact, capable of doing. Deaver said, "It is just as if the president were here in the

Oval Office. . . ."[37] Vice-President Bush said, "The power of decision has remained with President Reagan."[38] "He's going to call all the shots."[39]

What about the second question? Who was *actually* making the executive decisions?

Haig asserted at 4:15 P.M., while the president was in surgery, "As of now, I am in control here, in the White House. . . ."[40] It was clear as the day wore on, and even more so in the days that followed, that Haig was definitely *not* in command. He met with Bush and other cabinet members at 7:00 P.M. He continued to send messages to foreign leaders and prepared himself for his trip to the Middle East. He met briefly with the president on April 3, the day of his departure.[41]

Bush would make any necessary decisions if a crisis occurred, according to the White House staff. This directly contradicted their claim that Reagan would be "on top" of a really grave crisis.[42] Bush, meanwhile, went out of his way to disclaim any new authority. "There is no need", he said, "for any emergency procedures, the power of the vice-president to do anything. . . ."

He was asked, "You won't be assuming any special powers, Mr. Vice-President?"

He responded, "No. Absolutely not."[43]

Bush was anxious to avoid "upstaging the president." "The line we were [taking] on Monday was this: 'do nothing to appear presumptuous, but you don't want to appear in any state of panic either,' " his aide commented.[44]

But some perceived Bush as clearly acting for the president,[45] in spite of the absence of a transfer of power. For example, Speakes's announcement at a news conference that the vice-president had "automatically inherited 'national command authorities' "[46] accorded Bush presidential power. The next morning, Bush presided over a cabinet meeting, taking care to sit in the vice-president's rather than the president's chair. At 10 A.M., he met with congressional leaders; at noon, with the prime minister of the Netherlands. He was briefed by Meese, Baker, and Deaver, and subsequently by Richard Allen.[47]

On the following day, Wednesday, he had lunch with Casey, and on Thursday he held a cabinet meeting.[48]

Although the scope of Bush's activities clearly widened, there is no evidence that he was any more closely involved in the decision-making process. "It never occurred to me even for a fleeting moment that I was anything more than a stand-in," he said.[49]

Bush took pains to keep his conduct loyal, dutiful, and unassuming, which was quite consistent with both his personal style and the dictates of political prudence. Gergen recalled, "George Bush, given his nature, was very careful in how he handled himself during that time. He didn't want to be seen doing anything that might suggest arrogance or an arrogation of power. Do you remember how Don Regan got his wings clipped when Reagan was out at the hospital and Regan was chief of staff [in 1985], and he started taking the helicopter?"[50] Bush bent over backwards to avoid that kind of misstep.[51]

An appropriation of presidential authority by Bush might well have threatened the White House inner circle. Those closest to the president and most responsible for carrying out his wishes typically view the presidency not as one person but as what Martin Anderson has called a "pyramid of individuals who are built up under him." If the vice-president takes over, he will likely substitute his own radically different pyramid (that is, his own staff) for the existing one. "If the president is temporarily disabled, leave the presidency alone rather than risk the disorder from a group not aware of all the nuances of the problems confronting the country." In Anderson's view, to agree with the possibility that Bush might become the acting president at that time would have aroused concern on the part of those for whom Bush's loyalty was still suspect.[52] (Anderson, like Darman, was clearly willing to disregard the constitutional mandate embodied in the Twenty-fifth Amendment.)

Whatever Bush did, he cleared with Meese and Baker.[53] It was Baker, Meese, and Deaver who were actually running the White House. In the absence of an acting president, their daily meetings covered the range of foreign and domestic policy decisions. Meese was considered the "heavyweight" through his work with the cabinet, the National Security Council, and the domestic policy group. In the formulation of policy, he seemed to articulate the president's view as well as anyone. Baker played a critical role as the supervisor of other White House operations and the channel through which virtually all documentation reached the president (although there was little enough of that). In the short period of the Reagan presidency, the troika had already been assigned broad areas of responsibility by the distributive president, and in his disabled state, they did not hesitate to use their authority.[54]

During the period of trauma and convalescence, *they were the president of the United States.* They were not elected officials, nor were their appointments subject to the review and approval of the Congress. But they held the power of the president in their hands at a time when he might well have lacked the strength, energy, concentration, and clarity of focus essential to make the correct assessments. They believed that they were protecting the nation and the president; instead, the country and the government were unable to address a number of important problems. Reagan was legally in command, but actually so only when he was awake, alert, and capable of focusing on the issues, a matter of hours during the weeks that followed March 30, rather than days.

Reagan's slow recovery required a limited work schedule for many weeks. With the Polish crisis unresolved, the Middle East a potential source of mounting problems, the domestic agenda waiting for action, Meese and Baker pushed ahead as well as they could. Baker noted that the president "is being briefed on national security matters. He is signing legislation that has to be signed. He is signing nominations that have to be signed. But that's about it."[55]

"The important thing to note," Speakes said, "is that the White House did not skip a beat, the government did not skip a beat"[56] "The American government is functioning fully and effectively . . . ," said Bush.[57] "I want to make it clear that there was not one second . . . when there was . . . a lack of anybody being in charge," said Meese.[58]

But the president himself had raised a crucial question of state even as they wheeled him into the operating room. "Who's minding the store?" he asked his aides.[59] The question he did not ask was, Should I step aside temporarily?

If a crisis had erupted over Poland, the president would have been in no position to assess all of the facts independently and to arrive at a reasoned decision on the proper course of action. Weinberger, Haig, and Allen would all have had clearly defined points of view, but they would have been filtered through the mind and ideology of Meese, Baker, and, to a lesser extent, Deaver. Bush would have listened and agreed, as he had done up until then and as he did in the ensuing years. The elected president was less the national leader in full control than he was the follower.

Cynics voiced the belief that the situation after the shooting was much the same as before, given Reagan's unprecedented delegation of authority to his aides. If trauma rendered him incapable of rapid response to a crisis with his full capacities, if he lacked the energy and focus to direct the administration—"What difference would it make?" they asked.

A physician involved in his case commented, "I don't know how much of his lack of interest in what was going on was just Ronald Reagan, and how much was the attack he had suffered. I remember that Jaruzelski or possibly Walesa was on television in a major address. One of the surgical residents went into his room, and he was watching cartoons. There was this live action taking place on television with the Russians on the Polish border and the Solidarity movement possibly about to precipitate a military confrontation, and he was watching cartoons. He clearly wasn't very much interested in world events at that moment."[60]

Such a view is supported by the administration's conduct in other crises. In August 1981, Meese waited five hours to tell Reagan that the United States had shot down two Libyan warplanes over the Gulf of Sidra. Reagan then returned to sleep for an additional three and a half hours.[61] In September 1983, when the Soviets downed KAL 007, Secretary of State

George Shultz preferred to let Reagan get his normal amount of sleep rather than wake him with the news. Speaker of the House Tip O'Neill was shocked to discover that Shultz told him about the incident before Reagan had been notified.[62]

Ultimate authority cannot reside in the hands of aides when the president is asleep, let alone when he is disabled. If a new crisis had arisen after the assassination attempt, the government's credibility and accountability could have been seriously compromised.

No matter how wisely a president doles out responsibilities, the sheer volume of president-only decisions will eventually cause breakdowns in the executive system. Reagan's absence was felt as his disability continued. The Japanese were confused by a Haig letter strongly suggesting that they cut auto exports to the United States, a letter of which other administration officials were apparently unaware until after the fact. The transfer of education, health, and social programs to the states that was a part of the Reagan agenda was held up. Action to revoke the embargo on grain to the USSR—a campaign promise—was in limbo. Only "time urgent" matters were brought before him, with the result that numerous decisions were held in abeyance.[63]

Reagan's illness robbed certain policy efforts of the political impetus that only presidential involvement can provide. Nearly three weeks later, Reagan aides were saying that the president tired quickly during their discussions: "In a session dealing with the president's economic program . . . Reagan began alertly and was full of questions, but showed obvious signs of fatigue after half an hour."[64]

Reagan's greatest skill as president was not that of an administrator but that of a salesman. A defection by three con-

servative Republicans on the Senate Budget Committee resulted in the defeat of a resolution favored by the administration; it might have been reversed had Reagan been available
to urge their support.[65]

It may be argued that, in the emergency, there was no time
to consider all of the pertinent factors. Such a contention
neglects the evidence: no president under anesthesia can possibly make decisions about the fate of a nation, or about
anything else. In an attitude of genuine concern for leadership, Bush, Meese, or Baker might have inquired of Dr.
Aaron or Dr. Ruge how the potential complications of surgery—hemorrhage, infection, pulmonary embolism—could
affect the president. They might well have probed the impact
of the trauma, blood loss, drugs, anesthesia, and surgery experienced by Reagan on his concentration and decision-making ability. Deaver has said, "I do not deny that for 24 hours,
perhaps even 48, we were not certain of the president's survival. For a week, we may have worried about his effectiveness."[66]

Some of the physicians were asked whether the White
House staff had consulted with them on the president's competence to make decisions for the nation. Ben Aaron replied,
"Not once. They were there every morning, but none of
them communicated with me."[67]

Similarly, no one asked Dr. Ruge about the president's
cognitive capacity or about the possible need to use the
Twenty-fifth Amendment. "I think that it should have been
invoked during that time," he said. "Maybe I am responsible,
because I really hadn't thought about it too much, even
though I carried a copy of it with me at all times. They could
have talked to me, but they didn't. I was well prepared for

certain things. If he had become ill, I knew who to call and get things going. If he had been killed, it would have been pretty easy to know what to do; I wouldn't have had to do anything. And if he had had an injury like Brady's which made him completely disabled, my role would have been clear. Probing into relative degrees of competence is another matter."[68]

Ruge had considered the possibility not only of an injured president but also of a dead one. As early as December 17, 1980, one month before the inauguration, he had asked Dr. Paul Le Golvan, director of pathology at the Veterans' Administration, to determine the process that would follow a president's death in office. Le Golvan reported to him that the FBI was responsible for investigating the deaths of the president, the vice-president, and congressmen, while the Armed Forces Institute of Pathology would perform the autopsy (see the copy of the letter on page 194 from Dr. Le Golvan).[69]

Nobody questioned Dr. Dennis O'Leary or Dr. William Knaus[70] about Reagan's ability to make decisions. Knaus, the internist who took care of Reagan during the first few postoperative days, said, "You can make a strong case that when something this serious happens to the president, he ought to turn over the office temporarily to the next in line. I wasn't involved in any of those decisions. I didn't know whether they were taking place or not. No one even mentioned the Twenty-fifth Amendment. I just know that for Tuesday and Wednesday, there was no decision making going on. I was in that room more than I was out of it, and there was no discussion of politics or government except for that one farm bill."[71]

**Veterans
Administration**

Memorandum

Date: December 17, 1980

To: Dr. Daniel A. Ruge
Director, Spinal Cord Injury Service

Subj: Information Concerning Forensic
Sciences Services Available in
the U.S.

1. I made an inquiry to Dr. Robert L. Thompson, Captain MC, USN, Chairman of the Department of Forensic Sciences at the Armed Forces Institute of Pathology, Washington, D.C., regarding the subject above. His telephone number is 576-3287 and he would welcome any direct inquiries to him from you if you so desire.

2. By law, the Federal Bureau of Investigation investigates all deaths involving the President, Vice President, Congressman, etc.

3. The Federal Bureau of Investigation has an agreement with the Armed Forces Institute of Pathology by which the Armed Forces Institute of Pathology would provide forensic and other pathology support in conjunction with deaths of such individuals if so required. The Armed Forces Institute of Pathology would conduct the inquiry at the AFIP probably and would call in national consultants and local consultants as required.

PAUL C. LEGOLVAN, M.D.
Director
Pathology Service   (113)

The rush to pronounce Reagan healthy and capable ignored essential facts. His limitations were such that he was simply unable to keep pace with the presidential decisions that were required in the weeks that followed.

Some time later, Dr. Ruge was asked whether the need for invocation would have occurred to him if the shooting had taken place four years later. He was certain that it would have.[72]

Even if Ruge had thought of it and brought it up, there is no evidence that the White House staff or the vice-president was interested in probing fully the president's capacity to govern. In retrospect, Meese has said that the president should relieve himself of authority under Section 3 before going into surgery, or should be relieved of authority under Section 4 if unconscious. But he maintained that Reagan was not disabled during the recovery period and that it would have been improper to have Bush act as president during that time.[73]

Gergen, however, looked back at Reagan's condition with greater concern: "He was extremely weak; he was emaciated; he was much older, obviously a man who had had a grievous wound. . . . I did not feel that he was mentally out of it; I didn't sense that. I did feel in retrospect that a lot of effort was undertaken to shield the public from just how sick he was over in the hospital and after he came back to the White House."[74]

An administration should prepare itself and the country for possible presidential disability, in Gergen's view, with a "public discussion of when you are going to use the Twenty-fifth so that you are clear to the public before you start—what your general understandings are and what the operational rules are going to be. If you suddenly do it out of the blue, it may send the wrong message."[75]

We can only conjecture on the role of psychological "denial" in the response of the men around the president.

Still feeling their way in the pyramid of power, they may simply have refused to confront the seriousness of his condition. At a deeper level, below the surface of thought, conversation, and action, they may have felt a strong need to distance themselves from the temporary transfer of power. Who could predict the president's reaction to those who doubted his fitness to discharge the responsibilities of office, when he himself in retrospect might well have had no doubts at all?

Years later, Larry Speakes was asked if he believed the provisions of the amendment should have been invoked. "Looking back, I certainly do," he replied. "But at the time, there really wasn't that much thought of using it. The emphasis was on reassuring the American people."[76]

Seven years after the event, most of the doctors in charge of Reagan's care agreed with Speakes that the Twenty-fifth Amendment should have been used, at the very least during the first hours after surgery, and perhaps for several days thereafter.[77]

10

The First Use of the Disability Provisions of the Twenty-fifth Amendment

IN 1984, A SMALL POLYP WAS DISCOVERED IN PRESIDENT REAGAN'S large bowel during a proctoscopic examination. Biopsy showed that it was benign; thus, surgery was not required. Another polyp was found in March 1985, this one attached to the intestinal wall by a stalk. There were also traces of blood in stool samples. With a change in Reagan's diet, the stool examinations became negative. Nevertheless, he was placed on the surgical schedule for removal of the polyp at Bethesda Naval Medical Center. On the same day, July 12, the doctors would perform a colonoscopy to examine the full length of his colon.[1]

On the Monday before Reagan's polyp surgery and colonoscopy, White House Counsel Fred Fielding met in the

Oval Office with the president, Vice-President George Bush, and White House Chief of Staff Donald Regan to discuss the implications of Reagan's scheduled treatment and to consider the question of whether a transfer of presidential authority to Bush would be required. They reviewed the provisions of the Twenty-fifth Amendment and the National Command Authority.[2] On the basis of medical advice that the effect of the sedation would be similar to that of drinking a few martinis, they decided that a transfer would not be proper, unless unanticipated findings required the use of general anesthesia.[3]

On the afternoon of July 12, Dr. Edward Cattow removed the polyp and performed the colonoscopy, which revealed a second, more dangerous tumor: a larger, precancerous lesion called a villous adenoma. Because of its size, and because it was not on a stalk, it could be removed only by major surgery.[4] Reagan was told he could undergo surgery immediately or in two to three weeks. Although his wife apparently preferred to delay until the following week on the advice of her astrologer, he chose to return for surgery at Bethesda the next day to avoid going through the preparatory regimen once more.[5]

When Don Regan heard that surgery was planned, he immediately called Bush and National Security Adviser Robert McFarlane. McFarlane, in turn, notified Secretary of State George Shultz and Secretary of Defense Caspar Weinberger. A Regan staffer contacted the rest of the cabinet. Senate Majority Leader Bob Dole and Speaker of the House Tip O'Neill were also informed of the scheduled operation. Speakes briefed the news media at 6 P.M.[6]

George Bush was touring the Teradyne plant in Boston when the news reached him.[7] He had intended to go to his summer home in Kennebunkport, Maine, for the weekend.

He told Regan that he would remain there—about an hour from Washington by air—until he received further information.[8]

That afternoon, Regan called Fielding, who began considering the need for use of the Twenty-fifth Amendment to transfer power to the vice-president. Fielding and Bush consulted by telephone, debating the question of whether such a transfer would set an undesirable precedent. Their discussions continued on and off until 3 A.M. Saturday. Fielding also spoke with Attorney General Ed Meese and Regan.[9]

The decision to transfer authority to Bush was hampered by the difficulty of getting reliable medical advice from the president's physician, Dr. Burton Smith, a urologist who "couldn't articulate much about medicine outside of his specialty," according to Speakes. It was not until Speakes and Fielding consulted Dr. John Hutton from the surgical team that they got a realistic assessment of the effect of anesthesia on Reagan, and decided a transfer of power would be required.[10]

The administration was influenced by congressional criticism of the failure to transfer power after the 1981 assassination attempt. But Fielding knew that the president was reluctant to employ the Twenty-fifth Amendment for a "minor" surgical procedure, lest he create a precedent that might weaken the office. As in 1981, the possibility of alarming the public and of venturing into uncharted legal waters may also have concerned Fielding.[11] He therefore drafted two letters: an "optional" version that bypassed invocation, and a "normal" version that explicitly invoked Section 3 of the Twenty-fifth Amendment, adapted from the administration's "emergency book."

On Saturday morning, July 13, Fielding met with Don

Regan, at the hospital and showed him the letters. They then met with Nancy Reagan, McFarlane, and the president in his hospital room and discussed the issue. Reagan signed the "optional" letter (below) at 10:32 A.M.[12]

First Letter

I am about to undergo surgery during which time I will be briefly and temporarily incapable of discharging the constitutional powers and duties of the office of the President of the United States.

After consultation with my counsel and the Attorney General, I am mindful of the provisions of Section 3 of the 25th Amendment to the Constitution and of the uncertainties of its application to such brief and temporary periods of incapacity. I do not believe that the drafters of this amendment intended its application to situations such as the instant one.

Nevertheless, consistent with my longstanding arrangement with Vice President George Bush, and not intending to set a precedent binding anyone privileged to hold the office in the future, I have determined and it is my intention and direction, that Vice President George Bush shall discharge those powers and duties in my stead commencing with the administration of anesthesia to me in this instance.

I shall advise you and the Vice President when I determine that I am able to resume the discharge of the constitutional powers and duties of this office.

May God bless this nation and us all.

Sincerely,

RONALD REAGAN.

The letter was sent to the Speaker of the House and the president pro tem of the Senate, in accordance with the guidelines and requirements of the Twenty-fifth Amendment. But it was not a letter of invocation. Instead, Reagan said he did not "believe the drafters of this Amendment intended its application in situations such as the instant one." He concluded the letter with the comment that he would notify Congress when he was able to resume the powers and duties of his office.[13]

Surgery started at 11:48 A.M., but Bush became "acting" president at 11:28 A.M. when Reagan was anesthetized. (Although Bush arrived at his Washington residence at 11:35 A.M., nobody told him he was acting president until 11:50 A.M.[14] Fielding later said this mix-up occurred when eager doctors anesthetized Reagan early to get a "head start" on the operation.)[15] Bush's last minute return to Washington may have been delayed by Regan. Bush had been eager to return Friday evening so as to be in Washington during the surgery. Regan advised him to stay in Maine, contending that his return would alarm the public. Bush came back the next morning anyway. He later denied rumors that Regan wanted to shunt him aside or grab the spotlight; rather, he said, Regan merely wanted to avoid attracting unnecessary attention to a "routine operation." The president later added that it was originally his idea that Bush need not return to Washington.[16]

Before going into surgery, Reagan discussed legislative matters, including the budget deficit, with Regan and received his daily national security briefing.[17]

At 1:00 P.M., when Speakes appeared in the hospital press room to announce that the president had gone into surgery, he distributed copies of the letter dealing with the transfer of power. He refused to read it aloud, and some reporters became confused and thought that Reagan had resigned. The news conference became chaotic as television and radio journalists in the front row began reading the letter for live broadcast, while reporters in the back rows began booing because Speakes would not answer their questions.[18]

Surgery lasted two hours and fifty-three minutes. The seven-member surgical team, led by Dr. Dale Oller, resected the right half of the large bowel, removing approximately two feet of the colon. They also explored the abdominal cavity and found no other signs of cancer after checking the intestines, liver, spleen, and lymph nodes. The tumor removed was about five centimeters in diameter.[19] On pathological examination, it was found to be malignant. It was classified as a "Dukes B" lesion, one that had invaded the muscle of the colon but was confined to the bowel wall.[20]

Recovery and the Second Letter

When Reagan regained consciousness, he was somewhat disoriented. The most difficult time he had during the treatment, he later recalled, was "trying to reorient as to where I was and had I been operated on yet or not—and they said, 'Oh, yes, it's all over.' "[21] Mrs. Reagan and her brother, Dr. Richard Davis, visited and talked to the president at 4:30 P.M. He slept or dozed under the influence of the anesthetic until about 7:00 P.M.[22]

After the surgery, Fielding, Regan, and Speakes met with the surgeon to discuss the Twenty-fifth Amendment and the question of the president's competency to resume the powers and duties of office.[23] Although his postoperative course was satisfactory, his aides wondered whether Reagan was lucid and considered deferring the return of authority until the next morning. The surgeon told them there was no standard method of determining whether he had fully regained his faculties. They debated whether to delay, but then devised their own test: they brought Reagan the two-sentence statement (below) that he would sign to reclaim his office, to see if he could read it out loud coherently.[24]

Second Letter

Following up on my letter to you of this date, please be advised I am able to resume the discharge of the constitutional powers and duties of the office of the President of the United States. I have informed the Vice President of my determination and my resumption of those powers and duties.

Sincerely,

RONALD REAGAN.

Fielding described the process of choosing this "test": "I was asking questions about how you could know, what was the legitimate way to determine whether the President was capable, understanding, lucid, and that sort of thing. We hit upon several tests, one of which was that I said 'I'm going to ask him to sign a letter. How about asking him to read the letter and understand it? Wouldn't that be evidence that he was lucid?' And he [Dr. Oller] said, 'Yep.' " The White

House physician was not consulted at this stage: "Once we got into the surgery phase . . . we were dealing with the surgical team," Fielding said.[25]

The three aides and the surgeon went to the recovery room shortly after 7:00 P.M. The room had been cleared of all beds except Reagan's. He was attended by a team of doctors and nurses, together with Secret Service agents. White House communications specialists stood by in case of need, and the nuclear "football" was close at hand.[26]

By this time, the general anesthetic had largely worn off, but Reagan was still numb from the waist down. He was receiving intravenous antibiotics, and a nasogastric tube had been inserted through his nose. Earlier in the day, he had received an injection of morphine into the spinal canal, which doctors said would relieve pain while leaving mental functions unimpaired. His laboratory values were normal, and he had no fever.[27]

When Reagan first looked at the (second) letter, he blinked his eyes and faltered, and Fielding, Regan, and Speakes were concerned. Fielding recalled that he thought, "Uh oh, and Don Regan and I looked at each other and decided that maybe we were a little premature."[28] But then Reagan asked for his reading glasses and read the passage aloud. In this way, he passed the test devised by his aides, who discussed the letter with him and offered to bring it back in a couple of hours for his signature. But Reagan replied, "Heck no, I don't want you to wake me up later. I'll sign it now."[29] He did so at 7:22 P.M.,[30] when George Bush had been acting president seven hours and fifty minutes.

Perhaps the most extraordinary aspect of the episode is that no one bothered to ask Ronald Reagan whether he was genuinely ready and wished to assume the burdens of office. Under Section 3, the president initiates invocation, and the president terminates the period of the acting presidency. Not Fielding; not Regan; not Speakes—the president. To be sure, he was able to read the second letter, and did so. But he read it and signed it not because he had expressed to anyone the conviction that he could comfortably function fully as president once more; he did so because Fielding had decided that he should, and asked him to sign. All of Fielding's experience with the attack on Reagan in 1981 had not clarified for him the concept that *the decision must be made by the president,* not *for* the president.

Regan told reporters afterward that he had tested the president "to see that he was alert, at least from my layman's point of view, by asking him to read the letter he was about to sign."[31] Regan was impressed when Reagan took up a subject they had discussed that morning before surgery—the budget deficit.[32]

Speakes recounted the surgeon's belief that "if the president needed to make a decision, he could make it." The president was "doing beautifully." That evening, Reagan commented to his staff, "I feel fit as a fiddle."[33]

Fielding would have been willing to wait longer if the president had not seemed lucid—"I would have had no problem with going overnight"—but he also felt that "the sooner the better for any number of reasons. . . . The public out there needed reassurance the President was in fact really O.K." They were careful not to act too soon, he said. "The worst thing in the world would have been to have him transfer . . . the power to the vice president . . . and then later have to transfer it back again. . . . We had to be reassured by the doctors that the probabilities of that to occur were low."[34]

Dr. Steven Rosenberg, a member of the surgical team, said the president would be fully restored in six to eight weeks. By all accounts, his recovery was rapid. On Monday, July 15, he was moved from the recovery room to the presidential suite in a wheelchair. That day his bladder catheter was removed. He had a slight fever, but he planned to take on a light work load with selected meetings and briefings.[35]

On Tuesday, July 16, it was announced that the polyp was malignant, but that the president had a greater than 50 percent chance of living out a normal life span. When the president was informed that he had cancer, the meeting took all of five minutes. He told the surgeon, Dr. Oller, "Well, I'm glad that's all out."[36] Evidently, he asked the doctors few questions throughout the course of his treatment.[37]

On Wednesday, July 17, he was taken off intravenous feeding and placed on a liquid diet. He and Bush then had their first meeting since the surgery.[38] The next day, he began eating solid food. The staples binding his incision were removed and replaced by adhesive strips. Speakes told the press the president was "totally back to normal."[39]

Reagan returned by helicopter to the White House the following morning, five days after surgery. He had lost less than five pounds during his stay in the hospital. He began working 9:30 A.M. to 11 A.M. or noon every day, a schedule that would continue until he left for a trip to Santa Barbara in mid-August. On July 23, a week and a half after surgery, he met with President Li Xiannian of China, although the ceremony was limited to fifteen minutes to conserve Reagan's strength.[40]

Who Was in Charge?

George Bush told an interviewer that he felt the burden of responsibility more heavily during the bowel surgery than he had when Reagan was shot in 1981, explaining that his role was "more defined." But while Bush officially became acting president, his functions were peripheral. He exercised none of the constitutional powers of the office, passing the eight hours at his official residence, reading, playing tennis, and talking on the phone.[41]

He was not a participant in the discussion that led to the president's resumption of presidential authority—a decision made by Regan, Fielding, and Speakes. He filled in for the president on some occasions while Reagan was hospitalized: he met with members of the Senate Finance Committee in Reagan's stead, stood in for him at a ceremony announcing the name of the first teacher to ride in the space shuttle, and telephoned European leaders and the Japanese prime minister to assure them that the surgery was successful. It was announced that Bush would substitute for the president at cabinet and National Security Council meetings, but none were held during the hospitalization. At some White House meetings, it was Regan rather than Bush who stood in for the president, and the White House staff held two meetings without inviting Bush.[42]

In contrast to March 1981, this time there was little pretense that Reagan was actually running the administration. As Don Regan said the day after surgery, "We'll try to make as many decisions as we can without involving him [Reagan] where we can get an agreement. And if there is a difference of opinion and it can't be ironed out, we will make it crisp and succinct and take it to him to make a decision and spare him from having to listen to the debate of various people."[43]

Regan served as the link between the White House and Reagan's hospital suite, and only the first lady had equal access to the president. Each day, after an 8:00 A.M. meeting with his staff, Regan would travel to Bethesda to consult with the president, and also had phone contact with him during the day. He had his own office at Bethesda, just down the hall from the president's suite. He decided what paperwork and decisions would reach the president. He had drawn up a plan as to how the executive branch would operate in the president's absence, and he ran the White House.

His responsibilities during Reagan's recovery went beyond the day-to-day management of the White House: they included choosing a new budget director (James C. Miller III), trying to shape a legislative compromise to reduce the deficit, and overseeing a shuffle of key White House personnel. He took up the slack while the president enjoyed a lightened work load during the entire course of the anticipated seven- to eight-week recovery period.[44] Senator Dan Quayle remarked during the hospitalization that Regan "is the acting President."[45]

Regan and Mrs. Reagan sealed the president off from other visitors during his convalescence. Bush didn't see him until four days after surgery, on July 17; McFarlane saw him later on the eighteenth. Both men had been anxious to visit earlier, but Nancy Reagan refused to allow it, insisting on protecting him from the stress of additional visitors.[46] Some perceived Regan himself as relishing the limelight and his access to the president. Speakes recalled that Regan "would always make a strategic pause just outside the hospital to confer with either me or one of the advance men in full view of the photographers. [It] helped create the 'I'm in charge' image. . . ."[47]

Iran-Contra and Beyond

Over a year after Reagan's surgery, it was suggested that he made the decision on the first arms shipment to Iran—a decision he could not recollect—while weakened during his recovery from surgery.[48] This allegation originated in Meese's testimony in a closed-door session of the House Intelligence Committee. After the meeting, Representative George Brown, Jr., reported Meese's statement that Reagan might have approved the shipment while "recovering from a serious illness and that his memory could have been impaired as a result of postoperative medication."[49]

Another committee member recounted Meese's comment that the president's surgery might have affected his ability to concentrate on events, and that he may have given a "vague and unspecific approval" for the arms shipment in such a mentally unfocused condition. Meese's spokesman denied that he had implicated postoperative drugs, but refused to comment on whether Reagan's recollection may have been impaired for some other reason. It seems safe to conclude that Meese believed Reagan may have approved the shipment while partially incapacitated because of the surgery.[50]

The picture of an ailing, confused Reagan approving the disastrous action from his sickbed raises serious questions. How could Meese have known about this meeting, since he was not personally present? Did he hear about it, or was he just speculating? How and to what extent was Reagan impaired? Was he disabled by medication? Was he in pain, emotionally unstable, or simply fatigued?

Meese's statements were an attempt to explain Reagan's inability to recall whether he had given prior approval to the first shipment, a point on which the testimony of Regan and McFarlane had clashed, and on which Reagan himself had vacillated.[51] His account was supposed to resolve the dispute in McFarlane's favor, with Reagan giving prior approval to the arms shipment. But some of its features did not quite match McFarlane's version of events.

The first arms shipment took place in August 1985. McFarlane met with Reagan in his hospital room together with Regan on July 18, and Reagan gave McFarlane the approval to use an Israeli contact to reach Iranian officials in the hope of helping the hostages.[52] According to McFarlane, Reagan did not approve a particular arms shipment then, but rather the general principle of sending arms to Iran through Israel.[53] This seems to match the report of a "vague and unspecific" approval in Meese's testimony before the subcommittee.

McFarlane stated, however, that explicit approval of the first arms shipment came in a telephone call to McFarlane's home in early August.[54] If McFarlane was correct, Reagan sanctioned the arms transaction *twice*, with a vague assent to the principle in July, and an approval of the first shipment in August.

This belies the notion that his action was an aberration brought on by incapacity, or that he forgot about the episode because he was unfocused and detached. Alternatively, if he *was* disabled in July, some incapacity may have persisted into August, when he gave the second approval.

It is difficult to assess the cancer surgery's psychological impact on the president. After returning from the hospital on July 20, he told aides, "I appreciate all these cards, but I never suffered from cancer." Later he elaborated on this judgment: "I didn't have cancer. I had something inside of me that had cancer in it and it was removed."[55] It was almost as if he had been a bystander, both denying the nature of his illness and recounting it as an event that might have happened to someone else.

Nevertheless, the episode had a profound effect on the people in the president's entourage. "If they had been protective of him before, they now grew fiendishly so. If they had sometimes slyly made decisions without him before, they now justified doing so openly. They didn't want to strain him with the burdens of his office."[56]

It is fair to ask whether the president and the White House staff had learned from the experience of March 1981. They were clearly sensitive to the criticism that arose from the failure to transfer power to the vice-president at that time.[57] Aware that the president would be unconscious during surgery, they were prepared to implement the appointment of Bush as acting president. But the fear of establishing a "poor precedent" impelled the president to avoid the constitutional mechanism already in place. Instead, Reagan issued a strong disclaimer that the transfer of power to Bush had anything to do with the Twenty-fifth Amendment. Without defining the authority behind the contention, the letter stipulated anesthesia and surgery as conditions in which its application was not "intended" by its architects. This interpretation has been contradicted by former Senator Birch Bayh, the legislator who exerted the greatest influence on the final text of the draft. "If the president is going to be under anesthesia, why shouldn't he . . . turn his powers and duties over to the vice president?" Bayh asked. "To me, the argument is strongly in favor of going ahead." The White House staff should have said, "We're just doing what is required by the Constitution." "This was the time," he believed, "for a good precedent to be set." In Bayh's view, an important opportunity was lost. "There is a tenacious desire to hold on to presidential power and not to trust other people with it. I think the president botched it."[58]

The manner in which Bush's authority was terminated also illustrated a failure to come to grips with a central question of the Twenty-fifth Amendment, namely, the meaning of "inability." Regan, Fielding, and Speakes devised an extraordinary test to assess the cognitive competence of the president; on the basis of it they determined that his decision-making capacities were intact.

The notion that the ability to read a few lines of a letter was a credible test of a complex set of mental attributes was apparently first considered when Regan and Fielding were told by Dr. Oller that there were no standard methods of postoperative evaluation. It reflected the "take charge" chief of staff, fully confident of his common sense, ingenuity, and ability to explore this matter, operating in an arena totally outside his expertise.

To read is not necessarily to understand. Even if the president understood the two sentences, that says nothing about his ability to concentrate, attend, remember, reflect, deliberate, discriminate, comprehend, evaluate, and reason. All are involved in the decision-making process that presidents confront. As we have seen, a common sequel of surgery is confusion severe enough to impede a patient's ability to think clearly.

The president and the White House staff had the period from March to July 1985 to consider the coming surgery and to review the problems involved in the temporary replacement of an unconscious president. The lack of planning was evident in Fielding's last-minute scramble to prepare the letters and get adequate medical advice. The White House physician was not prepared for such a situation, and gave misleading information about the effects of anesthesia. The aides might well have discussed with knowledgeable surgeons, psychologists, and psychiatrists the length of time required by surgical patients to recapture their cognitive faculties fully. The staff might have looked into the available psychological tests to determine which might be applicable to the president's situation. They might have thought more broadly than "I would have no problem with going overnight"[59] to consider a period of days or weeks of recovery. This would have made the transfer of power to the vice-president more meaningful and would have allowed him to play the role as an official whom the American people had elected. It would have given the president more time to recuperate and might have avoided the fiasco of the Iranian arms deal.

The episode illustrates well one of the dangers of transferring power back to the president prematurely: "the decision and policies which had been attributed to the ailing President become suspect and the standing of the Presidency for that period in history becomes shaken."[60] Reagan's avowed failure to recall a key decision made after surgery raises the question of his competency during the postoperative period, as does the testimony of Regan, McFarlane, and Meese. Even if he was not disabled, even if he made no critical decisions, the early return of power, without proper safeguards and deliberation, ensured that a cloud of doubts and uncertainty would surround important policies formed during that period.

It is equally hazardous to turn the reins of government over to individuals who are not elected or accountable to the voters, and who have no constitutional authority to act. In sharp contrast to Bush, Regan made "as many decisions" as he could,[61] and seemed almost deliberately to short-circuit Bush, once the enabling letter had been signed by the president after surgery. Quayle's remark that Regan was "the acting president" undoubtedly reflected the reality of the situation.[62] It was certainly not what Herbert Brownell, Birch Bayh, and many others involved in shaping the Twenty-fifth Amendment had envisioned.

11

The Next Time

AS THE REAGAN EXPERIENCE DEMONSTRATED, IT IS DIFFICULT TO DEAL
with presidential inability on short notice or during a crisis.
For one thing, the Twenty-fifth Amendment holds no reliable
guidelines for determining fitness. This is hardly surprising,
because the amendment in its final form was already more
explicit than some of its architects would have liked.[1] "Inability" was framed primarily as an issue of politics and constitutional law. Any attempt to define it in detail was considered
unwise and unworkable. The presence of inability, it was
thought, was relative and depended on the contingencies of
the time: a fixed definition would fail to anticipate the varied
cases that might arise and might prejudge even those that
could be foreseen. As for medical guidelines, the framers felt

that these were unnecessary, since physicians' advice would be available when the need arose.[2]

Nevertheless, a good deal of deliberation was devoted to the issue. It was often emphasized that the term should be broadly construed as any inability to perform the powers and duties of office or to communicate decisions. This would exclude such factors as unpopularity, incompetence, impeachable conduct, poor judgment, and laziness.[3] On the other hand, it would include mental or physical disability, as well as incapacitating circumstances such as capture during wartime. Multiple potentially disabling conditions were mentioned during the congressional hearings, including heart attacks, coma, paralysis, mental illness, anesthesia, and the infirmities of old age.[4] But it was generally assumed that presidential inability would be obvious to an observer (as it probably would be in a "worst-case" situation), and there was virtually no detailed discussion of any specific medical condition. No medical authorities were called to testify in the congressional hearings. Birch Bayh later remarked on the lack of medical testimony: "We might have been in error there. We were willing to accept the worst case situation from a medical standpoint. [Our mission] was to design and create a structure that would go forward and take advantage of medical expertise at the time it would be needed."[5] During the Senate hearings, Charles S. Rhyne, president of the American Bar Association, expressed a widely held view: "Historically, the real problem of Presidential inability has not stemmed from a question of determining the existence of any Presidential inability. This is the error of those people who focus on some sort of a commission. . . . The inability usually has been clear and undisputed."[6]

Aside from Eisenhower, who was keenly aware of his own disabilities, the paradigmatic cases that loomed largest were those of Wilson and Garfield, in which the issue surely was not whether they were disabled but rather how to deal with it.

In any case, it is this question that remains the central dilemma of the Twenty-fifth Amendment. What is "disability"? What is "inability"? At what level of cognitive alteration is the country likely to be endangered? Senator Birch Bayh believes that the presidency is essentially a cognitive responsibility, requiring an intact ability to think and reason. "In the Eisenhower situation, if the Twenty-fifth Amendment had been in place, he would have turned the office over to Vice-President Nixon and then, when he got to feeling better, taken it back.

"It has to be a question of degree because it is only natural for the president's men to say, 'He's in bad shape, but compared to whom? Look who's going to succeed him.' There are other factors that are operative. In the Kennedy-Johnson period, because of the bitterness that existed, the people around President Kennedy probably would have been reluctant to invoke. It's the old business of balancing tickets, where you get some person whom you can't stand but if he can bring in California or New York, you put him in as vice-president and then expect to turn him out to pasture.

"I have heard some say that this president [Bush] would have to be a hell of a lot sicker than others before his office will be turned over to this vice-president [Quayle]. That is not my assessment; I heard it from people who are close to the administration. Of course, this should change as Vice-President Quayle grows, and people have fewer doubts than they have now or have had before. In a perfect world, you're going to have a vice-president fully as capable as the president whom he replaces."[7]

John Feerick, the dean of Fordham Law School and an important contributor to the American Bar Association version of the Twenty-fifth Amendment, agreed with the definition of inability as any state "that renders the president unable to handle the powers and duties of the office. It could be that he's unable to make a decision or to communicate it. It could be physical, it could be mental. If there was significant concern about mental capacity, judgments, or the ability to reflect and to deliberate, that would call for a careful review."[8]

The problem with the word "inability" lies precisely in its layers of meaning. The president may be able to sign a bill, or make an appointment, or greet a foreign visitor. If he cannot conduct his office at a satisfactory level, however, is he "unable"?

The complexity is further illustrated by an episode that occurred near the end of Reagan's second term. Donald Regan had resigned (or been dismissed) as the White House chief of staff at the end of February 1987, and former Senator Howard Baker was appointed to the post. Baker asked an aide, James Cannon, to look at the problems of internal disorder in the White House that had come to his attention. Cannon proceeded to interview fifteen to twenty of the White House staff, including senior officials. They informed him "how inattentive and inept the president was. He was lazy; he wasn't interested in the job. They said he wouldn't read the papers they gave him—even short position papers and documents. They said he wouldn't come over to work— all he wanted to do was to watch movies and television at the residence."[9]

Cannon was dismayed both by the breakdown of the staff system and by the evidence of Reagan's depressed mood in the aftermath of the Iran-Contra affair. Some officials felt free to sign Reagan's name to memoranda he had not reviewed. Cannon had actually seen a "significant" document in which the president's initials had been signed by someone else. In summarizing his impressions for Howard Baker, Cannon recommended that he should "consider the possibility that Section 4 of the Twenty-fifth Amendment should be applied" because the president was no longer discharging the duties of office. According to Michael Deaver, Cannon had concluded that the president "was at the brink of being physically and mentally incapable of carrying out his responsibilities."[10]

Baker took the report seriously and together with Cannon and two other aides met with the president the next day. By the end of the conversation, Baker was persuaded of the president's mental competence, and Cannon's recommendation was disregarded.[11]

Cannon was an official experienced in government. He had worked with Nelson Rockefeller, Gerald Ford, and Howard Baker over a period of many years. His perception of a depressed, inadequate president unfit to govern could not be dismissed lightly by Baker, and it was not. Yet Cannon was overruled in his assessment of the president's "inability." The evidence he had collected was undermined by the president's ability to rise to the occasion. His performance was enough to neutralize the perception that he was simply not functioning adequately in office.

Clearly, reasonable people can differ in judging all but the most obvious kinds of disability. "No one is going to act to interfere with the presidential exercise of authority unless the president drools in public or announces on television that he is Alexander the Great," according to George Reedy, Lyndon Johnson's press secretary. "Where presidents are concerned, the tolerance level for irrationality extends almost to the point of gibbering idiocy or delusions of identity."[12]

Four months before the attack on Reagan, the electorate of Connecticut had been asking, "When does a top official's illness constitute 'inability'?" Governor Ella T. Grasso had been hospitalized at Hartford Hospital with ovarian cancer; she confirmed on November 25, 1980, that it had spread to her liver. She had been on a reduced work schedule *for eight months,* and yet was said to be "overseeing the affairs of state from her hospital room." The lieutenant governor made the remarkable comment that "the Governor is not *fully* incapacitated in the slightest" (italics added). But important decisions were being deferred because the state constitution contained no mechanism for determining whether disability existed. Meanwhile, an obviously impaired governor was holding tightly on to office, to the detriment of her constituents.[13]

Such considerations underlay the issue of "guidelines" for the Twenty-fifth Amendment. Given the complexity of the political, legal, medical and psychological questions, some presumed that medical experts would not be qualified to determine presidential inability.[14] Brownell, for example, contended, "It [would be] unwise . . . to establish formal legal machinery for giving a President physical and mental examinations because this amounts to placing a president constantly on trial as to his health and this would give a hostile commission the power to harass him at all times. . . . Provision for such physical and mental examinations [would] be an affront to the president's personal dignity." Furthermore, such formal legal requirements could lead to harmful publicity, conflicting medical opinions, or a public stalemate.[15]

Others emphasized that a medical commission would encourage a vice-president to act when necessary by providing independent judgments.[16] Such action was the whole point of amending the Constitution in the first place.

The arguments for simplicity eventually won out over the various proposed guidelines, partly because of the pressing need for compromise and action. But the legislation left room for procedures and criteria to be developed later. Furthermore, the Congress was authorized to form some "other body" to determine inability in the event that the vice-president and the cabinet were deadlocked and could not grapple with the problem.

Guidelines for Invocation

Twenty-five years after the framing of the Twenty-fifth Amendment, its effective use in the future may well hinge on new congressional hearings to determine how well it has worked, and whether improvements can be designed.

The *Report of the Miller Center Commission on Presidential Disability and the Twenty-fifth Amendment* recommended that each new president, vice-president, the White House physician, and the chief of staff review medical contingencies during the transition. They suggested that guidelines be developed, agreed on in advance, for emergencies, planned surgical procedures, and chronic ailments.[17] Kenneth Crispell, a professor of medicine and law at the University of Virginia, and his co-worker, Carlos Gomez, expressed the belief in their book on presidential illness that the administration of anesthesia and narcotics should be preceded by a temporary transfer of power under Section 3.[18] Such studies and an analysis of presidential illnesses and other disabling episodes provide a basis for a more detailed set of guidelines.[19] A formalization of the scenarios in which invocation is justified may be considered restrictive. Perhaps a more forward-looking view is that it will provide a durable framework for thoughtful and rational application of the Twenty-fifth Amendment in the future.

The following conditions should almost invariably suggest the use of Section 3:

- Planned, minor surgical procedures that require general anesthesia. Presidential power could be transferred for a long enough period to allow the president to concentrate on his personal health and to recover fully from the effects of anesthesia. If the surgery proves more complex than anticipated, the transfer period should be extended on the advice of the president's physicians.

- Planned, major surgery. Major operative procedures represent a substantive insult to the human organism and affect many organ systems. Power could be transferred for a minimum of a few days to a week. On his physician's advice, the president should feel comfortable extending the transfer for up to two or three weeks, and delegating heavily to the vice-president after that. (The temporary transfer of power does not preclude the president from being consulted in a crisis, and his wishes given full consideration. But the pressure to be fully involved will be moderated at a time when his attention is focused on his pain, on postoperative problems, or even on his survival.)

· Any emergency surgery that requires general anesthesia, so long as there is time for the president to sign enabling letters while he is lucid and capable.

· The use of psychoactive drugs in significant amounts. Such medications as narcotics, tranquilizers, amphetamines, barbiturates, and anesthetics may profoundly alter consciousness, judgment, perception, and behavior. Power should be transferred for the period of time while the drug is being administered, as well as the subsequent period during which its effects persist. For example, the onset of congestive heart failure is sometimes accompanied by profound respiratory distress. Morphine plays an important role in providing symptomatic relief, together with oxygen and drugs (such as digitalis, diuretics, and anti-arrhythmic agents). Clearly, the president should not be expected to consider and make important decisions while under the influence of morphine, let alone while experiencing the impact of congestive heart failure. The example that stands out among recent presidents is Franklin D. Roosevelt, who was in chronic heart failure when he ran for his fourth term.[20]

· In any of the foregoing situations, if Section 3 is not invoked prior to surgery, anesthesia, or use of mind-altering drugs, it should be done as soon as the president is capable of signing the papers. If not, Section 4 may be utilized.

- The perception by the president or his physician that an illness, injury, or emotional condition is interfering with his judgment or ability to govern. For example, any sustained febrile illness—pneumonia or a serious bout of influenza—may be debilitating and relatively incapacitating, especially in elderly individuals.

- Serious presidential illness. The diagnosis of any life-threatening disease—heart attack, stroke—should prompt consideration of the use of Section 3. Transfer should remain in effect for several days so that the president, his family, physicians, and advisers have time to evaluate the condition and determine how best to cope. Once the period of adjustment is over, the president should resume the powers and duties of office unless there is reason to believe that the knowledge of his illness, the illness itself, or its treatment may impair his judgment.

- Death or serious illness in the president's immediate family. Such events consume attention, destroy concentration, and interfere with decision-making ability. The death of Woodrow Wilson's wife during his first term plunged the president into a deep depression, and he acknowledged to an aide that "he was unfit to be President because he could not think straight."[21]

- The diagnosis of Alzheimer's disease or of any other progressive, mentally disabling conditions. If the president is incapable of evaluating the seriousness of his illness, Section 4 may have to be utilized.

- Any anticipated situations in which the president will be unable to communicate with his government. Rarely, communication gaps may be caused by circumstances which are not health related, such as trips that bring him to turbulent areas outside the continental United States or, possibly, outside the Western Hemisphere. Delegation of requisite powers to the vice-president might represent a simpler mechanism than invocation, when problems in communication are anticipated.

While it is essential not to attach any stigma to the appropriate application of Section 3, it is equally important to avoid its overuse. Ronald Reagan had a propensity for making the presidency a nine-to-five job. It would be a misuse of the amendment for a president to become so comfortable with invocation that he would simply hand over the responsibility to the vice-president for weekends and holidays. The transfer of power is an action of profound importance. It must be limited to circumstances in which the president's ability to make or communicate rational decisions has been compromised.

Stipulating the use of Section 4 is still more complicated and delicate. The White House staff will view the removal of the president's powers with deep suspicion, perhaps as an effort by the vice-president to arrogate authority to himself. They will then draw a "protective screen" around him and consider "their number-one goal in life to be that of presenting their 'chief' in the most favorable possible light."[22] The use of Section 4 may encourage this mistrust, particularly if the president objects strongly to the act.

It is all the more important, therefore, to construct guidelines around which a consensus may develop. The most important of these include:

- Loss of consciousness, a comatose state, or general anesthesia, whenever the transfer of power under Section 3 has not already occurred.

- Significant alterations of the president's cognitive faculties or inability to communicate. If the president suffers a massive coronary occlusion or a stroke, as President Eisenhower did while in office, power could be transferred for the duration of hospitalization and probably much of the convalescent period. A president might also be physically prevented from governing by a plane crash or capture during wartime.

- Serious injury to the president following an accident or an attack on his person. Depending on the president's competence or level of consciousness, he may be able to sign the letter of transfer. If he is unable to do so, Section 4 should be used. (A fatally wounded president may be conscious prior to death, but so ill that it would be inappropriate to ask him to sign a letter of transfer.)

- Terminal illness, when the president refuses to resign. Section 4 should be considered only with the concurrence of his family and staff if it is known that the president will not recover and has a short time to live. The president deserves the opportunity of spending his remaining time with family and friends. The country requires the immediate transfer of the power and authority of the president to a competent vice-president.

- Alzheimer's disease, brain tumor, or other progressive, mentally disabling conditions in a president who is incapacitated but cannot or will not step aside voluntarily. In this case, the judgment of others that the president is no longer competent to "discharge the powers and duties of his office" may conflict with his wishes. A psychotic president confident of his own abilities would also fit into this difficult category, as would one with a physical illness so enervating that he cannot fulfill his obligations competently. Woodrow Wilson was in such a condition through the later period of his presidency. Failure to invoke under such circumstances may render the office a hollow vehicle, occupied by an individual who cannot adequately fulfill his mandate.

No set of guidelines can determine the action of the president, under Section 3, or of the vice-president, under Section 4, in implementing the Twenty-fifth Amendment. The guidelines serve as a coherent and rational list of the settings in which invocation must be considered. Whereas the guidelines are primarily *medical* in character, the final decision is *political* and will be made by the president and/or the vice-president and cabinet except under extraordinary circumstances.

Temporary removal is motivated not only by the best interests of the nation but also by concern with the best therapy. The amendment allows a president to be human, to get sick, and to exercise caution and good sense in responding to his disability without endangering himself or the nation. The president and the public are best served by the transfer of power to the vice-president until the president is fit.

The Role of
the White House Physician

In virtually all of the conditions described above, the president's physician must provide essential information. Yet the care of the president can suffer when public relations takes precedence over medical prudence. In Reagan's case, the efforts to shape an exaggeratedly upbeat image were enough to hamper Reagan's treatment, as Ruge later complained: "I believe that people like Ed Meese, Jim Baker, Mike Deaver, wanted the world to know that the president was very, very well; they had more darned visitors going in there than they should have. . . . Nobody is in good shape after being shot, having had an anesthetic, and having lost a lot of blood and had it replaced. I think the visitors were overdone."[23]

Some White House physicians have treated the president "as they would a wealthy old patient who had no responsibility for others."[24] They respected his demands for clandestine treatment and disregarded the potential impact of presidential illness. As a result, the president was often deprived of competent care and the country was stripped of able leadership.

It is at such a juncture that the physician's relationship with his patient may conflict with what his obligations to the country ought to be. Communications between doctor and patient are normally confidential unless the patient chooses to share them with others. The code of confidentiality works with other factors to politicize the physician. Nothing concerning the president is separable from responsibility to the nation. As Ruge put it, "First, he is the President. Then, he is my patient. He came to Washington to be President, not to be my patient."[25]

This attitude is understandable and necessary if it means that the physician should be as unobtrusive as possible. Carried to an extreme, it may result in situations that compromise his integrity and his medical judgment. He could conceivably be coerced by a president, especially if he were in the military. The president has the power to dismiss him, which could hurt the doctor's professional and public standing.[26]

The documented cases of medical cover-ups, however, indicate a willing participation on the part of physicians, whose professional judgment has often been colored by personal loyalty and the extraordinary status and power of their patient. As Ruge observed, "When you are dealing with the president, the roles could easily be reversed to produce a patient-physician instead of a physician-patient connection. . . ."[27]

Perhaps the most dramatic example is that of Cary Grayson, physician to Woodrow Wilson. Wilson's physical and mental deterioration at the end of World War I may have contributed importantly to the United States's failure to enter the League of Nations.[28] In 1919, Wilson had suffered a massive stroke and was completely incapacitated. For months he lay in a darkened room, completely isolated from the public and his cabinet, while the reins of government fell into the hands of Grayson and Mrs. Wilson. Grayson, Wilson's intimate friend as well as his doctor, helped orchestrate the cover-up of his condition, quashed an effort to replace Wilson, and even dissuaded the president from stepping down, all in the hopes of preserving Wilson's authority and alleviating his emotional burdens.[29]

Admiral Ross McIntire engaged in similar deceptions in caring for Franklin D. Roosevelt, arranging hospital visits under spurious names, encouraging him to seek a fourth term when he was already a dying man, and issuing persistently optimistic appraisals of his patient even as death became imminent. The president could not be shielded from the unremitting demands of office at the end of World War II; he had to cope with world-shaping challenges such as the Yalta negotiations while physically and mentally debilitated by hypertensive heart disease, congestive heart failure, and other ailments.

More recently, John F. Kennedy's physician, Dr. Janet Travell, refused to acknowledge that Kennedy suffered from Addison's disease. Meanwhile, Kennedy was dependent on regular corticosteroid treatments to control the illness.[31] Steroid therapy may produce profound alterations of mood and behavior. Although it may not have altered the course of Kennedy's administration, the illness behind it should have been known to the public.

Can the White House physician's dual responsibilities be reconciled with the ethical tenets of the medical profession? Professional standards reflect both the importance of confidentiality and the need to consider the national interest. The American Medical Association in 1957 adopted a set of "Principles of Medical Ethics" which allowed violations of confidentiality when required by law and when "necessary in order to protect the welfare of the individual or of the community."[32] In 1980, the rule was changed to say merely that a physician must safeguard confidences "within the constraints of the law."[33] In addressing mental health problems (an even more sensitive issue), the Group for the Advancement of

Psychiatry issued contradictory statements: "In the case of high ranking patients the need for confidentiality is absolute," but "the psychiatrist must nevertheless accept his responsibility not only to his patient but also . . . to the community and the national welfare. . . ."[34] Nothing was said about resolving potential conflicts between the national interest and the need for "absolute" confidentiality.[35]

Given the president's responsibilities and power, and the dictates of the Twenty-fifth Amendment, it is not defensible to preserve absolute confidentiality regarding the president's physical and mental health. Information that would tend to call into question his physical or mental capacity to hold office should be available to the vice-president and the cabinet. "The President's body is not wholly his own; that is why we go to such lengths to protect it."[36] Breaching the president's confidence on the grounds of national interest is essential, if the alternative is to allow a disabled president to retain authority.

The job of physician to the president has never been medically varied or stimulating. The boredom he has confronted has been justified by the urgency of his role in the rare medical emergency that may occur. Dr. Daniel Ruge was able to satisfy himself after the attack that the president was receiving the best medical and surgical care available. Although he blames himself for not recommending use of the Twenty-fifth Amendment, it is not at all clear that he was empowered to do so or could have influenced the decision. One might expect the White House physician, as the official responsible for the president's health, to play a key role in advising the president's men about the extent of disability and the need for a transfer of power. In fact, he has had no legal role in assessing a potentially disabled president, much less in suggesting his removal.

If this seems paradoxical, it becomes less so in light of the fact that the office of White House physician has traditionally carried little status and few well-defined duties. Working from a tiny office squeezed into the White House basement alongside that of the florist and decorator, and ranking near the bottom of the pecking order with the White House usher, the physician has had no official job description and few responsibilities. Ruge called it a "blue collar" job "so lacking in opportunities for creativity and medical skills that most physicians shy away from it."[37]

Furthermore, the choice of physicians to the president has never been systematized to assure the selection of the most competent person. Most have been drawn from the military, which has not always attracted the best medical professionals. Woodrow Wilson and Franklin D. Roosevelt picked naval officers who were "nice fellows" but whose medical skills were questionable.[38] Other physicians have attained the job through friendship with the president, or as friends of friends.

Reagan's physician, Dr. Ruge, was a neurosurgeon selected because of his former position as the partner of Dr. Loyal Davis, Nancy Reagan's stepfather. Ruge said, "Loyal was asked by Nancy and Ronnie to get a White House physician. He thought that they gave him carte blanche. He knew that I liked Ronald Reagan.

"On the Tuesday after the election, I went to New York for the 25th Anniversary celebration of the Hospital for Special Services. We checked into the Hyatt Hotel, and ten minutes later, Loyal Davis was on the phone. He asked me to take the job, and I said, 'Well, what you want is a bright young internist, somebody who wants to make a name for himself.' He hit the ceiling and said, 'That's exactly what we don't want.'

"This thing went on for two days. I finally had to leave the meeting because he was calling me all of the time. Two days later, I asked him, 'Why does it have to be me?' He said, 'Because you won't let anybody do foolish things to Ronnie.' I said, 'You finally gave me a good reason; I'll do it.' " (Once Ruge had agreed, however, he arranged to have a very bright and capable young internist appointed assistant physician.)[39]

The physician is unique among White House officials not only because of his medical training but because he is responsible for choosing outside experts to treat or evaluate the president. Reagan's physician saw his job less as the on-line caregiver for the president's every medical need and rather more as the coordinator of the services of other physicians and specialists. He had no hesitation about calling on outstanding authorities for consultation with the president.[40] By extension to the issue of invocation under the Twenty-fifth Amendment, the physician to the president should draw on the experience of the other White House physicians and of consultants from other medical centers.

Both the Miller Commission report and the study by Crispell and Gomez[41] emphasized the difficulties encountered by the White House physician, the need for a "code of conduct," and the importance of the information that he must supply if appropriate decisions on Section 3 and Section 4 are to be made. The following set of guidelines and procedures is based on their suggestions, the broader literature, and a consideration of the goals of the Twenty-fifth Amendment drawn from the congressional hearings.

- The president's physician should be fully aware of the cognitive, emotional, and psychological effects of illnesses such as heart disease, stroke, trauma, hypertension, cancer, prolonged infection, and metabolic disorders; of drugs and medications used or likely to be used by the president; and of common medical procedures, especially as they may relate to the president's current state of health. He should also be alert to the symptoms of common emotional, psychological, and personality disorders.

- The president's physician should, at all times, carry undated, unsigned letters invoking Section 3 of the Twenty-fifth Amendment which the president could sign in an emergency if necessary and appropriate.

- When the president undergoes any medical care that is not routine, his physician should inform him in person and in writing of the nature of the procedure and of any disability that may accompany it. For any episode involving surgery, anesthesia, mind-altering drugs, judgmental deficits, cognitive alteration, or a great deal of discomfort, or for which the effects are unknown, he should recommend to the president that he invoke Section 3 of the Twenty-fifth Amendment. In an emergency, the physician should offer the letters to be signed as soon as possible, while the president is lucid.

- In a medical emergency, the president's physician should advise the president whenever he is likely to be incapacitated and should recommend use of Section 3.

- If, in the physician's opinion, the president becomes incapacitated, the physician should inform him fully and recommend use of Section 3. If the president refuses to act, the physician should bring in expert consultants to review the president's condition. If they concur with the opinion of the White House physician, he should be empowered to inform the president that he will send letters indicating his opinion to the vice-president, the members of the cabinet, and the chief of staff.

- If the president is or will become incapacitated, but is *unable* to declare his incapacity under Section 3 of the Twenty-fifth Amendment, the physician should send letters to the appropriate officials, informing them of his opinion and advising them that the president's medical condition warrants use of Section 4 to invoke the amendment.

- If neither Section 3 nor Section 4 is employed following his letters to the vice-president, cabinet, and chief of staff, the physician should be empowered to draft letters to the Speaker of the House and the president pro tem of the Senate explaining his recommendation.

- If the president undergoes surgery or anesthesia without invoking Section 3, and if Section 4 is not invoked in the interim, the physician should recommend the invocation of Section 3 at the earliest possible time following the procedure. The president will be able to convalesce relieved of the day-to-day burdens of office, and certain that his responsibilities are being discharged by the constitutionally designated officer.

- The president's physician should be familiar with the constitutional provisions on succession, as well as all aspects of the Twenty-fifth Amendment, including its leg-

islative background and the intent of those who drafted
it. He should be prepared to explain the implications of
Sections 3 and 4 to other physicians called upon to treat
the president. Their judgments about the president's
health and competence might be important if the invocation of these sections is considered.

- When the president is no longer incapacitated by illness
  or medical treatment, his physician should inform him
  that there are no medical barriers to his resumption of
  office.

- If the physician had earlier sent informing letters to the
  vice-president and other officers of government, he
  should now communicate to them the changed state of
  the president's health.

Such a protocol would make clear the parallel responsibilities of the physician: to serve the nation as well as his patient.
Playing this dual role may present difficulties—challenges as
routine as trying to fit medical treatment into the president's
busy schedule, or as weighty as seeking to have him relieved
of his office temporarily for the protection of the national
interest. But in every instance the physician's function is to
provide *medical* advice to those who will make the *political*
decision. The potential conflict with the physician's need for
confidentiality has already been addressed and can never be
fully resolved. These recommendations bring this conflict
sharply in focus and weight the physician's responsibilities on
the side of the national interest.

Some of these suggestions have already been implemented
in the changing White House medical unit of the 1990s.[42]

For one thing, there are more personnel and a larger organization than before. The unit has one set of quarters in the White House and another at the Old Executive Office Building. Each of these can give care that is equal in most respects to that of a good emergency room.[43] Some changes began during the latter half of the Reagan administration under Dr. John Hutton, and were expanded during the Bush presidency. There are now four physicians, five physician assistants, and five nurses experienced in intensive care (figure 14). Dr. Burton Lee, III, an oncologist from Memorial Hospital and a personal friend of the president's is the "physician to the president," an appointive position. He has the overall responsibility for the health care of the president and sets the policy for how the unit operates. The White House physician, Dr. Lawrence Mohr, is the executive officer of the unit and runs most of the day-to-day operations under the general direction of Dr. Lee. Mohr is a career Army officer and has both an administrative coordinator and a military assistant attached to him.

The other two physicians in the unit share responsibility for making emergency calls to the president, with whom they also travel occasionally. Dr. Michael Nash, an Air Force physician, has primary responsibility for the care of the vice-president; in addition, he deals with preventive medicine and training matters. Dr. Alan Roberts is responsible for the operation of the clinic.

All of the physicians are board-certified internists, and they consult and teach at the local hospitals (Mohr is an associate professor of medicine at George Washington University). Their patients include not only the president and his family and the vice-president but also the chief of staff and the rest of

WHITE HOUSE MEDICAL UNIT

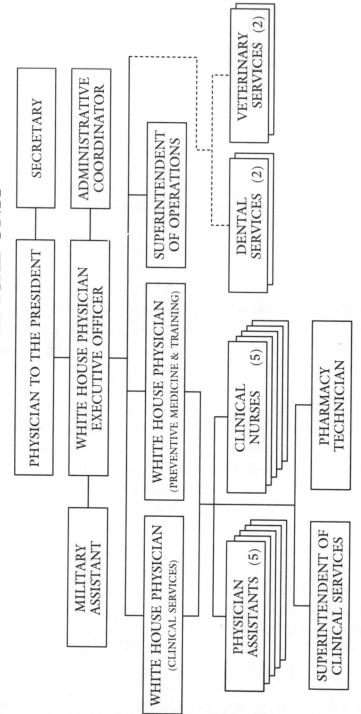

Figure 14 Table of Organization of the White House Medical Unit (1991).

the White House staff. It is customary for the White House medical unit to simulate a variety of exercises and scenarios with the Secret Service in an effort to be fully prepared for all eventualities. For example, what would happen if George Bush were in a boating accident at Kennebunkport, Maine? The exercise would include a rehearsal of the rescue of the president, mapping out the course to the nearest medical facility, and touching base with all professional and non-professional personnel who might be needed.

The overall tasks assigned to the White House medical unit include the following:

1. presidential medical support
2. emergency contingency planning
3. operation of the White House clinic
    (a) primary care
    (b) occupational medicine
    (c) emergency medicine
4. preventive medicine activities
5. staff activities

President Bush has traveled a great deal, covering 250,000 miles by the end of his second year in office. Two physicians always accompany him on *Air Force 1*, which is medically very well equipped. Virtually anything that can be done in an emergency room—except for X-ray and a few laboratory procedures—can readily be handled. All of the doctors are trained in emergency medicine. The medical facility on the plane is quite new, so that even life-saving surgery would be possible if the president became ill in a part of the world where surgical backup was poor.

One nurse or physician's assistant goes to any city to which the president will travel. There is a detailed protocol designed to identify physicians and surgeons to provide care for the president if needed. Hospitals of choice are also identified along the route of the president's flight, so that the plane would be one hour or less from an acceptable location in the United States. All hospitals are selected with an eye to the quality of the medical staff. Contingency plans are prepared for many kinds of events, including the choice of the most desirable hospital if the president were to come under attack. (In the local setting, the choice of George Washington University Hospital was made by Dr. Ruge not only because of its proximity to the White House but also because of the quality of emergency room care. Hence, Agent Jerry Parr had no problem shifting directions when the gravity of Reagan's condition became apparent.) If the president became ill in a foreign country, the White House physician would take pains to discuss his care with the health ministry but would retain the role of primary decision maker.

Whether in the United States or abroad, the appropriate letters of invocation to the Speaker of the House and the president pro tem of the Senate are now available to the president at all times.

Is the medical office of the White House better prepared now than in 1981 to respond to constitutional guidelines for presidential disability? Dr. Lee has expressed his understanding of his responsibility to the public as well as to the president. He has said that he would resign if he "had to hide a serious medical problem for political reasons for any length of time."[44] Dr. Mohr, when asked how he would react if an impaired president refused to relinquish power under Section

3, replied that he was sworn to uphold the Constitution. In pursuit of that commitment, he would live up to his responsibility to facilitate invocation of the Twenty-fifth Amendment when required. The same question was broached about Alzheimer's disease. He again indicated that the White House physicians would fulfill their constitutional responsibility. Whether the succession provisions of the Constitution would be operative ("inability to discharge the powers and duties of the office"), rather than the Twenty-fifth Amendment, might depend on the presentation of the illness and the extent of the disability.

During the presidential campaign, Bush noted that he had not even considered the possibility of presidential disability and the need to transfer power under the Twenty-fifth Amendment. "It never occurred to me to do that," he said.[45] After the election, however, a series of "nuts and bolts" working meetings were held at the staff level between November 4, 1988, and January 20, 1989, on the mechanisms for implementing the provisions of the Twenty-fifth Amendment. Additional staff work in the White House followed the inauguration and resulted in the delineation of the circumstances under which the provisions of the Twenty-fifth Amendment would be enacted. Both before and after the inauguration, there was White House physician involvement in the process. Many of the guidelines described earlier in this chapter were addressed.[46]

The culmination of these working sessions was a historic meeting in the White House on April 18, 1989. Dr. Lee played the major role in arranging the discussion, following a meeting with Dr. Kenneth Crispell and Kenneth Thompson at the Miller Center. At the time of his appointment, Lee had mentioned such a meeting as one of the first tasks he would address.[47] President Bush, together with his wife, met with Vice-President and Mrs. Quayle, Dr. Lee, Counsel C. Boyden Gray, John Sununu, the White House chief of staff, Susan Porter Rose, Mrs. Bush's chief of staff, and a representative of the Secret Service. The purpose of the meeting was to familiarize all present with the important provisions of the Twenty-fifth Amendment. In particular, the participants reviewed the procedures required if Bush were incapable of signing the letters himself.[48]

Clearly, the country has come a long way. The president now understands that he has a constitutional obligation to implement the Twenty-fifth Amendment if the circumstances warrant it.

Prospects

Even an administration fully familiar with the Twenty-fifth Amendment might have confronted a difficult decision in 1981. After President Reagan was anesthetized, he was unable to declare himself disabled. The subtleties of determining the president's functional capacity during the postoperative period required an understanding of the gray areas of cognitive competence.

But if the amendment did not work in the shooting, would it ever be used in the most difficult (and often the most dangerous) situations? What would happen if the existence of disability were disputed or concealed—or if it were viewed as a stigma by much of the public, such as mental or neurological illnesses? If a disability appears to be temporary, it will be tempting to "ride it out," especially when a decision to invoke may be controversial.[49]

The success of any preparedness measures relies entirely on the willingness of the president and the president's men to use the Twenty-fifth Amendment when necessary. The letter and intent of the law require its use in cases like the Reagan shooting. Unfortunately, political expediency often argues against it. Reagan's presidency was strengthened by the rosy media coverage of his recovery. Bush's political currency increased in value when he assumed the role of steady, loyal, and cautious second in command. In contrast, Haig's career was derailed by his seeming to make an unwarranted claim of power and authority. Above all lay the rational but partially self-serving desire of Reagan's men to avoid alarming the public and to present a reassuring picture of a chief executive who never lost command.

Thus, there are strong political and organizational pressures to suppress or avoid use. The vice-president and the cabinet are well positioned to judge presidential inability, having access to the president, an understanding of the demands of the office, and the medical expertise that the White House physician can provide. But they may prefer to forgo the impression that the president is weak or unable to govern, that they have turned against him, or that they are overreacting to the situation.

The hesitancy of the cabinet and the vice-president will be heightened by the assertiveness of the White House inner circle. The staff is quite willing to take charge in a crisis: its members have no special, constitutionally defined duties regarding presidential inability, no obligation to ensure that the nation is always in the hands of a capable chief executive. In their view, their job is to respond pragmatically to the situation at hand by seeing to the president's personal needs, shaping a favorable public image for him, and managing the day-to-day affairs of government in his absence. This mentality was in evidence in 1981, from Darman's removal of the papers on the Twenty-fifth Amendment to the deliberately upbeat portrayals of the president's health.

The attack on Reagan brought renewed attention to the importance of the vice-president—the one elected official who should be chosen specifically for his ability to take the president's place on a moment's notice. Yet a recent study of the vice-presidency noted, "Vice-presidents who wish to make the most of the position . . . are encouraged to keep their views anonymous, their behavior loyal . . . and their deportment self-effacing. (Those who deviate even slightly from this code may be regarded as untrustworthy by the president and, especially, by the White House staff.)"[50] Bush followed this pattern, remaining passive throughout the episode and allowing himself to be excluded from the highest levels of decision making.

He would have done well to assert his constitutional authority, under the Twenty-fifth Amendment, to initiate a cabinet review of the president's capacities. Fewer demands on a recovering president would have been made; the "business as usual" façade would have been unnecessary. When he had access to Reagan in the hospital in the days following the shooting, he said that he had limited his meetings with the president to just "a minute or two" so as not to "overload his circuits."[51] If a two-minute meeting was so stressful, then Reagan's condition was clearly worse than indicated by official pronouncements. While Bush was airborne, he was obviously in no position to judge Reagan's illness or to assert his own leadership. But on his return, he should have requested a full discussion with Ruge, Aaron, Giordano, and other outside experts as to the potential medical and psychological consequences of trauma and surgery. He would then have been far better prepared to consider his constitutional obligation to initiate invocation of the Twenty-fifth Amendment.

Authentic whistle-blowers have received a decidedly stormy response, no matter how selfless and well-intentioned their actions. Those who raise the issue of presidential inability risk attacks on their motives and condemnation of their actions. An aggressive White House staff provides ready sanction for a cabinet and a vice-president unwilling to assume a difficult responsibility. Jealous of threats to the president and to their own status, the staff may consider their power in jeopardy. The vice-president not only initiates the removal of the president but may also bring in his own staff—whom he has chosen—to run the White House. Facing that possibility, the president's staff have weapons that make them intimidating adversaries—the president's trust, their contacts with the media, and their ability to control access and the flow of information to the president.[52]

Although a well-prepared, scrupulous White House physician with a well-defined role should be able to trigger the consideration of disability, he cannot resolve all of the related problems. For one thing, his very willingness to breach confidentiality might encourage the president to avoid seeking treatment for a condition, or to seek it elsewhere. Kennedy's need for the lift provided by injections from Dr. Max ("Dr. Feelgood") Jacobson, which apparently contained amphetamine, illustrated how a president could easily obtain secret, and possibly dangerous, treatment by circumventing the official physician.[53]

It has been suggested that a formal commission might represent the best mechanism for monitoring the president's health and for bringing the proper authorities automatically into the process whenever a question of presidential disability arises (see chapter 8).[54] It could function as an advisory body or might, as the "other body" designated in Section 4, replace the cabinet. It would be activated under certain specified conditions, such as the administration of anesthesia, or at the initiative of one or more members. The presence of "outsiders" would ensure that it would become operative at times when the cabinet and the vice-president might hesitate to act. Such a commission might have forced consideration of the Twenty-fifth Amendment while Reagan was in surgery, and would probably have reached a recommendation soon afterward.

The White House chief of staff should be included so that invocation of the Twenty-fifth Amendment would be viewed less as a threat than as an official duty. The commission should also include the White House physician and civilian medical experts, two or three cabinet members, and a Justice Department official. This would moderate the physician's burden of determining disability—given his conflicting obligations—and place it in the hands of a public body. Independent civilian experts would ensure greater objectivity than the cabinet or the vice-president possesses, while representation from the cabinet and the White House would preserve the perspective of the executive branch.

In addition to responding to crises, the commission could arrange and monitor periodic medical examinations for the president, to guarantee that no disabling or potentially disabling conditions escape notice. The president would then have medical consultation available without attracting undue public comment. In the absence of such a mechanism, a president might avoid contact for certain kinds of medical problems, such as needed psychiatric evaluation or care.[55]

The commission could serve other functions—screening the health of presidential and vice-presidential candidates, advising the president's physician on medical and legal questions, reviewing information for general release, and educating the public on pertinent medical matters.[56]

Park has elaborated a persuasive argument for a presidential disability commission, to include physicians trained and skilled in the determination of disability. The physicians would be appointed by the elected president prior to inauguration, divided equally between the major political parties. They would represent a core of expertise in the essential clinical disciplines. Such a commission would underscore the degree to which "inability" reflects physical or mental impairment and therefore can best be evaluated by physicians rather than by political figures. It would incorporate and support the judgments of the White House physicians, while ensuring the independence of the appraisal and its nonpolitical character.[57]

Strong arguments against such a commission were advanced by Brownell during the congressional hearings. It might be unwieldy, an affront to the presidency, a departure from the system of checks and balances. It could result in divisive partisan battles, conflicting medical testimony, or a public stalemate. It might even become an instrument for harassing the president. In a disputed case, it would place the power to decide the president's fate in the hands of anonymous civilian experts.[58]

None of these contentions is persuasive. Instead, the advantages far outweigh the risk.

Furthermore, Congress could legislate some elements of a presidential health commission without enacting all. Its responsibilities could be designated individually or in combination.

Guidelines that strengthen the role of elected and cabinet officials relative to the White House staff would also be useful in achieving legislative goals. After Reagan's shooting and his cancer surgery, the cabinet and the vice-president hovered on the sidelines, leaving the key decisions to presidential aides. The framers knew that the cabinet and the vice-president might hesitate to act. But they were not aware of how aggressive the White House staff could be in protecting the president's "interest," as they construed it, and identifying it with their own.

Even if a consensus cannot be forged on all of these guidelines in the near future, many will command broad support. Changes directed at the president's physician are less controversial and potentially more important, and should be adopted after adequate congressional consideration. Review and analysis of a "physician protocol," together with renewed careful consideration of the potential effectiveness of a presidential health commission, would surely represent some of the most important elements in congressional hearings on the Twenty-fifth Amendment.

12

Looking Back
and Looking Forward

In many respects, the president and the nation were fortunate. Reagan was close to a hospital with adequate trauma
facilities. He received prompt and excellent care at a time
when delay might well have been fatal.

With his prospects for survival enhanced, the extent of his
disability should have been confronted directly. The most
knowledgeable medical evaluation was required, with a full
presentation of all the pertinent information and judgments
to a vice-president and cabinet acquainted with the laws on
succession and temporary replacement. But Reagan's men
were neither ready nor willing to face the issue.

That Reagan's team was caught unprepared is not surprising in light of the brevity of its tenure. Seventy days was not a

long time in which to learn how to handle a federal bureaucracy. Nevertheless, in the 145 days from November 4, 1980, to March 30, 1981, there was ample time to find a few hours to discuss the possibility of disability and succession.

The president can never be made invulnerable, but his office can. Among the key roles of a president is that of final arbiter of a nuclear launch release. While free to delegate his responsibilities as he sees fit, he always remains the ultimate "safety catch."[1] Confronting a decision that might have to be made in minutes, the president must be capable of exercising clear-minded judgment; in the event of presidential incapacity, a clear chain of command must exist. This should be the top priority of any administration.

On March 30, the staff of the White House counsel was still compiling its "emergency book," a guide to appropriate responses to crisis scenarios.[2] Haig was nursing ego wounds incurred during the previous week when Vice-President Bush had been appointed head of crisis management. He was brooding on the fact that "the Vice President had no adequate staff to support him for the time being," a state of affairs which would "delay the essential painstaking work of planning, staffing, and activating a mechanism that would automatically spring to life in time of crisis."[3] Speakes was planning a meeting between White House Press Office staffers and the Secret Service to discuss the handling of a presidential assassination attempt.[4]

As for the Twenty-fifth Amendment, many cabinet members were ignorant of the statutory stipulations regarding succession, temporary replacement, and the chain of command.[5] "I kept wondering at what point some alert staffer would remember that a doomsday book, in which guidelines and contingencies had been outlined, was locked up in a safe in somebody's office and would run upstairs and fetch it," Regan later said. "No such guide to policy, law, and behavior in a time of extreme danger to the state was ever produced; as far as I know, none existed."[6]

No one can view Hinckley's attack on Reagan in a vacuum. It is part of a continuum, a discrete example of a series of events that have characterized American history from the earliest days of the Republic. It is predictable that it will happen again. Not long after Hinckley's attack on Reagan, a young man was picked up in New York because of threats that he had made against the president. His parents, when told of their son's expressed intentions, found it hard to believe. Their son had told them that he "liked" President Reagan.[7]

In a society in which mental illness abounds, in which drug and alcohol abuse are virtually insoluble social problems on a wide scale, and in which political fanaticism and terrorism exist as in all nations, we must anticipate that the assassin will appear again. The word "assassin" goes back to medieval times, when a secret Islamic order known as the Hashhashin (addicted to hashish) systematically murdered prominent Christians. The "assassin" became identified with political murder,[8] which has in the late twentieth century grown virtually into an international industry.

No degree of protection of the president can possibly immunize him against attack in a free society such as ours. Furthermore, there is a continuing conflict between the efforts of the White House staff (and the requirements of a democratic system) to maximize presidential exposure to the public, on the one hand, and the implementation of the precautions of those responsible for his security, on the other.

"Physically surrounding the president is not sufficient protection. The president's ultimate shield must be the ability of the Secret Service to keep him out of dangerous environments." This requires effective intelligence regarding unstable individuals. When Hinckley was stalking Jimmy Carter in the autumn of 1980 before the election, and was picked up in the Nashville airport with three guns, we might have assumed that his name would have appeared on the Secret Service list of 400-odd persons who posed potential threats to the president. Instead, although the FBI was well aware of his presence and the event was duly noted, it was never communicated to the Secret Service.[9]

Beyond trauma to the president as the cause of disability, there are strokes, heart attacks, cancer, and Alzheimer's disease. All are prevalent in the age group of the majority of those who have sought the presidency in this country. Eisenhower's heart attack, intestinal obstruction, and stroke were not unusual. Reagan's trauma to the chest, prostatic surgery, and partial colectomy for cancer were not unique. (The vulnerability of any individual in his seventies is nowhere better shown than by the collection of blood in Ronald Reagan's head, apparently following trauma, that had to be evacuated at the Mayo Clinic six months after he left the presidency. This "subdural hematoma" was one of two that the president suffered, possibly but not certainly related to a horseback riding accident.)[10]

The impact of William Casey's brain tumor on the decisions made during his final period as director of CIA has been a subject of speculation. Concern that a president might develop a brain tumor has also been expressed, and with it the suggestion that magnetic resonance imaging (MRI) of the brain should be made available for presidents and candidates alike.[11] MRI would detect not just brain tumors but prior brain hemorrhage and other kinds of damage as well.

During the past two hundred years, the American people have exercised the right to choose, in a process that has been remarkably stable and durable, based in a singular constitutional framework devised by men of genius and foresight as the country began. One of the gaps in the Constitution was its failure to provide for procedures for replacement of a temporarily disabled president. What was needed to fill that gap was a set of measures that were structured, guarded against a coup, and assured the American people continuity of stable, capable leadership. After two centuries, perceiving the importance of devising a remedy, a legislative process was initiated and pursued with remarkable intelligence and sensitivity to the complex problems and differing interests involved. The process ended in 1967 with the ratification by the states of the Twenty-fifth Amendment to the Constitution. A mechanism was now in place. But would it work as those who crafted the amendment hoped?

The attack on Reagan was the first opportunity to test the provisions. It came at a time of potential crisis for the United States, with the possibility of a Soviet invasion of Poland hanging in the air.

This crucial test of the amendment was a failure. An opportunity was lost. Neither Section 3 nor Section 4 was invoked; Reagan was said to be in charge and making all of the decisions; and Vice-President Bush and the cabinet ignored their constitutional obligation to assess the president's capacity to function at his normal level of competence.

Why was the amendment not invoked? Because of ignorance, caution, concern, and guile.

The *ignorance* reflected most cabinet members' lack of

awareness of the provisions of the amendment. There is no firm evidence that Bush himself was fully cognizant of his delegated role, although Fielding and Smith briefed him on the provisions on his return to Washington. The White House staff believed—or wanted to believe—that the president's *survival* necessarily implied cognitive competence, without bothering to explore the president's postoperative state with his physicians.

Caution was apparent in Bush's own unwillingness, as the legal initiator of invocation, to be perceived as arrogating power to himself and preempting the president's role. Still the outsider in a new presidency, he deferred to the wishes of the White House staff.

Concern over the president's condition and how it might be viewed by the public and the international community were evident in the decision by Meese, Baker, and Deaver not to consider the amendment even before the president had undergone surgery, let alone afterwards. "We didn't want people in the country as a whole to get unduly exercised and alarmed," Meese said. Use of the Twenty-fifth Amendment might "put limitations on the power of the presidency and set a precedent for future presidents," in Meese's words.[12] "No one wants to activate it, because in effect you are expressing less than full confidence in your chief executive," according to Gergen.[13]

Guile was manifest in the refusal to demand a careful review of the president's capacities. *The staff knew best.* "If the president is temporarily disabled, leave the presidency alone rather than risk . . . disorder," in Martin Anderson's view.[14] Darman's audacious removal of the pertinent letters of invocation to a safe in his office was based on his desire to preclude consideration, regardless of what the Constitution required.[15]

The men around the president were not alone in their disregard of the constitutional mandate. One of our great national newspapers commented two days after the shooting, "The President's excellent prognosis rendered academic the sections of the 25th Amendment that provide for continuing firm government when a President is disabled and unable to execute his duties."[16] This confusion of survival with fitness, of prognosis with cognitive competence, and of convalescence with the capacity to make decisions was a central element in the failure to invoke. It raised once more the unanswered question of the Twenty-fifth Amendment: the meaning of the word "inability."

Some of the lessons of 1981 had been learned by 1985, at the time of Reagan's cancer surgery. Here was another situation that required invocation. In fact, the provisions of the Twenty-fifth were employed, though fogged by caveats that warned against the potential for setting a precedent if the amendment was actually utilized. This, of course, was precisely the kind of precedent that individuals like Birch Bayh and Herbert Brownell had envisioned. It would have provided the basis on which prudent application could be achieved in the future without a sense of panic and with a common understanding by the American people that this was the constitutional process in action, government rising to the occasion, rather than the breakdown of central authority.

As the first test under fire of the disability provisions, the response to the attack on Reagan provided important insights for the future. From its first day in office, and preferably during the transition, the new administration must prepare for the possibility of a disabled president. At the least, the following actions should be taken:

- Transfer of the "emergency book" from the outgoing White House counsel during the transition, with immediate review, updating, and modifications as appropriate.[17]

- Declassification and standardization of *all* succession procedures—including the National Command Authority—to the greatest possible extent. Secret directives about command delegation are probably more confusing to our own authorities than to potential adversaries.

- Simulations of possible succession scenarios. This would familiarize the president, vice-president, cabinet, and White House staff with the procedures of succession and the roles they would be called upon to play.

- Strengthening of emergency communications, particularly those between the White House and the various forms of vice-presidential transportation.[18] (This safeguard may already have been implemented in part.)[19]

The president and vice-president should agree in advance on those circumstances that will require medical evaluation and reporting, and explicit decisions regarding the use of the Twenty-fifth Amendment. Congressional leaders and key executive branch personnel should be informed of the agreements. When the need arises, the amendment's use will then be viewed not as an indication of weakness or a void in leadership but rather as a sign that the government is functioning according to plan.[20] The White House can prepare the public by briefing the media on its crisis procedures and simulations. This would help prevent the kind of confusion over the succession process that was evident after the Reagan shooting.

The central figure in the final approval of the Twenty-fifth Amendment was Senator Birch Bayh. Today he thinks, "It is the best that we could do. It's not perfect. We knew it wasn't perfect at the time we passed it. . . . When you are dealing with presidential power, probably more than with any other issue, a number of complex peripheral issues cloud the picture. Given the worst-case scenario, such as an assassination attempt, failure to transfer power was totally inconsistent with the intention of the Twenty-fifth Amendment.

"It is characteristic of many White House staffers to consider their own turf more important than the well-being of the country. They probably believe they are being conscientious, on balance. But some people have a selfish motive and don't want to give up power. And they can rationalize the devil out of it. 'We've got it all put together; we can make it function. Don't bring in this other group. Our boy will be well before they find their way to the men's room'—and that kind of thing. If you have a president who can't function— and President Reagan was darn near dead—not to turn it over to George Bush was totally irresponsible. I think it violated the Constitution. Fortunately, Reagan recovered and the country was none the worse for it.

"People don't like to talk about the fact that a president may become ill enough to have to step down temporarily, or that he may die. We should be willing to say that our president may get sick; and if he does, we should be able to treat him like any other human being. . . . We have to let the president's people know that he's not going to go down ten points in the polls just because he has a hernia and needs an anesthetic and is out of it for six hours or six days. That's not the end of the world."[21]

A president who is mentally alert and capable and able to function fully in his decision-making role has never been more important to the future of our interconnected world. The shortening of the time for decision making in crisis places unique demands on the leader of the Western world.

It is contended that institutional safeguards will always operate to prevent disastrous presidential mistakes because the decisions are inherently collective. No president could unleash the nuclear arsenal in a moment of irrational response to provocation. One example of presidential leadership all too frequently cited for its favorable outcome is the Cuban Missile Crisis, in which all of the apparatus of the executive branch was involved in analyzing the changing situation and the options available. In the final analysis, however, it was President Kennedy alone who made the decision, and in that terrible moment of risk, it might have gone either way.

Much of the analytic framework that supports national policy—for example, deterrence theory—has been based on the assumption of human rationality and predictable decision making. The theory is that rational man will choose the best possible course after weighing the probabilities and the potential gains and losses of alternative courses of action.

If this is how decisions should be made, it is not necessarily how they *are* made. Decision making in foreign policy is not a science. Too often, the opaque screen of hope and wishful thinking obscures the facts. Nations miscalculate and go to war believing that national goals will surely be attained. In the recent past, this was true of the United States in Vietnam; of the USSR in Afghanistan; and of Vietnam's invasion of Cambodia. It applies equally to Iraq's attack on Iran and, more recently, on Kuwait. All of these major national decisions proved to be catastrophes. The great fiascoes in U.S. foreign policy have resulted from human errors in assessing other countries. The Bay of Pigs, the Korean invasion of 1950, Pearl Harbor, and the escalation of the Vietnam War each exemplifies failure in our top decision-making processes.

Decision making in crisis has been subjected to careful assessment. Such studies have demonstrated major perceptual problems, narrowing of the cognitive process, increasing errors under the pressure of time, and a group dynamic that ultimately substitutes consensual validation for critical assessment. The degradation of the analytic process reflects the confluence of many factors, including the quality and quantity of available information, the powerful effects of stress, the strength of individual needs, and the personality traits of the leaders.

Most studies of crisis behavior have accepted the premise that it represents the response of "normal" or "stable" individuals to stress. The assumption of rational decision making loses credibility, then, if the behavior of "stable" individuals changes significantly in crisis, as we know it does; and perhaps more significantly, if the leadership responsible for decisions is impaired by physical, psychological, or drug-induced disability.

If we look only at U.S. presidents in the twentieth century, it is apparent how numerous and significant their illnesses have been while in office. FDR and Harding died, and Wilson, FDR, Eisenhower, Johnson, and Reagan were incapacitated by illness and/or surgery over varying periods. There were seven assassination attempts on the seventeen presidents, two successful (McKinley and Kennedy). Three presidents (Wilson, Coolidge, and Johnson) died within four years after leaving office.

McKinley, Taft, Wilson, Harding, Coolidge, FDR, Truman, Eisenhower, and Johnson suffered from heart disease, ranging from thin heart walls to progressive arteriosclerosis. Taft, Wilson, Harding, FDR, and Eisenhower had high blood pressure. Wilson, Harding, FDR, and Eisenhower experienced strokes.

T. Roosevelt, FDR, Truman, Eisenhower, Johnson, and Reagan underwent surgery at least once. FDR, Johnson, and Reagan had forms of cancer. Truman, Eisenhower, and Johnson had gall bladder disease. Wilson and Johnson had kidney disease.

Wilson, Harding, Coolidge, FDR, Truman, Eisenhower, and Kennedy suffered from gastrointestinal disorders, ranging from ulcers and enzyme deficiency to chronic ileitis and obstruction.

T. Roosevelt, Coolidge, Wilson, FDR, and Johnson suffered from various kinds of chronic respiratory illness.

Other major health problems included diabetes (Harding), Addison's disease (Kennedy), prostatic disease (Wilson and Reagan), phlebitis (Nixon), periodic alcohol abuse (Harding, Nixon, and Johnson), and obesity (McKinley, Taft, Harding, and Johnson).

The most recent episode of illness in office involved President George Bush. It is a measure of the progress that has been made—and a tribute to the usefulness of the Bush-Quayle meeting on the topic of disability, on April 18,

1989—that the sudden onset of Bush's atrial fibrillation was handled as it was. On May 4, 1991, the president became short of breath while jogging and was quickly found to have an irregular heartbeat. Transferred by helicopter to the Naval Hospital in Bethesda, he was placed on drug therapy to reverse his atrial fibrillation and attain normal rhythm once more. According to the doctors' plan, if the drugs failed to affect the arrhythmia—as initially they did—an electrical shock would be administered the following day, a common way of returning a patient's rhythm to normal.[22]

When it was announced that Dan Quayle would be acting president under the Twenty-fifth Amendment provisions while Bush was under anesthesia for the cardioversion[23]—if it was required—a different kind of shock reverberated across the nation. The prospect of Quayle as president brought home sharply the electorate's lack of confidence in his ability to lead.[24]

As it happened, the drugs were ultimately effective, and the president had a normal rhythm by 10:25 P.M. on May 5. Early on the following morning, just before 5:00 A.M., he began to fibrillate once more. The decision was made to continue drug therapy rather than use electrical cardioversion, and the president returned to the White House on Monday, May 6.[25]

Serious questions remained, however, as to whether this was an isolated episode or whether there were would be further bouts. Patients in chronic atrial fibrillation are known to have an increased incidence of strokes; small pieces of clot may move from the atrium to arteries in different organs. Furthermore, sustained drug therapy with one of the two drugs Bush was receiving—procainamide—has caused significant side effects, including muscle aches, arthritis, and blood abnormalities.[26] Hence, the nation's pleasure at seeing the president back in the White House was tempered by the knowledge that this single episode was not necessarily the last. The fact that it was associated with hyperthyroidism did nothing to calm those concerned with succession, nor did the use of anticoagulants, with their associated risk of hemorrhage.

It was important, as the episode unfolded, that the appropriate plan was already in place for invocation. In spite of the reservations about Quayle, there was wide acceptance of the propriety of using the Twenty-fifth Amendment if the president went under anesthesia. If this means that future presidential illnesses, trauma, or surgery will also initiate the temporary replacement process, it will surely be the response that Bayh and the other architects of the amendment hoped for.

FDR was sixty-three when he died and was in chronic heart failure when he ran for a fourth term as president of the United States. Eisenhower was sixty-two when he became president and then had a heart attack in 1955, bowel obstruction and surgery in 1956, and a stroke in 1957. George Bush was almost sixty-seven when he developed his arrhythmia, an age in which the incidence of heart attacks, strokes, and malignant neoplasms is appreciable. Beyond temporary replacement under the Twenty-fifth Amendment, if the experience of other vice presidents of the twentieth century repeats itself, Vice-President Quayle has a 35 percent chance of becoming President Quayle, either by succession of by election.*

---

*The twentieth-century vice-presidents who became president were Theodore Roosevelt, Calvin Coolidge, Harry Truman, Lyndon Johnson, Richard Nixon, Gerald Ford, and George Bush (7 out of 20).

This brings up the point once more that the person next in line really does matter in the affairs of the great powers and the international community. It may be his or her decision in crisis and his or her finger on the button that we will all have to rely on.

Exercising greater wisdom in our choice of vice-presidents is one thing; assuring cognitive competence in office is another. It is in the light of our knowledge that presidents are only human that the wisdom of forging the Twenty-fifth Amendment as a secure bridge is manifest. Used with judiciousness but also with a scrupulous regard for its original intent, it offers an impressive defense of continuity in government that the founding fathers would surely have considered a proper adaptation to the twentieth century and beyond.

Appendix 1:

Laws on Succession

The Original Constitutional Provision

The Constitutional Convention met on May 25, 1787, and the thirty-nine delegates signed the Constitution on September 17, 1787. The provision on succession had gone through a series of revisions before reaching its final form. It was not until the spring of 1790 that ratification by Rhode Island—the last state to do so—completed the process with the approval of all thirteen states. Article II, Section 1, Clause 6, reads as follows:

> In Case of the Removal of the President from Office, or of his Death, Resignation, or Inability to discharge the Powers and Duties of the said Office, the Same shall devolve on the Vice President, and the Congress may by Law provide for the Case of Removal, Death, Resignation or Inability, both of the President and Vice President, declaring what Officer shall then act as President, and such Officer shall act

accordingly, until the Disability be removed, or a President shall be elected.

The Twentieth Amendment

The Twentieth Amendment was passed by the Congress on March 2, 1932, and ratified by the states on January 23, 1933. It provided for the vice-president-elect to become president in the event that the president-elect died before inauguration, the date of which was fixed as January 20 of the year following election. The text of the Twentieth Amendment follows:

SECTION 1. The terms of the President and Vice President shall end at noon on the 20th day of January, and the terms of Senators and Representatives at noon on the 3d day of January, of the years in which such terms would have ended if this article had not been ratified; and the terms of their successors shall then begin.

SEC. 2. The Congress shall assemble at least once in every year, and such meeting shall begin at noon on the 3d day of January, unless they shall by law appoint a different day.

SEC. 3. If, at the time fixed for the beginning of the term of the President, the President elect shall have died, the Vice President elect shall become President. If a President shall not have been chosen before the time fixed for the beginning of his term, or if the President elect shall have failed to qualify, then the Vice President elect shall act as President until a President shall have qualified; and the Congress may by law provide for the case wherein neither a President elect nor a Vice President elect shall have qualified, declaring who shall then act as President, or the manner in which one who is to act shall be selected, and such person shall act accordingly until a President or Vice President shall have qualified.

SEC. 4. The Congress may by law provide for the case of the death of any of the persons from whom the House of Representatives may choose a President whenever the right of choice shall have devolved upon them, and for the case of the death of any of the persons from whom the Senate may choose a Vice President whenever the right of choice shall have devolved upon them.

SEC. 5. Sections 1 and 2 shall take effect on the 15th day of October following the ratification of this article.

sec. 6. This article shall be inoperative unless it shall have been ratified as an amendment to the Constitution by the legislatures of three-fourths of the several States within seven years from the date of its submission.

The Twenty-fifth Amendment

The Twenty-fifth Amendment was passed by Congress July 5, 1965, and finally ratified by the states on February 10, 1967. The full text follows:

SECTION 1. In case of the removal of the President from office or of his death or resignation, the Vice President shall become President.

sec. 2. Whenever there is a vacancy in the office of the Vice President, the President shall nominate a Vice President who shall take office upon confirmation by a majority vote of both Houses of Congress.

sec. 3. Whenever the President transmits to the President pro tempore of the Senate and the Speaker of the House of Representatives his written declaration that he is unable to discharge the powers and duties of his office, and until he transmits to them a written declaration to the contrary, such powers and duties shall be discharged by the Vice President as Acting President.

sec. 4. Whenever the Vice President and a majority of either the principal officers of the executive departments or of such other body as Congress may by law provide, transmit to the President pro tempore of the Senate and the Speaker of the House of Representatives their written declaration that the President is unable to discharge the powers and duties of his office, the Vice President shall immediately assume the powers and duties of the office as Acting President.

Thereafter, when the President transmits to the President pro tempore of the Senate and the Speaker of the House of Representatives his written declaration that no inability exists, he shall resume the powers and duties of his office unless the Vice President and a majority of either the principal officers of the executive department or of such other body as Congress may by law provide, transmit within four days to the President pro tempore of the Senate and the Speaker of the House of Representatives their written declaration that the President is unable to discharge the powers and duties of his office. Thereupon

Congress shall decide the issue, assembling within forty-eight hours for that purpose if not in session. If the Congress, within twenty-one days after receipt of the latter written declaration, or, if Congress is not in session, within twenty-one days after Congress is required to assemble, determines by two-thirds vote of both Houses that the President is unable to discharge the powers and duties of his office, the Vice President shall continue to discharge the same as Acting President; otherwise, the President shall resume the powers and duties of his office.

Statutory Succession Laws

Act of March 1, 1792

Sec. 9. *And be it further enacted,* That in case of removal, death, resignation or inability both of the President and Vice President of the United States, the President of the Senate pro tempore, and in case there shall be no President of the Senate [pro tempore], then the Speaker of the House of Representatives, for the time being shall act as President of the United States until the disability be removed or a President shall be elected.

Sec. 10. *And be it further enacted,* That whenever the offices of President and Vice President shall both become vacant, the Secretary of State shall forthwith cause a notification thereof to be made to the executive of every state, and shall also cause the same to be published in at least one of the newspapers printed in each state, specifying that electors of the President of the United States shall be appointed or chosen in the several states within thirty-four days preceding the first Wednesday in December then next ensuing: *Provided,* There shall be the space of two months between the date of such notification and the said first Wednesday in December, but if there shall not be the space of two months between the date of such notification and the first Wednesday in December; and if the term for which the President and Vice President last in office were elected shall not expire on the third day of March next ensuing, then the Secretary of State shall specify in the notification that the electors shall be appointed or chosen within thirty-four days preceding the first Wednesday in December in the year next ensuing, within which time the electors shall accordingly be appointed or chosen, and the electors shall meet and give their votes on the first Wednesday in December, and the proceedings and duties of the said electors and others shall be pursuant to the directions prescribed in this act.

Act of January 19, 1886

Be it enacted by the Senate and House of Representatives of the United States of America in Congress assembled, That in case of removal, death, resignation, or inability of both the President and Vice-President of the United States, the Secretary of State, or if there be none, or in case of his removal, death, resignation, or inability, then the Secretary of the Treasury, or if there be none, or in case of his removal, death, resignation, or inability, then the Secretary of War, or if there be none, or in case of his removal, death, resignation, or inability, then the Attorney-General, or if there be none, or in case of his removal, death, resignation, or inability, then the Postmaster-General, or if there be none, or in case of his removal, death, resignation, or inability, then the Secretary of the Navy, or if there be none, or in case of his removal, death, resignation, or inability, then the Secretary of the Interior, shall act as President until the disability of the President or Vice-President is removed or a President shall be elected: *Provided,* That whenever the powers and duties of the office of President of the United States shall devolve upon any of the persons named herein, if Congress be not then in session, or if it would not meet in accordance with law within twenty days thereafter, it shall be the duty of the person upon whom said powers and duties shall devolve to issue a proclamation convening Congress in extraordinary session, giving twenty days' notice of the time of meeting.

Sec. 2. That the preceding section shall only be held to describe and apply to such officers as shall have been appointed by the advice and consent of the Senate to the offices therein named, and such as are eligible to the office of President under the Constitution, and not under impeachment by the House of Representatives of the United States at the time the powers and duties of the office shall devolve upon them respectively.

Sec. 3. That sections one hundred and forty-six, one hundred and forty-seven, one hundred and forty-eight, one hundred and forty-nine, and one hundred and fifty of the Revised Statutes are hereby repealed.

Act of July 18, 1947

(a) (1) If, by reason of death, resignation, removal from office, inability, or failure to qualify, there is neither a President nor Vice-President to discharge the powers and duties of the office of President, then the Speaker of the House of Representatives shall, upon his resignation as Speaker and as Representative in Congress, act as President.

(2) The same rule shall apply in the case of the death, resignation, removal from office, or inability of an individual acting as President under this subsection.

(b) If, at the time when under subsection (a) of this section a Speaker is to begin the discharge of the powers and duties of the office of President, there is no Speaker, or the Speaker fails to qualify as Acting President, then the President pro tempore of the Senate shall, upon his resignation as President pro tempore and as Senator, act as President.

(c) An individual acting as president under subsection (a) or subsection (b) of this section shall continue to act until the expiration of the then current presidential term, except that—

(1) If this discharge of the powers and duties of the office is founded in whole or in part on the failure of both the President-elect and the Vice-President-elect to qualify, then he shall act only until a President or Vice-President qualifies; and

(2) If his discharge of the powers and duties of the office is founded in whole or in part on the inability of the President or Vice-President, then he shall act only until the removal of the disability of one of such individuals.

(d) (1) If, by reason of death, resignation, removal from office, inability, or failure to qualify, there is no President pro tempore to act as President under subsection (b) of this section, then the officer of the United States who is highest on the following list, and who is not under disability to discharge the powers and duties of the office of President shall act as President: Secretary of State, Secretary of the Treasury, Secretary of Defense, Attorney General, Postmaster General, Secretary of the Interior, Secretary of Agriculture, Secretary of Commerce, Secretary of Labor.*

(2) An individual acting as President under this subsection shall continue so to do until the expiration of the then current presidential term, but not after a qualified and prior-entitled individual is able to act, except that the removal of the disability of an individual higher on the list contained in paragraph (1) of this subsection or the ability to qualify on the part of an individual higher on such list shall not terminate his service.

(3) The taking of the oath of office by an individual specified in the list in paragraph (1) of this subsection shall be held to constitute his

*The position of Postmaster General was abolished in 1970, and the Secretaries of Health, Education and Welfare, of Housing and Urban Development, and of Transportation have been added to the line of succession.

resignation from the office by virtue of the holding of which he qualifies to act as President.

(e) Subsections (a), (b), and (d) of this section shall apply only to such officers as are eligible to the office of President under the Constitution. Subsection (d) of this section shall apply only to officers appointed, by and with the advice and consent of the Senate, prior to the time of the death, resignation, removal from office, inability, or failure to qualify, of the President pro tempore, and only to officers not under impeachment by the House of Representatives at the time the powers and duties of the office of President devolve upon them.

(f) During the period that any individual acts as President under this section, his compensation shall be at the rate then provided by law in the case of the President.

Appendix 2:

The National Command Authority

On the evening of the attack on Ronald Reagan, Larry Speakes, acting as White House spokesman, said that there had been an "automatic assumption of command authority" by Vice-President Bush.[1] James Baker later appeared to repudiate this statement, claiming that it referred to a procedure known as the "National Command Authority," to be employed "only in a very narrow, narrow, limited range of circumstances."[2] Baker said that the National Command Authority had, with the president's approval, been "established at the inception of the [Reagan] administration, as it always is."[3]

Secretary of Defense Weinberger later confirmed that "the chain of leadership under the National Command Authority" was clarified in one of the first directives he had presented to the president-elect a few days before the inauguration. If the president were disabled, the vice-president would be next in line to command the military and, after him, the secretary of defense.[4]

Baker maintained that the cabinet discussed and rejected the use of the

National Command Authority on the evening of the shooting because it did not apply to the circumstances they confronted. In other words, Bush would not actually assume any additional authority unless a military emergency arose. Meanwhile, with Reagan on the operating table and under anesthesia, an "informal" agreement had been worked out by the cabinet and White House staff that the vice-president would assume presidential power in the event of a major crisis.[5]

The situation was complicated by the fact that when Reagan went into surgery, Bush was two hours away from Washington on an aircraft which lacked secure communications. Accordingly, there was some initial uncertainty over whether command would devolve on Bush or on Weinberger.[6] Nevertheless, the airborne communications capabilities were apparently considered sufficient for Bush to assume command. In congressional hearings the day after the shooting, Air Force Chief of Staff Lew Allen indicated that Bush was in control of the military while Reagan was incapacitated, even when airborne. When asked who had authority to "launch on warning" while the president was anesthetized, he said, "As soon as we had contacted the vice president, that confirmed the fact that the authority was there and that he was in an aircraft with appropriate communications."[7]

The question that General Allen responded to—who had authority to "launch on warning"?—obviously referred to the nuclear weapons forces. If the vice-president was empowered to act as Allen described, it represented a predelegation of presidential authority. The vice-president would assume the president's control over nuclear weapons if the president was "incommunicado" when a military crisis arose.[8]

The Defense Department's publicly released definition of the term "National Command Authorities" makes no mention of nuclear command or emergency procedures. According to the legal office of the department, the term is "just a general expression" to refer to the "principal authorities with respect to the military establishment"—that is, the president and the secretary of defense.[9] But the Joint Chiefs of Staff (JCS) dictionary of military terms states, "National Command Authorities— (DOD) The President and the Secretary of Defense *or their duly deputized alternates or successors.* Commonly referred to as NCA" (emphasis added).[10] Those individuals listed in the presidential directive—the "chain of leadership under the National Command Authorities," as Weinberger put it[11]—apparently constitute the president's list of "duly deputized alternates or successors" who control the "button" in the event of a military emergency and incapacity of those higher up on the list.

It is difficult to get a clear and consistent picture of the composition and operational aspects of the National Command Authority. The term has no statutory or constitutional basis,[12] which may explain why its usage often varies. Although always abbreviated as NCA, it is sometimes given as singular ("National Command Authority") and sometimes as plural ("Authorities").[13] It has been said to include "the President and his military advisers, the JCS"[14] but has also been described as "the top U.S. national security decision makers . . . which includes the President and the Secretary of Defense."[15] There is general agreement that it designates the locus of nuclear decision-making power. Officially, only the president has this power. "The lines of command and control merge at the White House, where the President, with his constitutionally mandated powers as commander in chief of the armed forces, sits as the national command authority (NCA)."[16] Nevertheless, most definitions depict both the president and the secretary of defense as NCA, responsible for "final decisions about the use of U.S. nuclear weapons."[17]

The definition of the "NCA" has gone through a number of permutations over the years. It was first alluded to in 1960 in a classified Joint Chiefs of Staff paper entitled "Department of Defense Emergency Plan."[18] A definition appeared as early as 1962, in Defense Department Directive S-5100.30.[19] It was distinguished by its inclusiveness, ambiguity, and vagueness: the National Command Authorities "include the President, the Secretary of Defense, the Joint Chiefs of Staff and their authorized successors and alternates."[20] This differed from the current definition in that the individuals designated were not exclusively civilian: the Joint Chiefs of Staff were included. Also noteworthy is that it designated the president, secretary of defense, the Joint Chiefs, *and* their alternates and successors (the current version says *or*). Thus, the vice-president and any other successors or alternates would have been included; if taken literally, this would give potential authority over nuclear weapons to a fairly large group of individuals. The language of the directive specified a sequence in the line of nuclear command: "the order of succession due to incapacity of any of the centers is established by the rank of the National Command Authority present in the surviving command facilities. . . ."[21]

By 1967, the "and" had been changed to "or," so that the alternates or successors could not be considered essential elements in the NCA: "The NCA consist of the President, the Secretary of Defense, the Joint Chiefs of Staff or the duly deputized alternates or successors."[22] Thus, the Joint Chiefs were still included. However, when the first JCS dictionary was issued, in 1972, it derived a still narrower definition from DOD Directive 5100.30, dated December 2, 1971.[23] This directive was a descendant of the 1962 document and is often cited as the standard DOD source for the official descriptions of the NCA and the chain of command. The section reads, "The NCA consists only of the President and the Secretary of Defense or their duly deputized alternates or successors. The chain of command runs from the President to the Secretary of Defense and through the Joint Chiefs of Staff to the commanders of Unified and Specified Commands."[24] After defining the NCA and the chain of command, the directive appears to link the two: "The channel of communications for execution of the Single Integrated Operational Plan (SIOP) and other time-sensitive operations shall be from the NCA through the Chairman of the Joint Chiefs of Staff, representing the Joint Chiefs of Staff, to the executing commanders."[25] The last sentence is usually construed as an alternative chain of command for the execution of SIOP (the nuclear war plan) and other "time-sensitive matters." The executing orders for SIOP issue "from the NCA," rather than "from the President." This distinction is reiterated in the DOD's emergency plans, which call upon unified and specified commands to ensure their capability "to implement the SIOP execution order of the National Command Authorities (NCA)."[26] It seems reasonable to assume that orders issued "from the NCA" encompass emergency arrangements involving delegation of authority to alternates or successors.

This special SIOP hierarchy is called a "channel of communications," a wording perhaps chosen to suggest that the normal chain of command was unaltered. Indeed, the chairman of the JCS is legally prohibited from exercising "military command over the Joint Chiefs of Staff or any of the armed forces"[27] and yet is included in the SIOP "channel of communications." This same distinction is made in the description of the role of the JCS in the regular chain of command, where they serve as a "channel of communications." Nevertheless, it may be that the "differentiation [between channel of communications and chain of command] is marginal" for practical purposes.[28]

Hence, the National Command Authority is both a line of succession and a conduit for orders to move through the system. The line of succession, then, runs from the civilian leadership to military commanders, so that the chairman of the Joint Chiefs of Staff, and after him the commander of the Strategic Air Command, could become the center of release authority if it were impossible to get in touch with the president, the vice-president, and the secretary of defense.[29]

It is difficult to reconcile what is known about the National Command Authority with the constitutional and statutory guidelines for command authority. Do the members of the NCA, the president and the secretary of defense or their alternates and successors, somehow share jurisdiction over nuclear command? If so, is this in conflict with the understanding that the president, as commander in chief, holds the sole authority to order the use of nuclear weapons? (That stipulation was made unequivocal in the language of the National Security Council in 1948: "The decision as to the employment of atomic weapons in the event of war is to be made by the Chief Executive when he considers such decision to be required.")[30] If not, why is the SIOP order said to originate from the NCA?

Under the National Security Act of 1947 and its amendments, the operational chain of command runs from the president through the secretary of defense to the commanders of the specified and unified commands, and the Joint Chiefs of Staff do not exercise operational command. The NCA, by inserting the vice-president and possibly the chairman of the Joint Chiefs, appears to run counter to these provisions. (This may be the least problematic of the issues surrounding the NCA, because the president has the authority to alter the chain of command under the Goldwater-Nichols Department of Defense Reorganization Act of 1986.)[31]

More important, how can the NCA be reconciled with the succession laws? The NCA puts the secretary of defense and members of the military next in line, after the president and the vice-president, to inherit nuclear command authority, while the legal succession runs from the vice-president to the Speaker of the House, the president pro tem of the Senate, the secretaries of treasury and state, *then* the secretary of defense and the other cabinet members.

The National Command Authority may represent a purposeful effort to avoid passing command authority down the line of succession defined by the Constitution and related statutes. Perhaps it would be undesirable for the secretary of education to issue orders, for example.[32] Unfortunately, if the president and vice-president are killed, dual succession lines might pass the president's authority to two different individuals simultaneously: the secretary of defense and the Speaker of the House. The president's legal successor could presumably revoke such arrangements but might have insufficient time to take such action and assume command during a nuclear war.

Finally, is the NCA intended to short-circuit the Twenty-fifth Amendment? The reports from the executive branch after the Reagan shooting indicate that the NCA provisions would have allowed successors to act if the president had been incapacitated. There was no implication whatsoever that this would have followed the constitutional determination of incapacity under the Twenty-fifth Amendment. Perhaps this reflected the belief that the amendment is too time-consuming or cumbersome for use in an emergency.

It was not only Speakes and Baker who were confused about these matters. Reagan, who approved the NCA plans, was later surprised to learn that the Joint Chiefs of Staff kept a duplicate of his nuclear authorization code card.[33] Shortly after the shooting, Defense Department lawyers issued a statement saying that "the chain of command runs from the President, who at all times is the Commander in Chief of the Armed Forces under the Constitution, directly to the Secretary of Defense," and that this arrangement held "at all times" on March 30. The Pentagon spokesman who issued the statement added that "only the President can order the use of military weapons" and said that he saw "no problem" or disagreement with earlier White House statements that the vice-president precedes the secretary of defense in the National Command Authorities.[34]

If, on March 30, the chain of command continued to run from the president to the secretary of defense, perhaps that meant only that the National Command Authority provisions were never actually in effect. No military emergency arose during the period after the attack on the president; hence, the vice-president or secretary of defense never took command. But it is surely a misstatement that only the president can "order the use of military weapons." At the very least, the National Command Authority apparently provides for the exercise of nuclear weapons control by the vice-president or others if the president is unavailable and the missiles are flying.

Looking back at the changes in definition of the NCA and the varied interpretations of its meaning and structure, we can hardly find it surprising that there was uncertainty in the executive branch about its role at the time of the attack on Reagan. The ambiguity may have been deliberate;[35] a more precise explanation may have been contained in classified directives of the executive branch. No published documents place the vice-president in the NCA. Nevertheless, Jimmy Carter apparently included Vice-President Mondale in the NCA, and there is evidence that Vice-President Bush was included during the Reagan administration.[36] Certainly, he had his own "football" and his own code card.[37]

Although the public believes that only the president has the right to authorize the use of nuclear weapons, there are clearly circumstances in which release authority would devolve on others. There seems little purpose in the failure to clarify this matter and to make certain that there is a common understanding both within the executive branch—so as to avoid confusion—and in the public at large as to the locus of power to authorize nuclear weapons use. The concept that ambiguity may diminish the chance of a successful "decapitation" strike surely underestimates the adversary's capacity to understand and reconstruct the likely chain of Nuclear Command Authorities in the United States.

Appendix 3:

The Situation Room

At the center of the activities of the executive branch following the attack on Reagan, the Situation Room of the White House was overburdened by the sheer numbers of cabinet and staff in a relatively small space. Furthermore, its facilities proved to be inadequate for the purpose of crisis management.[1]

An adjunct to the Situation Room was subsequently built. The Crisis Management Center (or Situation Room Support Facility) was established in the Executive Office Building. Designed for the use of senior White House and departmental staffs while the president uses the original Situation Room, it contains high-tech communications and display equipment to improve "connectivity."[2] Data from national security agencies are now instantly available and can be synthesized and projected for group discussion. Bradley Patterson, a scholar who studied the organization of the White House while serving under three presidents, has described the present resource: "A digital information and display system (DIDS) can fill the screen with choropleth maps (demographic/economic data pro-

jected as colored segments of geographic units); war games can be arranged. Secure voice and video lines connect to the smaller Situation
Room across the street; any displays in the National Military Command
Center can be projected onto the White House screen simultaneously.
Tape and television recorders are there to film every moment of a crisis
situation. . . . Each message, telephone call, and decision would be logged
as well. . . . Computers will permit telegrams the Sit Room readers have
identified as important to be switched directly to the consoles of the
geographic or functional NSC staff members."[3]

Why were these changes made? On this matter, Richard Allen, the
national security adviser in 1981, has been explicit: "The events surrounding the attempt on President Reagan's life motivated the creation of the
Crisis Management Center."[4] The idea for the adjacent room, however,
apparently originated with Martin Anderson, the head of the Office of
Policy Development.[5] He felt the need for an analogue for domestic
policy of the Situation Room as the focus of national security. He noted a
large old room on the second floor of the Executive Office Building
(Room 208) that had served until 1948 as the office of the secretaries of
state from Hamilton Fish (1869–77) until George Marshall.[6] It was in sad
disrepair, with old carpeting and a serious need for renovation and resto-
ration, but it had large tables and comfortable chairs. He thought it might
become a supplemental conference room in which visual presentations
could readily be made. The rest of the meeting rooms were thirty to forty
years behind the times in his view. He spoke to Richard Allen about it,
since the funds available to him were very limited, and Allen agreed that
the money could be put up by the National Security Council with shared
utilization. Anderson reviewed it with Ed Meese, and, with his agreement,
the concept of a shared domestic and national security area was accepted.
A joint memorandum was initiated, describing the project.[7]

But the wheels turned slowly, and at the time Anderson left the White
House in 1983, the room was completely torn up, and the computer
experts had entered the scene. Ultimately, according to Anderson, "it
became a communications room with an enormous amount of high-
powered electronics and data processing capacity. It has now been transformed into a national security cave, and I was amazed to hear that Ollie
North had used it for his shenanigans."[8]

Anderson's account was confirmed by Richard Allen: "Concerning
Room 208 EOB: Indeed, Meese did want a domestic counterpart to the
NSC Situation Room, but never had in mind the monster that ultimately

evolved. Martin Anderson began the discussion with me concerning Room 208, and he and I reviewed the actual physical layout of the offices and visited them. I then agreed to provide a small amount of funding from the NSC budget to assist in the process, as the Situation Room is not always the most suitable or accessible room even for important meetings dealing with foreign policy and national security considerations, and the new briefing room could be used for less sensitive national security discussions. It was my practice to keep the Situation Room essentially for its original purpose."

"What we had in mind was a reasonably secure briefing room, but not one that would replace the Situation Room. The mere location of Room 208 precluded any reasonable degree of security, or at least any security that could be achieved at reasonable cost."[9]

A similar but slightly different version of what happened has been given by Patterson:

"What really stimulated the creation of the second crisis center (Room 208 EOB) was not so much the assassination attempt (although that event was a stimulus) as a conclusion which Ed Meese had reached on his own that there was no facility in the White House—comparable to the NSC Sit Room in the lower level of the West Wing—which could handle domestic crises. Meese at that time was Counsellor to the President and Chairman of the Domestic Policy Council. Meese wanted to have a parallel structure to the NSC Sit Room. Richard Beal was an assistant to Meese at the beginning. Meese in effect told Beal to get moving on it, and the first $25,000 of the funding for the second Sit Room came from the Domestic Policy Council. Later, Beal was assigned to the NSC staff and the rest of the funding came from the national security side of the policy machinery."[10]

The importance of the added facility as a focus for crisis management is not uniformly acknowledged. David Gergen, for example, has expressed his belief "that if the same thing happened in the next few years to George Bush that happened to Ronald Reagan, people would still go to the Situation Room. Very little use was made of the second room, at least when I was there. Maybe they made more extensive use after I left. There were a lot of people on the White House Staff who thought the new room was a joke. It had all the makings of something—a lot of slide shows and stars and light, and sound and music, and it was strange in the beginning. Maybe it's more functional now."[11]

What has not yet been fully resolved is the question of who is in charge in the Situation Room if the president is disabled. Is it the vice-president, as in Reagan's choice of Bush for head of crisis management? If the vice-president is in Texas, or China, or even in Washington, D.C., is it the secretary of defense, as Weinberger believed when arguing with Haig on March 30, 1981? Or is it the senior cabinet officer, the secretary of state, as Al Haig so forcefully contended when he stated to the nation, "I am in control here at the White House"? The National Security Act of 1947 provided that "the Secretary of Defense shall be the principal assistant to the president on all matters relating to the national security."[12] It was President Truman's decision, however, that the secretary of state would preside as the second-ranking member of the National Security Council, in the president's absence.[13]

During the Johnson administration, when the president used the Situation Room to plan targeting missions for the Vietnam War, the defense secretary was in charge of operations and responsible for passing along instructions, even when the secretary of state was present.[14]

The Bush administration and future presidents must address this issue and define more sharply than earlier the distribution of power in the Situation Room during domestic and international crises that require informed, prudent, and firm leadership for the nation. Until this matter is clarified, the tensions that produced the Haig-Weinberger argument will surely recur.

Appendix 4:

The Interregnum
—Election Day to
Inauguration

After the attack on the president, the issue of preparation for such an event was raised repeatedly. Why had it not been undertaken during the transition? What had occupied those on the massive roster of the executive branch from November 4, 1980, through January 20, 1981?

In fact, a whirlwind of activity took place. During those seventy-seven days, there was a huge investment of people and energy in a host of areas essential to a smooth takeover by the administration. This interval between the election and the inauguration was crucial for many reasons. A process for initiating policy had to be developed, personnel recruited, the budget reviewed, and a central point of contact for the news media created. Internationally, the country was vulnerable: President Carter's power and personal leverage were dwindling, but Reagan had no authority and was inexperienced in foreign policy.[1] Errors, delays, or missed opportunities might have been difficult to correct or modify.

Inept or inexperienced spokesmen of the new administration were sending misleading signals to foreign countries, and sudden policy shifts could have resulted in lasting resentments. The nation's security, trade, and diplomatic relationships might have been damaged. As Eisenhower emphasized in his memoirs, an emergency early in a new administration may be dangerous simply because the new officials are unfamiliar with their duties and authority.[2]

In spite of the mixture of risk and opportunity, a president-elect may enter this interval with confidence that borders on arrogance. But he must live with the incumbent. If he has attacked him sharply, the relationship may be colored by resentment, and effective cooperation blocked. Ironically, at a time when so many crucial decisions confront him, he is least equipped to make them. Exhausted by the campaign, he may have difficulty developing a blueprint for implementing his slogans, promises, and inclinations. Many of our recent presidents have had little knowledge of foreign affairs prior to their election.[3]

Excessive and arbitrary secrecy surrounding foreign affairs presents a special problem. Whether justified or not, there is a powerful sense that the proper information must be provided to loyalists who need it—but only to those people. Even when classified material should be made available to others, especially party opponents, inertia derived from reluctance impedes a rapid transfer of knowledge.[4]

Transitions are shaped by many elements, including the state of domestic and international affairs, the team, and the president himself. Such factors—the scope of Reagan's victory, the sense of mission of his supporters and his team, and his executive style—played large roles in defining the transformation. Reagan's administrative motif favored a collegial staff in which people could voice opposing viewpoints without developing resentments and hard feelings. He preferred to work with small groups of aides. Because he envisioned his position as that of chairman of the board, he frequently left lesser decisions to others.[5]

Paradoxically, the beginning of the "transition" occurred even before the nominating convention. Throughout the election year, Reagan asked advisers and supporters for their suggestions on the critical items he should address if he won. At a Washington meeting on April 8, 1980, he spoke with almost seventy defense and foreign policy advisers and requested that they make policy and budget recommendations for the first hundred days in office.[6] A similar planning effort was initiated to review domestic and economic issues.

While E. Pendleton James conducted the search for personnel,[7] Robert

Freer, a former associate of Caspar Weinberger's, established a volunteer group to focus on government departments and agencies. From July to October, Freer saw to it that detailed reports were prepared on government agencies. Key offices were identified, and the principal policy issues were delineated. After the papers were complete, Freer proposed the formation of agency transition teams that could inform Reagan of important findings immediately following the election.[8]

Other groups were laying the groundwork for a Reagan presidency. The Heritage Foundation, a conservative think tank in Washington, initiated an extensive study of government programs, personnel, and agencies. The result was a 3,000-page report intended to guide administration policies after the election.[9]

Many transition advisers on foreign policy came from the Center for Strategic and International Studies (CSIS) at Georgetown University. Another leading source of advice was the Hoover Institution at Stanford University. Both Martin Anderson and Darrell Trent were associated with Hoover; Glenn Campbell, the Hoover director, and Richard T. Burress, the associate director, gave their assistance. The aerospace and defense industries also provided many consultants.[10]

Years before the event, in preparation for the election of a conservative Republican, staff and fellows at the Hoover Institution, the Center for the Study of the Presidency, the Heritage Foundation, the Institute for Contemporary Studies, the American Enterprise Institute, and the Georgetown Center for Strategic and International Studies were all working on the themes and issues to be addressed.[11]

Although Reagan avoided some of Carter's problems with internal fighting during his transition, the organization of the team was complicated. Anne Armstrong, for example, moved from the post of campaign cochairman to that of cochairman of the executive group. Senator Paul Laxalt, who had been campaign chairman, became chairman of the congressional advisory group,[16] acting to promote communication between the new administration and the Congress. Problems arose because of the ambiguous position of some staff members. Many would have no job in the new administration, while others would be appointed to important agency roles. By early December, some staffers began to act as if they were members of the new administration. Instead of gathering information for incoming appointees, a few began articulating policy even before a cabinet secretary was named. At the State Department, Robert Neumann led a transition team that upset and annoyed the staff with its intrusiveness. When the new secretary of state, Alexander Haig, received the team's report, he immediately dismissed it.[12]

Meanwhile, using a computer-based system for classifying and recording resumes, James's preelection personnel group listed five to ten names for each of eighty-seven positions at the deputy and under secretary ranks. They did the same for the one hundred positions that would be open at the assistant secretary level. Their goal was to make their choices by the inauguration, but filling so many government posts was a complex and demanding task.[13]

Thousands of résumés arrived daily. By December 1, thirty thousand job applications had been received at the headquarters. There were several categories of potential appointees. The "public men" were accomplished individuals in their fifties and sixties who signaled their availability in ways other than that of sending résumés. They had been successful professionally and were willing to set aside financial and other personal ambitions to serve in the government.

Another type included a far larger group of young lawyers, economists, sociologists, writers, publicists, and policy analysts, many of whom were committed to their careers and hence not job seekers in government. This put Reagan in a catch-22 situation: although he could form a distinguished cabinet from the group of "public men," those who were needed for subcabinet posts were frequently unwilling to sacrifice their current positions.[14]

The decision-making process for the cabinet and top White House appointments began with the "kitchen cabinet." It was composed of conservative millionaires who had originally been impressed by Reagan's speech for Goldwater at the 1968 convention and who had later helped persuade him to run for the governorship of California. Holmes P. Tuttle, a wealthy Ford dealer in Los Angeles, led the group, which also included Justin Dart, an industrialist; Charles Wick, a wealthy filmmaker; and William French Smith, Reagan's personal attorney (and subsequently, his attorney general).[15] During their meetings, each participant held a top-secret notebook of résumé summaries gathered over the past six months by James, who had outlined the strengths and weaknesses of about seventy candidates.

On November 21, twenty-one senior advisers listed recommendations on the basis of their desire to have a cabinet made up of men with typical corporate managing qualities. The next day the group met with Reagan in William French Smith's office. Although the meeting lasted for three hours, the president-elect mostly listened to the others' opinions. In later meetings at his home, however, he presided over the kitchen cabinet and indicated his own evaluations.[16]

Final decisions were left largely to top staff and advisers who would have key positions in the new administration: Bush, Meese, Baker, Deaver, Laxalt, Casey, and a few others. The primary considerations were philosophical commitment to Reagan, integrity, competence, toughness, and team play. Nevertheless, Reagan wanted the cabinet to exhibit some diversity in geographical background, race, and gender.[17]

The advisers in the kitchen cabinet based their choices largely on the candidate's ideology. But James looked for prior government experience and paid equal attention to ideology and competence. Many of his candidates were from past Republican administrations. Reagan's bias was towards businessmen. By and large, the officials were selected more for their loyalty to the president-elect than was true of any other recent administration. Subcabinet positions were filled by people with little government experience: 59 percent had none.[18]

The transition was the most expensive in history, with one thousand to twelve hundred people (five hundred on the payroll) occupying nine floors of a downtown Washington building. Private contributions paid for preelection planning, while federal funds provided $2,000,000 after the election. This amount was depleted rapidly, and another $1,000,000 in private contributions was spent.[19]

Reagan contended that he ran over budget only because the federal contribution was unchanged from four years ago and did not account for inflation. Nevertheless, because of his opposition to big government, the high cost and large staff were a target for criticism in Washington. Carter officials recalled that they achieved the same end with a staff of 350 people and returned one-fourth of the federal funds to the Treasury.[20]

A mountain of policy proposals had been produced by the end of November. Some of these preliminary recommendations were unexpected: they included the possible declaration of a national economic emergency and reconsideration of the proposed MX missile system.[21]

A small but important group decided what actions Reagan should take after the inauguration. Headed by the former professor Richard Real, they developed the "Initial Actions Project" for Meese. In their report, they identified strategic objectives and suggested a desirable sequence and timing of events for the first weeks and months of the new administration.[22]

Shortly after the election, Communications Director David Gergen assembled a book entitled "The First 100 Days." He believed that there should be a single focus on the economy, which, in fact, became the top objective. A paper by David Stockman, known as the "Stockman Manifesto," was widely circulated. It called for a reduction in government spending by using "supply-side economics," which combined nondefense reductions, tax cuts, control over the money supply, and deregulation designed to stimulate the economy and lead to a balanced budget. Stockman's appointment as director of the Office of Management and Budget on December 1 enabled him to delve immediately into budgetary data. As discussions progressed through December and early January, expectations from the cutting of fraud and waste lessened, and a greater emphasis was placed on tax reduction and controlled expenditure over a two- to three-year period.[23]

Begun earlier than usual, the appointments process took more time to complete than in the past. One consequence of the delay and of the fixation on the economy was a virtual guarantee that foreign policy would be secondary to domestic issues. Positions at intermediate levels in foreign affairs were frequently filled months after the inauguration. One of the central appointees in national security policy was chosen in August—six and a half months after the administration took office.[24] Almost all of these new people needed training, experience, and indoctrination. These factors converged to create a six- to nine-month hiatus. When added to Carter's declining influence during the interval, there was a one-year period when the United States was "running at half throttle or less in its conduct of foreign affairs."[25]

The slow pace of appointments was partly caused by the requirements of the Ethics in Government Act of 1978. Officials were now required to make far more extensive financial disclosures than previously and were not permitted to contact their old agencies for at least one year after leaving their federal positions.

The government clearance system also included security checks, fingerprinting, and numerous questions about past and present associates. This arduous process dissuaded some potential subcabinet nominees from accepting appointments. Still another element was the salary structure, which had failed to keep up with private-sector earnings.[26]

But the large number of advisers and their elaborate clearance system probably deserved most of the blame for the delays. A further convolution was an intricate sign-off procedure; only Meese, Baker, Deaver, and Reagan could veto a nomination. By the first week in May, fewer than 60 percent of the top four hundred government officials had been announced, 36 percent formally nominated, and 21 percent confirmed.[27]

Reagan met with most cabinet secretaries shortly after he assumed office. These early meetings were to signal his desire to work quickly in order to get his program passed. He also met with sixty senators and congressmen during the first three weeks of his administration. On March 10, only forty-nine days after his inauguration, the new administration submitted a complete revision of Carter's 1982 budget to Congress. Within six months, Reagan's budgetary goals were reached: large increases in defense spending, large tax cuts, and reductions in domestic programs. By focusing on a single task, he avoided overwhelming Congress with too many programs too soon.[28]

Unfortunately, he also neglected important international issues. When Reagan was criticized for ignoring foreign affairs, he replied that foreign policy would not be effective until the economy was sound. He intended to make U.S.-Soviet relations and relations with Western Europe the centerpiece of his foreign policy. In the light of the Afghan and Polish crises and hostile Soviet activities in developing countries, he viewed the Soviet Union as a power that must be deterred, even if it required military action. But for the moment, foreign policy initiatives, especially controversial ones, were avoided.[29]

In early January, Reagan asked Haig to draft an organizational plan for foreign policy. With the help of the Defense Department, the CIA, and Richard Allen, the new national security adviser, it was completed shortly after the inauguration. But its implementation was deflected by differences in the policy coalition; the delay exacerbated early rivalries, distrust, and uncoordinated statements on foreign policy. The Chinese were incensed by an administration adviser's suggestion that the United States might increase contacts with Taiwan.[30] Allen finally demanded that all members of Reagan's Foreign Advisory Board and the teams in national security withhold comments on international affairs. A special unit was set up to monitor communications between Reagan advisers and representatives of foreign governments.

Haig went through a grueling set of confirmation hearings, which left little time to make plans for the State Department. While the president failed to assume command over foreign policy, he refused to delegate control to Haig.[31] Thus, the development of foreign and national security policy was slower and less conclusive than that of economic policy.

Like Nixon and Carter, Reagan promised cabinet government throughout his campaign. But he raised false expectations among his appointees. In reality, he made his decisions in private with the help of trusted advisers—not in a chairman-of-the-board style with the help and in the presence of his cabinet. The cabinet became a communication channel through which the president received and transmitted information. Seldom involved during early stages of policy debate, Reagan did not mind being uninformed on issues and controversies within the administration.[32]

Meanwhile, Carter and his officials were responsible for effective governing during the interregnum. Carter had agreed to limit executive initiatives and refrain from making major policies and appointments in his final days in order to allow Reagan maximum flexibility. Hence, a number of key bills were deferred until the new administration took office.[33] But there were certain tasks that Carter had to handle. He was kept busy with the Iranian hostage problem, the budget, the State of the Union Message, and the annual economic message.

There were no in-depth discussions between the outgoing and the incoming administrations until well into December, when Stuart Eizenstat, Carter's assistant for domestic affairs and policy, met with his designated replacement, Martin Anderson. At the same time, Zbigniew Brzezinski, assistant for national security affairs under Carter, met with Richard Allen.[34]

When Carter met Reagan late in December, he described him as "detached and uninterested" in the information he received. Asked if he would like a pad of paper in order to take notes, Reagan responded that it was unnecessary because he would remember the complexities of the discussion.[35]

The hostage crisis, the defining preoccupation of Carter's last year in office, remained at the top of his agenda. Negotiations were slow until the Carter administration offered the Iranians $7.8 billion for the safe return of the hostages. On January 19, Carter, convinced that final arrangements had been made, announced that the hostages would be released. Additional obstacles delayed the exchange until January 20, when Carter telephoned Reagan in the morning to tell him that the transaction was complete. Even then, he did not receive the good news of the hostages' release until the inauguration was over.[36]

The transition, then, was a period that made tremendous demands on the executive team. Its members were confronted not only by a host of competing priorities but also by the deadline of January 20, 1981, when the responsibility for governing would truly rest in their hands. The answer to the question "Why was there no preparation for a disabled presidency?" was straightforward: it was not considered an important priority. There was no interest in addressing the possibility that the seventy-year-old president might be incapacitated, or in exploring the mechanism for responding to such an eventuality.

Commenting on this matter, David Gergen said that he was "not aware of any planning that went on between Reagan and Bush, or between Carter and Mondale. But it should be done during the transition. It should be initiated when you get a general counsel and an attorney general."[37]

It was not. As a consequence, Reagan's trauma was framed in a series of actions well outside the orderly manner prescribed by the Twenty-fifth Amendment to the Constitution. In Senator Bayh's view, the president's men "were acting unconstitutionally when they did not invoke it when the president went under anesthesia."[38]

Notes

Abbreviations

LAT   *Los Angeles Times*
NYT   *New York Times*
WP   *Washington Post*
WSJ   *Wall Street Journal*

CHAPTER 1: The Assassin

1. Ed Magnuson, "Six Shots at a Nation's Heart," *Time*, April 13, 1981, 25; Sam Donaldson, *Hold On, Mr. President!* (New York: Random House, 1987), 199.
2. "Building and Construction Trades Department, AFL-CIO: Remarks at the Union's National Conference, March 30, 1981," in Office of the Federal Register, *Weekly Compilation of Presidential Documents* (Washington, D.C.: National Archives and Records Service, April 6, 1981), 367–72.
3. Ibid., 372.
4. Howell Raines, "Reagan Wounded in Chest by Gunman," *NYT*, March 31, 1981, 1; Magnuson, "Six Shots," 25.
5. Aaron Latham, "The Dark Side of the American Dream," *Rolling Stone*, Aug. 5, 1982, 20.
6. James M. Perry, "Reagan Shot in Chest on Washington Street; Undergoes Surgery," *WSJ*, March 31, 1981, 1.
7. Richard D. Lyons, "Witnesses to Shooting Recall Suspect Acting 'Fidgety' and 'Hostile,' " *NYT*, March 31, 1981, 4; Raines, "Reagan Wounded," 1.
8. Michael K. Deaver and Mickey Hershkowitz, *Behind the Scenes* (New York: William J. Morrow, 1987), 17.
9. Raines, "Reagan Wounded," 1.
10. Lincoln Caplan, "The Insanity Defense," *New Yorker*, July 2, 1984, 46.
11. Priscilla Johnson McMillan, "An Assassin's Portrait," *New Republic*,

July 12, 1982, 17; Caplan, "Insanity Defense," 55, 63; Latham, "Dark Side," 20.

12. Francis X. Clines, "Agents Tracing Hinckley's Path Find a Shift to Violent Emotion," *NYT,* April 5, 1981, 1; Kurt Anderson, "A Drifter Who Stalked Success," *Time,* April 13, 1981, 40.

13. Lincoln Caplan, *The Insanity Defense and the Trial of John W. Hinckley, Jr.* (Boston: David R. Godine, 1984), 33; Anderson, "Drifter Who Stalked Success," 40.

14. Caplan, *Insanity Defense,* 33; Neil Henry and Chip Brown, "An Aimless Road to a Place in History," *WP,* April 5, 1981, 18; Anderson, "Drifter Who Stalked Success," 40.

15. Lang, "John Hinckley—A Misfit Who Craved Fame," *U.S. News & World Report,* April 13, 1981, 26.

16. Jo Ann Hinckley, in "Jo Ann Hinckley's Story," *Newsweek,* May 17, 1982, 54; McMillan, "Assassin's Portrait," 17.

17. Anderson, "Drifter Who Stalked Success," 40.

18. Lang, "John Hinckley," 26.

19. McMillan, "Assassin's Portrait," 17.

20. Jo Ann Hinckley, "Jo Ann Hinckley's Story," 54.

21. Joseph B. Treaster, "A Life That Started Out with Much Promise Took Reclusive and Hostile Turn," *NYT,* April 1, 1981, 19; Michael Posner, "America's High Noon Mentality," *Maclean's,* April 13, 1981, 24.

22. Treaster, "Life," 19.

23. Latham, "Dark Side," 18.

24. McMillan, "Assassin's Portrait," 17.

25. Latham, "Dark Side," 19.

26. Ibid.

27. Ibid., 20.

28. Henry and Brown, "Aimless Road," 18.

29. Treaster, "Life," 19.

30. Latham, "Dark Side," 19.

31. Treaster, "Life," 19.

32. Caplan, "Insanity Defense," 55.

33. Latham, "Dark Side," 20; Athelia Knight and Neil Henry, "Love Letter Offers Clue to Motive in Shooting," *WP,* April 1, 1981, 1.

34. Clines, "Agents Tracing Hinckley's Path," 1.

35. Latham, "Dark Side," 20.

36. Ibid., 20, 51.

37. Ibid., 51.

38. Ibid.; Clines, "Agents Tracing Hinckley's Path," 30.

39. Clines, "Agents Tracing Hinckley's Path," 30.

40. Philip Taubman, "Suspect Was Arrested Last Year in Nashville on Weapons Charge," *NYT,* March 31, 1981, 2.
41. Richard D. Lyons, "F.B.I. Notice on Hinckley Arrest at Issue," *NYT,* April 3, 1981, 17.
42. UPI, "Webster Defends Actions," *NYT,* April 9, 1981, 17.
43. Taubman, "Suspect Was Arrested," 2.
44. Caplan, "Insanity Defense," 56.
45. Ibid.
46. Ibid., 50, 56.
47. Latham, "Dark Side," 20, 52; McMillan, "Assassin's Portrait," 18.
48. Matthew L. Wald, "Yale Police Searched for Suspect Weeks before Reagan Was Shot," *NYT,* April 5, 1981, 32.
49. Jack Hinckley, Jo Ann Hinckley, and Elizabeth Sherrill, "The Secret Life of John Hinckley, Jr.," *Redbook,* May 1985, 158.
50. Mike Sager and Eugene Robinson, "A Drifter with a Purpose," *WP,* April 1, 1981, 1.
51. Latham, "Dark Side," 54. An extraordinary "look-alike" was reported about a week after the attack. See Joseph B. Treaster, "Man, 22, Is Arrested in New Haven for Threatening the President's Life," *NYT,* April 8, 1981, 1. Edward Richardson threatened the lives of both President Reagan and Jodie Foster on April 6, 1981, while in New Haven. He was arrested in New York, in possession of a .32-caliber revolver.
52. Latham, "Dark Side," 54.
53. Matthew L. Wald, "Teen-Age Actress Says Notes Sent by Suspect Did Not Hint of Violence," *NYT,* April 2, 1981, 24.
54. "Text of Letter in Suspect's Room," *NYT,* April 2, 1981, 25.
55. Latham, "Dark Side," 54.
56. Lyons, "Witnesses to Shooting," 1.
57. Ibid., 4.
58. James M. Perry, "Reagan Shot in Chest on Washington Street; Undergoes Surgery," *WSJ,* March 31, 1981, 1.
59. Latham, "Dark Side," 54.
60. Raines, "Reagan Wounded," 1; Donaldson, *Hold On, Mr. President!* 199–200; Philip Taubman, "Explosive Bullet Struck Reagan, F.B.I. Discovers," *NYT,* April 3, 1981, 1.
61. Lou Cannon, "The Day of the Jackal in Washington," *WP,* April 5, 1981, 1; Department of the Treasury, Office of the General Counsel, *Management Review on the Performance of the U.S. Department of the Treasury in Connection with the March 30, 1981 Assassination Attempt on President Ronald Reagan* (Washington, D.C.: Department of the Treasury, Aug. 1981), 56, 57.

62. Lyons, "Witnesses to Shooting," 4.
63. Ibid.
64. Taubman, "Suspect Was Arrested," 1–2; Raines, "Reagan Wounded," 1; Department of the Treasury, *Management Review,* 70.
65. Hinckley and Hinckley, "Secret Life," 119.

CHAPTER 2: Before the Attack

1. Frederick M. Kaiser, "Presidential Assassinations and Assaults: Characteristics and Impact on Protective Procedures," *Presidential Studies Quarterly* 11, no. 4 (Fall 1981): 545–58.
    Only the attack on Franklin D. Roosevelt took place at a relatively earlier date. Giuseppi Zangara fired at Roosevelt in Miami, Florida, three weeks prior to his inauguration on Feb. 15, 1933.
2. "TRB from Washington," *New Republic,* Nov. 15, 1980, 3; Hedrick Smith, "A Turning Point Seen," *NYT,* Nov. 19, 1980, 1.
3. Peter Goldman, "The Republican Landslide," *Newsweek,* Nov. 17, 1980, 27, 30; David S. Broder, "A Sharp Right Turn," *WP,* Nov. 5, 1980, 1.
4. Carl M. Brauer, *Presidential Transitions, Eisenhower through Reagan* (New York: Oxford Univ. Press, 1986), 256.
5. Ibid., xvi.
6. Frederick C. Mosher et al., *Presidential Transitions and Foreign Affairs* (Baton Rouge: Louisiana State Univ. Press, 1987), 35.
7. Ibid.
8. James P. Pfiffner, *The Presidency in Transition* (New York: Center for the Study of the Presidency, 1989), 91.
9. Brauer, *Presidential Transitions,* 221.
10. Adam Clymer, "Manager of Only Show in Town," *NYT,* Nov. 7, 1980, 14; Thomas C. Hayes, "The Reagan Team's Chief Recruiter," *NYT,* Nov. 7, 1980, D-1; James P. Pfiffner, "The Carter-Reagan Transition: Hitting the Ground Running," *Presidential Studies Quarterly* 13, no. 4 (1983): 632; Brauer, *Presidential Transitions,* 225; Dick Kirschten, "The Reagan Team Comes to Washington, Ready to Get Off to a Running Start," *National Journal* 12 (Nov. 15, 1980): 1925.
11. "Key Aides on Reagan's Transition Panel," *NYT,* Nov. 7, 1981, 14; Clymer, "Manager of Only Show in Town," 14; George C. Church, "The Organization Man," *Time,* Dec. 15, 1980, 18.

12. Brauer, *Presidential Transitions,* 227.
13. Pfiffner, "Carter-Reagan Transition," 634.
14. John Osborne, "White House Watch: Without Joy," *New Republic,* Jan. 24, 1981, 8.
15. Allan J. Mayer, "Changing of the Guard," *Newsweek,* Nov. 24, 1980, 41.
16. Steven R. Weisman, "Reagan Names His Chief of Staff and His Counselor," *NYT,* Nov. 15, 1980, 1.
17. Edwin Meese III, interview with author, Stanford, Calif., June 2, 1989.
18. Brauer, *Presidential Transitions,* 262; Norman A. Graebner, "From Carter to Reagan: An Uneasy Transition," *Australian Journal of Politics and History* 27, no. 3 (1981): 319.
19. Osborne, "White House Watch," 8.
20. "TRB from Washington," *New Republic,* Jan. 31, 1981, 2; Graebner, "From Carter to Reagan," 319.
21. Pfiffner, "Carter-Reagan Transition," 623, 636.
22. Tom Morganthau, "Hail to the New Chief," *Newsweek,* Feb. 2, 1981, 47–48.
23. Pfiffner, "Carter-Reagan Transition," 636.
24. Howell Raines, "Reagan Chops Wood as Top Aides Prepare to Sell His Budget Cuts," *NYT,* Feb. 21, 1981, 9; Steven V. Roberts, "Weinberger Approved, 97–2," *NYT,* Jan. 22, 1981, B-8; Juan de Onis, "U.S. Halts Nicaragua Aid over Help for Guerillas," *NYT,* Feb. 19, 1981, 1; Ed Magnuson, "More Signals to the World," *Time,* Feb. 16, 1981, 17; Hedrick Smith, "White House Hit a Last-Minute Snag on Canada Trip," *NYT,* March 11, 1981, 11; George C. Wilson, "Reagan Asks 16% Boost in Spending for Defense," *WP,* March 5, 1981, 1; Peter Behr and Jane Seaberry, "Haig Taking Charge of Talks with Japan on Auto Import Curb," *WP,* March 25, 1981, 1; Morganthau, "Hail to the New Chief," 48.
25. Richard Halloran, "Allies Said to Agree with U.S. on Poland," *NYT,* March 28, 1981, 5.
26. "Key Accords Announced in Poland," *LAT,* Jan. 31, 1981, 1; Michael Dobbs, "Polish Leadership Replaces Premier with Top General," *WP,* Feb. 10, 1981, 1. The discontent in Poland was long in the making. Although it began well before 1970, on Dec. 15 of that year it took the form of "Bloody Tuesday," when workers at the Lenin Shipyards in Gdansk declared a strike and then burned down the party headquarters in a free-form battle throughout the town. As

a result of those events, Wladyslaw Gomulka had been forced to resign and was replaced as Polish party chief by Edward Gierek.

Throughout the seventies, labor protests in Poland continued. With an increase in meat prices of nearly 100 percent in July 1980, a strike took place in Lublin, near the Soviet border, followed by a walkout of 50,000 workers in Gdansk on Aug. 15. The sustained unrest spawned reports that a crackdown on dissidents and Soviet troop movements into Poland were planned. (Almost a decade later, in 1990, evidence was published in Poland supporting the belief that military intervention had been prepared for late 1980.) See Lawrence Weschler, *Solidarity* (New York: Simon and Schuster, 1981), 160, 169–72; Zbigniew Brzezinski, "White House Diary, 1980," *Orbis* 32, no. 1 (Winter 1988), 39; and Craig R. Whitney, "Historians Dig Up Dark Hints of 1980 Plan to Invade Poland," *NYT,* Jan. 13, 1990, 5.

27. "East Bloc Exercises Begin in Poland," *LAT,* March 19, 1981, 22; "Union Says Polish Police Beat Farmers," *LAT,* March 20, 1981, 12.

28. "Reagan Fears Soviet Move," *LAT,* March 26, 1981, 1; "U.S. Warns Russians and Poles on Force against the Unions," *LAT,* March 27, 1981, 1; Halloran, "Allies"; Oswald Johnston, "U.S. Concern Grows over Possible Invasion of Poland," *LAT,* March 30, 1981, 6; John Darnton, "Sense of Despair in Poland," *NYT,* March 24, 1981, 1; "Soviet Bloc Stages Landing in Poland," *NYT,* March 24, 1981, 3; "Poles Stage Warning Strike," *LAT,* March 27, 1981, 1; John Darnton, "Millions in Poland Go on 4-Hour Strike to Protest Violence," *NYT,* March 28, 1981, 1. Weinberger stated that Soviet military intervention would prompt "concerted efforts" by the Western powers in retaliation. On March 29 (the day before the assassination attempt), the Soviet press accused Solidarity of trying to intimidate the Polish security forces and wrest control from the government. Haig was troubled by indications that fresh Soviet, East German, and Czech troops had been introduced along the Polish border. See Halloran, "Allies"; Anthony Austin, "Soviet Accuses Union of Seeking Control of Poland," *NYT,* March 30, 1981, 9; Bernard Gwertzman, "Haig Is Troubled by Troop Moves on Polish Border," *NYT,* March 30, 1981, 1.

29. John Darnton, "Polish Union Approves and Calls Off a Threatened Strike," *NYT,* April 1, 1981, 1; Edward Walsh and George C. Wilson, "U.S. Concern about Poland Growing," *WP,* April 3, 1981, 1.

30. "Surviving in the Bull's-Eye," *Time,* May 27, 1974, 19.

31. Ronald Brownstein and Nina Easton, *Reagan's Ruling Class: Por-*

traits of the President's Top 100 Officials (Washington, D.C.: Presidential Accountability Group, 1982), 539; Allan J. Mayer, "Master of the Power Game," *Newsweek*, Dec. 29, 1980, 13.

32. Mayer, "Master of the Power Game," 13.

33. "The Presidential Cleanup Crew," *Time*, May 14, 1973, 30; Mayer, "Master of the Power Game," 13.

34. Brownstein and Easton, *Reagan's Ruling Class*, 540–42. In the early days of the Nixon administration, Haig was frequently assigned to tasks which Kissinger found distasteful. One such job was the ordering of wiretaps (called "technical surveillance") on government officials and journalists. He was in charge of reading through the transcripts produced by the taped conversations and giving those containing important information to Kissinger. During the one-and-a-half-year project called "June," thirteen government officials and four reporters had their phones tapped.

35. Ibid., 542–43; "The Army: Shooting Stars," *Newsweek*, Sept. 18, 1972, 45.

36. Mayer, "Master of the Power Game," 14; Hugh Sidey, "A Loyalist's Departure," *Time*, Sept. 30, 1974, 31; Tom Oliphant, "Alexander Haig: Nixon's New Go-Fer," *Ramparts*, Jan. 1974, 17.

37. Christopher Buckley, "Saving the West with General Haig," *Esquire*, Sept. 26, 1978, 25.

38. "Haig: 'Events That Led to the Fire Storm,' " *U.S. News & World Report*, Nov. 5, 1973, 66; Mayer, "Master of the Power Game," 14. Leon Jaworski, *The Right and the Power: The Prosecution of Watergate* (New York: Reader's Digest Press, 1976), 7. When Special Prosecutor Archibald Cox was ordered to relinquish the tapes and refused, Haig told Attorney General Elliot Richardson to fire him. Rather than do so, Richardson resigned, as did Deputy Attorney General William Ruckelshaus when confronted with Haig's demand.

With Cox and Richardson out of the way, Nixon had to find replacements quickly—before Congress did so for him. He chose William Saxbe for attorney general, and persuaded Leon Jaworski to become the Watergate special prosecutor.

39. Mayer, "Master of the Power Game," 15.

40. Ibid., 14; "Surviving in the Bull's-Eye," 19; Buckley, "Saving the West," 25.

41. Mayer, "Master of the Power Game," 15.

42. Morton Kondracke, "Alexander the Great," *New Republic*, Oct. 7, 1978, 8; Tom Mathews, "Why Al Haig Resigned," *Newsweek*, Jan. 15, 1979, 27.

43. Don Oberdorfer, "Deterrent Force Cited Repeatedly," *WP,* Jan. 10, 1981, 1.

44. Hedrick Smith, "Haig Moves Fast in Effort to Win Key Policy Role," *NYT,* Jan. 27, 1981, 1; Tad Szulc, "Dateline Washington: The Vicar Vanquished," *Foreign Policy,* no. 43 (Summer 1981): 175.

45. Richard Halloran, "Battle Being Waged on Military Policy," *NYT,* Jan. 29, 1981, 17.

46. Bernard Gwertzman, "Haig Says Teheran Will Not Get Arms," *NYT,* Jan. 29, 1981, 1; Juan de Onis, "Test For Haig Seen in Dispute over Aid," *NYT,* Feb. 1, 1981, 1.

47. Juan de Onis, "Primary Foreign Aid Servives in Budget," *NYT,* Feb. 22, 1981, 9; Richard Halloran, "Weinberger Asserts U.S. Will Help Saudis to Buttress Forces," *NYT,* Feb. 4, 1981, 1.

48. Michael Getler, "The Tough-Talking Haig Takes on the Role of Pragmatist at State," *WP,* March 14, 1981, 14.

49. Hedrick Smith, "Haig Is Given Broad Policy Power, But Less Than He Initially Sought," *NYT,* Feb. 27, 1981, 1.

50. Walter Pincus, "Weinberger's Concerns about Land-Based MX's Deepen Policy Rift," *WP,* March 14, 1981, 5; Getler, "Tough-Talking Haig."

51. Robert C. Toth and Oswald Johnston, "Haig: 'The Vicar' Inspires, Misfires," *LAT,* April 5, 1981, 1; Martin Schram, "Bush to Head Crisis Management," *WP,* March 22, 1981, 1.

52. Alexander M. Haig, Jr., *Caveat: Realism, Reagan, and Foreign Policy* (New York: Macmillan, 1984), 144.

53. Edwin Warner, "Trouble on the Team," *Time,* April 6, 1981, 8.

54. Haig, *Caveat,* 144.

55. Peter Goldman, "Haig vs. the White House," *Newsweek,* April 6, 1981, 26, 28; Don Oberdorfer and Lee Lescaze, "Haig Loses Out in Dispute over Key Policy Role," *WP,* March 25, 1981, 1; Hedrick Smith, "Foreign Policy: Costly Feud," *NYT,* March 26, 1981, 1.

56. Haig, *Caveat,* 146–47; Oswald Johnston, "Reagan Says Haig Is Top Foreign Aide," *LAT,* March 26, 1981, 1.

57. Goldman, "Haig," 26–31; Bernard Gwertzman, "Aide Terms Haig 'Wounded Lion' over Bush's Role," *NYT,* March 28, 1981, 1.

CHAPTER 3: The Shooting
and Its Aftermath

1. Jerry Parr, phone interview with author, July 23, 1990.

2. Department of the Treasury, Office of the General Counsel, *Management Review on the Performance of the U.S. Department of the Trea-*

sury *in Connection with the March 30, 1981 Assassination Attempt on President Ronald Reagan* (Washington, D.C.: Department of the Treasury, Aug. 1981), 43.

3. Ibid., 44, 45.
4. Ibid., 46, 47.
5. Ibid.
6. Michael K. Deaver and Mickey Hershkowitz, *Behind the Scenes* (New York: William J. Morrow, 1987), 24.
7. Department of the Treasury, *Management Review*, 55.
8. Parr interview.
9. Ibid.
10. Department of the Treasury, *Management Review*, 48.
11. Ibid., 49.
12. Parr interview.
13. FBI ballistics tests subsequently indicated that the bullet skidded for an inch along the car's armored right panel before it hit Reagan. See Laurence I. Barrett, *Gambling with History* (Garden City, N.Y.: Doubleday, 1983), 107.
14. Anastasia Toufexis, "Emergency in Room 5A," *Time*, April 13, 1981, 44; Victor Cohn, "Bullet Lodged an Inch from Reagan's Heart," *WP*, April 16, 1981, 1.
15. Department of the Treasury, *Management Review*, 56.
16. T. R. Reid, "Agent Tells of the Blood-and-Guts Getaway," *WP*, April 3, 1981, 1.
17. Deaver, *Behind the Scenes*, 18.
18. Quoted in "Transcript of an Interview with the President on His Wounding and Recovery," *WP*, April 23, 1981, B12.
19. Parr interview. Three days later, on April 2, Parr's actions were publicly acclaimed by a Senate subcommittee. After his testimony, Senator Paul Laxalt shook his hand and said, "If it weren't for you, I think our guy might not have been around." "Well," Parr replied, "God was on our side." See Reid, "Agent Tells." See also Ronald Reagan, *An American Life* (New York: Simon and Schuster, 1990), 260; and Lou Cannon, "The Day of the Jackal in Washington," *WP*, April 5, 1981.
20. "Agent Said He Knew Reagan Had a Lung Wound," *NYT*, April 3, 1981, 17.
21. Department of the Treasury, *Management Review*, 59.
22. Ibid.
23. Dr. Joseph M. Giordano, interview with author, Washington, D.C., Dec. 2, 1988. Dr. Daniel Ruge, the president's physician, said in an interview on Dec. 11, 1988, "He could have ended up at Bethesda

and if so, he would have died. The White House is close to George Washington University. It was the hospital that the Secret Service was accustomed to going to for other things. Jerry Parr talked with me that morning about where the president should be taken in an emergency. He asked me, "Are we going to be using GW?" and I said, "Yes, we're going to use GW."

Question: "He brought it up by coincidence?"

Dr. Ruge: "Yes. But we had discussed it even before the inauguration."

Question: "Wouldn't the Naval Medical Center in Bethesda have been the usual hospital for the president?"

Dr. Ruge: "Yes, but not for emergencies. Emergencies are taken to the nearest facility. No matter where the president goes, there are plans for emergencies. If the president went to Chicago, there would be a hospital selected near O'Hare; there might be another one en route, and there would be another one where the main event occurs. The White House is close to George Washington University Hospital. If something happens at the national capital, we would still head to GW."

"Let's assume that he had an acute illness in the White House at night. I lived in Georgetown two miles from the White House. The understanding with the Secret Service was that they would take the president to GW, then call me—I had three White House phones in my home—and I would be picked up and meet him there."

24. Reid, "Agent Tells."
25. Susan Okie, "Reagan's Risk May Have Been Much Greater Than Believed," *WP*, April 2, 1981, 1.
26. Cannon, "Jackal."
27. Okie, "Reagan's Risk."
28. David Treadwell, "Hospital Intern Says President Was in 'Acute Distress,' " *LAT*, April 2, 1981, 18.
29. Susan J. Kelley, "The President in the Emergency Department: A Nursing Perspective," *Journal of Emergency Nursing* 11, no. 1 (Jan./Feb. 1985): 15A.
30. Treadwell, "Acute Distress."
31. Dr. Wesley Price, "An Eyewitness Account by the First Doctor to Get to the President," *Washingtonian*, Aug. 1981, 116.
32. Ronald Reagan, "Why I'm for the Brady Bill," *NYT*, March 29, 1991, 15.
33. Dr. Daniel Ruge, personal communication, April 15, 1991.

34. Joseph Giordano et al., "Delay Could Have Been Fatal," *LAT,* April 4, 1981, 1; Lawrence K. Altman, "Doctor Says President's Life Was in Danger at First," *NYT,* April 4, 1981, 18.

35. Dr. Sol Edelstein, comments at the conference on the topic "Medical Care of the VIP: The Special Problems of Special Patients" (Washington, D.C., Dec. 7, 1990).

36. Giordano, "Delay."

37. Dr. Daniel Ruge, interview with author, Denver, Colo., Dec. 11, 1988.

38. Giordano, "Delay."

39. Reagan, *American Life,* 261.

40. Nancy Reagan, *My Turn* (New York: Random House, 1989), 6.

41. Robert Rheinhold, "A Bullet Is Removed from Reagan's Lung in Emergency Surgery," *NYT,* March 31, 1981, 1; John Pekkanen, "The Saving of the President," *Washingtonian,* Aug. 1981, 113. Pekkanen, a Washington journalist and medical writer, wrote a superb account of the handling of the president, James Brady, and Tim McCarthy at George Washington University Hospital after the attack. It is replete with important details based on exhaustive interviews, probably in excess of fifty, by his account in an interview with the author, in Washington, D.C., Dec. 2, 1988. In the interview, his comments on the events and on the people involved, as well as his views on the media coverage, were invaluable in providing a useful perspective and important insights.

42. Giordano, interview; Giordano, "Delay."

43. Pekkanen, "Saving of the President," 116; Barrett, *Gambling with History,* 111.

44. Dr. Dennis O'Leary, interview with author, Chicago, Ill., Nov. 30, 1988.

45. Raines, "Reagan Wounded"; Cannon, "Jackal"; Giordano, "Delay"; Reinhold, "Bullet Is Removed"; Giordano, "Delay."

46. Pekkanen, "Saving of the President," 118; Dr. Daniel Ruge, personal communication, Sept. 26, 1990; Giordano, "Delay."

47. Throughout surgery, he was at a relatively light level of anesthesia. See Sandy Rovner, "Healthtalk: Anesthetics," *WP,* May 1, 1981, D5.

48. Toufexis, "Emergency in Room 5A," 44.

49. Cannon, "Jackal."

50. Dr. Benjamin Aaron, interview with author, Washington, D.C., Dec. 2, 1988.

51. George Skelton and Rudy Abramson, "Reagan Has 'a Little Bit of a Setback,' " *LAT,* April 4, 1981, 1 (hereafter referred to as "Set-

back"); John Pekkanen, interview with author, Washington, D.C., Dec. 2, 1988.

52. Cohn, "Bullet Lodged," A5; Skelton and Abramson, "Setback."

53. Lawrence K. Altman, "Doctor Says President Lost More Blood Than Disclosed," *NYT,* April 3, 1981, 17.

54. The crowd in the recovery room included doctors, interns and residents, nurses, members of the hospital administration, Secret Service men, Meese, Baker, and family members at times. But even in the wake of the shooting of the president and the security concerns it provoked, there were others: in particular, a short man who walked in and went right over to the president's bed. One of the doctors noticed him and said, "Who the hell is that guy?" Nobody knew, until he was finally identified as a part-time staff doctor who claimed to have a patient in the hospital (but did not) and was apparently simply curious to see the injured president. He refused to leave until hospital security officers removed him from the building. See Pekkanen, "Saving of the President," 121–22.

55. Dr. David Rockoff, personal communication with author, May 31, 1988.

56. Pekkanen, "Saving of the President," 122.

57. Cannon, "Jackal."

58. Howell Raines, "Reagan Making Good Recovery, Signs a Bill; White House Working, Bush Assures Senate," *NYT,* April 1, 1981, 1; Pekkanen, "Saving of the President," 122; Barrett, *Gambling with History,* 121.

59. Price, "Eyewitness Account," 117. An effort had been made to wean him from the respirator earlier, but his blood gases dropped, indicating he was not getting enough oxygen into his lungs. See Lawrence K. Altman, "Physicians Move Reagan out of Intensive Care Unit," *NYT,* April 2, 1981, 22.

60. Marlene Cimons, "Despite Fortitude, Reagan Had Fears," *LAT,* April 3, 1981, 1.

61. Ibid.

62. James M. Perry, "President, in High Spirits, Signs Legislation; Bush's Role as a Substitute Is Being Expanded," *WSJ,* April 1, 1981, 2.

63. Dennis L. Breo, "MDs, Hospital Ready for Reagan," *American Medical News,* April 10, 1981, 2, 17.

64. Deaver, *Behind the Scenes,* 23.

65. Perry, "President"; Barrett, *Gambling with History,* 121.

66. Pekkanen, "Saving of the President," 124.
67. Dr. William Knaus, interview with author, Washington, D.C., Dec. 2, 1988.
68. Rudy Abramson, "Reagan 'Doing Well,' Signs Bill in Hospital," *LAT,* April 1, 1981, 1.
69. Altman, "Physicians Move Reagan."
70. Knaus, interview.
71. Pekkanen, "Saving of the President," 125. It was now thought that his scheduled trip to Mexico on April 20 would have to be postponed. See Lou Cannon, "President's Condition Continues to Improve; Brady Shows Gains," *WP,* April 2, 1981, 1; Lee Lescaze, "President Exercising Regularly," *WP,* April 3, 1981, 1.
72. George Skelton and Don Irwin, "Hospital Official Denies Report Reagan Was Ever near Death," *LAT,* April 3, 1981, 6; Howell Raines, "Reagan Eager to Return to Work on Fiscal Plans," *NYT,* April 3, 1981, 16; Pekkanen, "Saving of the President," 125.
73. Aaron interview.
74. Lawrence K. Altman, "Reagan's Condition Called 'Good'; He Sees Aides as Fever Goes Down," *NYT,* April 5, 1981, 1.
75. Dr. David Rockoff, interview with author, Washington, D.C., Dec. 2, 1988.
76. The White House requested that heavy sedation be avoided because of the possibility of a Soviet invasion of Poland. As it turned out, systemic sedation was not required. See Barrett, *Gambling with History,* 121–22.
77. Altman, "President's Fever"; Skelton and Abramson, "Setback"; Susan Okie and Lee Lescaze, " 'A Little Bit of a Setback' for Reagan," *WP,* April 4, 1981, 1; Dr. David O. Davis, interview with author, Washington, D.C., Dec. 1, 1988.
78. Bill Peterson, "President Is Lively, Alert; Fever Abates," *WP,* April 5, 1981, 1; Pekkanen, "Saving of the President," 126; George Skelton, "Reagan Watches Poland, Responds Well to Therapy," *LAT,* April 5, 1981, 1.
79. Lawrence K. Altman, "Physician Says Reports on Reagan Were Optimistic But Hid Nothing," *NYT,* April 6, 1981, 1; Steven R. Weisman, "Reagan, Now Taking 2 Antibiotics, Continues to Register Slight Fever," *NYT,* April 7, 1981, 1.
80. Lee Lescaze, "Reagan Release from Hospital Delayed," *WP,* April 7, 1981, 1; "Doctors Say Reagan Shows No Infection," *NYT,* April 8, 1981, 16.

81. Steven R. Weisman, "Reagan's Workload up to 2 hours a Day," *NYT*, April 9, 1981, 1; Lou Cannon, "Reagan Gains, Won't Rush Return to Job," *WP*, April 8, 1981, 1.

82. Howell Raines, "Reagan Is Taken Off a Drug and Found in 'Good Shape,' " *NYT*, April 10, 1981, 15.

83. Steven R. Weisman, "Reagan's Return to White House Expected Today," *NYT*, April 11, 1981, 1.

84. Timothy D. Schellhardt, "Reagan Plans Restful First Week at Home Despite His Eagerness to Push Legislation," *WSJ*, April 13, 1981, 3.

85. Lee Lescaze, "Feeling 'Great,' " *WP*, April 12, 1981, 1.

86. Barrett, *Gambling with History*, 123. ("This robust, vital man had been horribly drained.")

87. Howell Raines, "Reagan Sees Launching on TV at White House," *NYT*, April 13, 1981, 11; Schellhardt, "Reagan Plans."

88. Bob Woodward, *Veil: The Secret Wars of the CIA* (New York: Simon and Schuster, 1987), 122.

89. The White House misrepresented Reagan's condition to the public, according to Haig. See "Haig Backs Up Woodward's Story of Reagan Recovery," *San Jose Mercury News*, Oct. 4, 1987, 14A.

90. Howell Raines, "Bush Hints Veto of One-Year Cut in Federal Taxes," *NYT*, April 16, 1981, 1.

91. Howell Raines, "Reagan Strolls in Garden; Budget Disputed," *NYT*, April 17, 1981, 14; "White House Seeks Report on Allegation of Anti-Semitism," *WP*, April 18, 1981, 3.

92. Steven R. Weisman, "President, Comfortable at Home, Delays His Return to Oval Office," *NYT*, April 19, 1981, 1.

93. Steven R. Weisman, "Reagan Tells of Initial Pain and Panic after Being Shot," *NYT*, April 23, 1981, 1.

94. Aaron interview.

95. Steven R. Weisman, "Reagan Ends Curbs on Export of Grain to Soviet Union," *NYT*, April 25, 1981, 1.

96. Dr. Daniel Ruge, personal communication, Sept. 26, 1990; "Daughter of President Is Married in California," *NYT*, April 25, 1981, 37.

97. "Reagan Now Oldest President," *NYT*, May 17, 1981, 28.

98. Howell Raines, "Reagan Is Welcomed on Notre Dame Trip, First since Shooting," *NYT*, May 18, 1981, 1.

99. Steven R. Weisman, "Reagan Steps Up His Work Schedule," *NYT*, June 4, 1981, B15.

100. " 'I Have Recovered,' President Declares," *NYT*, June 17, 1981, 27.

101. Ruge interview, Dec. 12, 1988.
102. Ibid.

CHAPTER 4: The President's Men

1. Prosperi's call cut about a minute from the time it would have taken for Baker and Meese to get word through normal Secret Service channels. See Laurence I. Barrett, *Gambling with History* (Garden City, N.Y.: Doubleday, 1983), 112.
2. Ed Magnuson, "Six Shots at a Nation's Heart," *Time*, April 13, 1981, 30. " 'He went totally white,' said an aide." See Tom Mathews, "Reagan's Close Call," *Newsweek*, April 13, 1981, 34. " 'Meese was like a rock. Baker was shaken,' said a participant." Alexander M. Haig, Jr., *Caveat* (New York: Macmillan, 1984), 150; Donald T. Regan, *For the Record: From Wall Street to Washington* (New York: Harcourt Brace Jovanovich, 1988), 163.
3. Lou Cannon, "The Day of the Jackal in Washington," *WP*, April 5, 1981, 1.
4. Michael K. Deaver and Mickey Hershkowitz, *Behind the Scenes* (New York: William J. Morrow, 1987), 19.
5. Mathews, "Reagan's Close Call," 34.
6. One of Bush's previous tasks on this trip had been to dedicate as a national monument the Hotel Texas, where President John F. Kennedy had spent his final night. See Cannon, "Jackal." See also Margot Hornblower, "Bush, on Swing through Texas, Returns to Quietly Take Command," *WP*, March 31, 1981, 11.
7. Because the Secret Service is part of the Treasury, Regan, as secretary of the treasury, had been alerted less than two minutes after the shooting. See Cannon, "Jackal."
8. Deaver, *Behind the Scenes*, 19; Barrett, *Gambling with History*, 113.
9. Mathews, "Reagan's Close Call," 34; Cannon, "Jackal," 2.
10. Jack Nelson and George Skelton, "Reagan Shot; Condition 'Good,' " *LAT*, March 31, 1981, 1.
11. Haig, *Caveat*, 150–51; Mathews, "Reagan's Close Call," 34.
12. Haig's account has it that he arrived after Baker and Meese left. See Haig, *Caveat*, 151. Other accounts suggest that it was immediately before their departure. See Cannon, "Jackal," Magnuson, "Six Shots," 34.
13. Haig, *Caveat*, 151–52.
14. Deaver, *Behind the Scenes*, 29; Barrett, *Gambling with History*, 113; Cannon, "Jackal."

15. Edwin Meese, interview with author, Stanford, Calif., June 2, 1989.
16. Martin Anderson, interview with author, Stanford, Calif., June 12, 1989.
17. David Gergen, interview with author, Washington, D.C., June 16, 1989.
18. Caspar W. Weinberger, *Fighting for Peace: Seven Critical Years in the Pentagon* (New York: Warner Books, 1990), 82–83.
19. Steven R. Weisman, "White House Aides Assert Weinberger Was Upset When Haig Took Charge," *NYT,* April 1, 1981, 20; Regan, *For the Record,* 164; Haig, *Caveat,* 153; Cannon, "Jackal," 1.
20. Bromley K. Smith, *Organizational History of the National Security Council during the Kennedy and Johnson Administrations* (Monograph prepared for the National Security Council) (n.p., Sept. 1988); Haig, *Caveat,* 152–53.
21. Henry A. Kissinger, *White House Years* (Boston: Little, Brown, 1979), 315.
22. Smith, *Organizational History,* 37.
23. Bradley H. Patterson, *The Ring of Power* (New York: Basic Books, 1988), 48, 120; Kissinger, *White House Years,* 315; Richard V. Allen, letters to author, April 7 and June 27, 1989; Bradley H. Patterson, letter to author, May 31, 1989.
24. Patterson, *Ring of Power,* 119; Smith, *Organizational History,* 37.
25. Larry Speakes with Robert Pack, *Speaking Out: The Reagan Presidency from Inside the White House* (New York: Charles Scribner's Sons, 1988), x.
26. Patterson, *Ring of Power,* 119.
27. Steven Strasser, " 'I am in Control Here,' " *Newsweek,* April 13, 1981, 40.
28. Haig, *Caveat,* 153.
29. Laurence I. Barrett, *Gambling with History* (Garden City, N.Y.: Doubleday, 1983), 116; Speakes, *Speaking Out,* 7.
30. Kissinger, *White House Years,* 315, 601.
31. Haig, *Caveat,* 153; Cannon, "Jackal," 1.
32. Regan, *For the Record,* 165, 167; Cannon, "Jackal," 1; Haig, *Caveat,* 153; Lawrence K. Altman, "Doctor Says He Erred on Presidential Power after '81 Shooting," *NYT,* Feb. 20, 1989, 8.
33. Regan, *For the Record,* 164; Haig, *Caveat,* 153; Walter S. Mossberg, "Confusion over Who Was in Charge Arose following Reagan Shooting," *WSJ,* April 4, 1981, 31.
34. Barrett, *Gambling with History,* 113–14.
35. Mathews, "Reagan's Close Call," 36.
36. Hornblower, "Bush."

37. Hedrick Smith, "Bush Says He Sought to Avoid Acting like Surrogate President," *NYT,* April 12, 1981, 1.
38. Mathews, "Reagan's Close Call," 36.
39. Steven R. Weisman, "Bush Flies back from Texas Set to Take Charge in Crisis," *NYT,* March 31, 1981, 1.
40. Haig, *Caveat,* 154.
41. Ibid., 155.
42. Cannon, "Jackal."
43. Deaver, *Behind the Scenes,* 22.
44. Barrett, *Gambling with History,* 114–15.
45. "Report by Aide in White House after Shootings," *NYT,* March 31, 1981, 5; Cannon, "Jackal"; Haig, *Caveat,* 155, 157–58. Normally, the head of the Joint Chiefs of Staff was included, but on this occasion, Haig thought, his presence would have been ominous.
46. Barrett, *Gambling with History,* 115–16.
47. Haig, *Caveat,* 157.
48. Speakes, *Speaking Out,* 7; Barrett, *Gambling with History,* 117; Haig, *Caveat,* 158–59.
49. Barrett, *Gambling with History,* 117; Terrell Bell, *The Thirteenth Man* (New York: Free Press, 1988), 66; Magnuson, "Six Shots," 30.
50. Haig had undergone triple-bypass surgery recently but had taken up smoking again.
51. "Attempted Assassination of President Reagan, March 30, 1981," in *Historic Documents of 1981* (Washington, D.C.: Congressional Quarterly, 1982), 354.
52. Ibid.
53. Cannon, "Jackal," 3.
54. Regan, *For the Record,* 167.
55. Gergen interview.
56. Regan, *For the Record,* 167.
57. Cannon, "Jackal," 3.
58. Barrett, *Gambling with History,* 119.
59. Regan, *For the Record,* 167.
60. Barrett, *Gambling with History,* 119; Cannon, "Jackal," 3.
61. Haig, *Caveat,* 161.
62. Ibid.; Meese interview.
63. Haig, *Caveat,* 161.
64. Hornblower, "Bush"; Speakes, *Speaking Out,* 9; Regan, *For the Record,* 168.
65. Cannon, "Jackal," 3; Haig, *Caveat,* 162.
66. Speakes, *Speaking Out,* 10, 11.
67. Hornblower, "Bush."

68. Nelson and Skelton, "Reagan Shot."
69. Weisman, "Bush Flies Back"; Fred Barbash, "At White House, a Flurry over Who's in Charge," *WP*, March 31, 1981, 14.
70. Stewart W. Taylor, Jr., "Disabling of Reagan Provokes Debate over Nuclear Authority in Such Cases," *NYT*, April 4, 1981, 9.
71. Mathews, "Reagan's Close Call," 37.
72. Edward Walsh, "Bush Assumes Ceremonial Duties, But Not Powers, of the Presidency," *WP*, April 1, 1981, 12; James M. Perry, "President, in High Spirits, Signs Legislation; Bush's Role as a Substitute Is Being Explored," *WSJ*, April 1, 1981, 2; "The President's Recovery Period: Informal Exchange between the Vice-President and Reporters, March 31, 1981," in Office of the Federal Register, *Weekly Compilation of Presidential Documents* (Washington, D.C.: National Archives and Records Service, April 6, 1981), 373–74.
73. John Darnton, "Polish Union Approves Agreement and Calls Off a Threatened Strike," *NYT*, April 1, 1981, 1. Solidarity voted to abandon its general strike plans. The agreement signed by Solidarity and the Polish government called for referral of the case of the police violence to a prosecutor.
74. Tad Szulc, "Dateline Washington: The Vicar Vanquished," *Foreign Policy*, no. 43 (Summer 1981): 178.
75. Bernard Gwertzman, "U.S. to Aid Poland with Surplus Food Worth $70 Million," *NYT*, April 3, 1981, 1.
76. Drew Middleton, "Russians in Poland: Signs of Alertness," *NYT*, April 5, 1981, 3; R. W. Apple, Jr., "Soviet Warns Warsaw Again about Unrest," *NYT*, April 4, 1981, 5; "U.S. Asserts Soviet Steps Up Readiness to Move on Poland," *NYT*, April 4, 1981, 1.
77. Benjamin Aaron, interview with author, Washington, D.C., Dec. 2, 1988; Barrett, *Gambling with History*, 122.
78. "U.S. Asserts."
79. Richard Halloran, "U.S. Is Weighing Aid to China If Russians Act against Poland," *NYT*, April 5, 1981, 1; Richard Halloran, "Weinberger, on Europe Trip, Is Wary over Brezhnev Role," *NYT*, April 6, 1981, 10; Drew Middleton, "Poland's Geography: Russia's Gateway to the West," *NYT*, April 6, 1981, 11; Edward T. Pound, "A Reagan Note to Brezhnev Tells of Concern on Poland," *NYT*, April 6, 1981, 10.
80. Steven R. Weisman, "Reagan, Now Taking 2 Antibiotics, Continues to Register Slight Fever," *NYT*, April 7, 1981, 1.
81. Lee Lescaze, "Reagan Release from Hospital Delayed," *WP*, April 7, 1981, 1.

82. Richard Halloran, "Weinberger Sees Poles Threatened with Soviet Invasion 'by Osmosis,' " *NYT,* April 7, 1981, 1.
83. R. W. Apple, Jr., "Bloc Means to Back Polish Communism, Czech Leader Says," *NYT,* April 7, 1981, 1.
84. "Doctors Say Reagan Shows No Infection," *NYT,* April 7, 1981, 16; Sara Fritz, "Taking Up the Slack," *U.S. News & World Report,* April 20, 1981, 23.
85. R. W. Apple, Jr., "Brezhnev Expresses View That Poland Can Solve Its Crisis," *NYT,* April 8, 1981, 1.
86. Steven R. Weisman, "Reagan's Workload up to 2 Hours a Day," *NYT,* April 9, 1981, 1.
87. Richard Halloran, "NATO Defense Aides Issue Joint Warning to Soviet on Poland," *NYT,* April 9, 1981, 1.
88. Richard Halloran, "Weinberger Says Invasion Is Still a 'Real Possibility,' " *NYT,* April 10, 1981, 8; Bernard Gwertzman, "U.S. Is Still Concerned on Poland But Slightly Relieved, Haig Says," *NYT,* April 10, 1981, 9; Fritz, "Taking Up the Slack," 23.
89. John Darnton, "Polish Parliament Votes a Strike Ban to Last Two Months," *NYT,* April 12, 1981, 1.
90. Steven R. Weisman, "President, Comfortable at Home, Delays His Return to Oval Office," *NYT,* April 19, 1981, 1.
91. John Vinocur, "Poles Say West Exaggerated 'Modest' Maneuvers," *NYT,* April 23, 1981, 15.
92. "Reagan Given Ovation on Returning to Offices," *NYT,* April 25, 1981, 7.

CHAPTER 5: Confusion:
In the White House and the Hospital

1. White Burkett Miller Center of Public Affairs at the University of Virginia, *Report of the Miller Center Commission on Presidential Disability and the Twenty-fifth Amendment* (Lanham, Md.: Univ. Press of America, 1988), 7.
2. Larry Speakes with Robert Pack, *Speaking Out* (New York: Charles Scribner's Sons, 1988), 4.
3. Ibid., 4–5.
4. Judy Woodruff, *This Is Judy Woodruff at the White House* (Reading, Mass.: Addison Wesley, 1982), 23; Alexander M. Haig, Jr., *Caveat* (New York: Macmillan, 1984), 160.
5. Speakes, *Speaking Out,* 7.
6. Haig, *Caveat,* 158–59.

7. Donald T. Regan, *For the Record* (San Diego: Harcourt Brace Jovanovich, 1988), 166.

8. Caspar Weinberger, *Fighting for Peace* (New York: Warner Books, 1990), 86.

9. Haig, *Caveat,* 159–60.

10. "Attempted Assassination of President Reagan, March 30, 1981," *Historic Documents of 1981* (Washington, D.C.: Congressional Quarterly, 1982), 354.

11. Weinberger, *Fighting for Peace,* 89.

12. Regan, *For the Record,* 167.

13. Woodruff, *This Is Judy Woodruff,* 23.

14. William Safire, "One Fell Short," *NYT,* April 2, 1981, 27.

15. Lawrence I. Barrett, *Gambling with History* (Garden City, N.Y.: Doubleday, 1983), 118.

16. Regan, *For the Record,* 167.

17. Speakes, *Speaking Out,* xii, x.

18. Martin Anderson, interview with author, Stanford, Calif., June 12, 1989.

19. Martin Anderson, *Revolution* (San Diego: Harcourt Brace Jovanovich, 1988), 316.

20. David Gergen, interview with author, Washington, D.C., June 16, 1989.

21. Haig, *Caveat,* 164.

22. Ibid., 164, 165.

23. Michael K. Deaver with Mickey Herskowitz, *Behind the Scenes* (New York: William J. Morrow, 1987), 29.

24. Haig, *Caveat,* 160, 161.

25. Weinberger, *Fighting for Peace,* 85.

26. National Security Act, July 26, 1947, Ch. 343, 61 Stat. 495 (amended through Sept. 30, 1973); Department of Defense Directive 5100:30, "World Wide Military Command and Control System (WWMCCS)," Dec. 2, 1971.

27. Jimmy Carter, *Keeping Faith: Memories of a President* (New York, Bantam Books, 1982), 40; Paul Bracken, personal communication, July 17, 1990.

28. "Attempted Assassination," 354.

29. John D. Feerick, *The Twenty-fifth Amendment: Its Complete History and Earliest Applications* (New York: Fordham Univ. Press, 1976), 251–53.

30. Weinberger, *Fighting for Peace,* 90.

31. Mark S. Hoffman, ed., *The World Almanac and Book of Facts* (New York: Pharos Books, 1990), 289–93.

32. Stuart W. Taylor, Jr., "Disabling of Reagan Provokes a Debate over Nuclear Authority in Such Cases," *NYT,* April 4, 1981, 9; Fred Barbash, "At White House, a Flurry over Who's in Charge," *WP,* March 31, 1981, 14.
33. Barbash, "At White House," 14.
34. Speakes, *Speaking Out,* 11.
35. George Skelton and Don Irwin, "Government Is Functioning—But It's on Hold," *LAT,* April 1, 1981, 1; Walter J. Mossberg, "Confusion over Who Was in Charge Arose following Reagan Shooting," *WSJ,* April 1, 1981, 31.
36. Steven R. Weisman, "Bush Flies back from Texas Set to Take Charge in Crisis," *NYT,* March 31, 1981, 1.
37. Woodruff, *This Is Judy Woodruff,* 23.
38. Barbash, "At White House," 14.
39. Regan, *For the Record,* 167.
40. Steven R. Weisman, "White House Aides Assert Weinberger Was Upset When Haig Took Charge," *NYT,* April 1, 1981, 20.
41. Lou Cannon, "The Day of the Jackal in Washington," *WP,* April 5, 1981, 3; Haig, *Caveat,* 165.
42. Weisman, "White House Aides," 20.
43. Taylor, "Disabling of Reagan," 9.
44. Speakes, *Speaking Out,* x.
45. Robert Shogan, "Attention Is Focused on Presidential Disability Law," *LAT,* March 31, 1981, 3; Taylor, "Disabling of Reagan," 9.
46. Regan, *For the Record,* 169.
47. Haig, *Caveat,* 155–56.
48. Weinberger, *Fighting for Peace,* 83.
49. Ibid., 86.
50. Haig, *Caveat,* 156–57.
51. Ibid., 159.
52. Ibid., 160.
53. Weinberger, *Fighting for Peace,* 86–87.
54. Ibid., 89–90.
55. Cannon, "Jackal," 3.
56. Barrett, *Gambling with History,* 119.
57. Deaver, *Behind the Scenes,* 20.
58. Speakes, *Speaking Out,* 8.
59. Haig, *Caveat,* 152.
60. Regan, *For the Record,* 178.
61. Mathews, "Reagan's Close Call," 31.
62. Barrett, *Gambling with History,* 116.
63. Weinberger, *Fighting for Peace,* 85–86.

64. Haig, *Caveat,* 161.
65. John Pekkanen, "The Saving of the President," *Washingtonian,* Aug. 1981, 113, 120.
66. Haig, *Caveat,* 161; Regan, *For the Record,* 167; Barrett, *Gambling with History,* 120.
67. Sam Donaldson, *Hold On, Mr. President!* (New York: Random House, 1987), 203; Speakes, *Speaking Out,* 8.
68. Speakes, *Speaking Out,* 8.
69. Deaver, *Behind the Scenes,* 21.
70. Pekkanen, "Saving of the President."
71. Deaver, *Behind the Scenes,* 16.
72. Jack Nelson and George Skelton, "Reagan Shot; Condition Good," *LAT,* April 1, 1981, 1.
73. Donaldson, *Hold On, Mr. President!* 201; "Nuclear Code Briefcase Remained near Reagan," *NYT,* March 31, 1981, 5.
74. Rudy Abramson, "Wherever President Goes, the Nuclear 'Football' Is beside Him," *LAT,* April 3, 1981, 10.
75. Bill Gulley with Mary Ellen Reese, *Breaking Cover* (New York: Simon and Schuster, 1980), 188.
76. Bill Gulley, quoted in Daniel Ford, *The Button* (New York: Simon and Schuster, 1985), 90.
77. Abramson, "Wherever President Goes," 10; William Manchester, *The Death of a President* (New York: Harper & Row, 1967), 230; George Church, "Business As Usual—Almost," *Time,* April 13, 1981, 22–23.
78. Manchester, *Death of a President,* 62.
79. Ron Rosenbaum, "The Subterranean World of the Bomb," in Norman Sims, ed., *The Literary Journalists* (New York: Ballantine Books, 1984), 280.
80. Ford, *Button,* 89; Gulley, *Breaking Cover,* 188.
81. Gulley, *Breaking Cover,* 188.
82. "F.B.I. Took Reagan Code Card," *NYT,* Dec. 14, 1981, sec. 4, p. 14.
83. Patrick Tyler and Bob Woodward, "Reagan N-code Taken by FBI in Hospital," *Boston Globe,* Dec. 13, 1981, 26; "F.B.I. Took Reagan Code Card," 14.
84. Skelton and Irwin, "Government Is Functioning," 1.
85. Tyler and Woodward, "Reagan N-code," 26.
86. Bob Woodward, *Veil* (New York: Simon and Schuster, 1987), 123.
87. Paul Bracken, "Delegation of Nuclear Command Authority," in Ashton B. Carter, John D. Steinbruner, and Charles A. Zraket, eds., *Managing Nuclear Operations* (Washington, D.C.: Brookings Institution, 1987), 359.

88. Pekkanen, "Saving of the President," 115.
89. Barrett, *Gambling with History,* 111.
90. David Rockoff, interview with author, Washington D.C., Dec. 2, 1988.
91. Pekkanen, "Saving of the President," 116.
92. Dr. Benjamin Aaron, interview with author, Washington D.C., Dec. 2, 1988.
93. Pekkanen, "Saving of the President," 116–17.
94. Barrett, *Gambling with History,* 111.
95. Aaron interview.
96. Ibid.
97. John W. Warner, Jr., "Letter to the Editor," *Washingtonian,* Nov. 1981, 30.
98. John Pekkanen, response to Warner letter, ibid.
99. Rockoff interview.
100. Haig, *Caveat,* 157.
101. Department of the Treasury, Office of the General Counsel, *Management Review on the Performance of the U.S. Department of the Treasury in Connection with the March 30, 1981 Assassination Attempt on President Ronald Reagan* (Washington, D.C.: Department of the Treasury, Aug. 1981), 10.
102. Donald P. Baker, "Book with Confidential Reagan Data Is Found on Phone Booth in Virginia," *WP,* April 7, 1981, 4; "Agent Who Left Book Identified," *WP,* April 8, 1981, C3.
103. Department of the Treasury, *Management Review,* 61, 62.

CHAPTER 6: How Well Was the
President's Condition Reported to the Nation?

1. Susan Okie, "Reagan's Risk May Have Been Greater Than Believed," *WP,* April 2, 1981, 1; Victor Cohn, "Bullet Lodged an Inch from Reagan's Heart," *WP,* April 16, 1981, 1.
2. Lawrence K. Altman, "Doctor Says President's Life Was in Danger at First," *NYT,* April 1, 1981, 18.
3. Kenneth R. Crispell and Carlos F. Gomez, *Hidden Illness in the White House* (Durham: Duke Univ. Press, 1988); Bert Edward Park, *The Impact of Illness on World Leaders* (Philadelphia: Univ. of Pennsylvania Press, 1986), 13, 227; Chauncey D. Leake, "Presidential Responsibility, Succession, and Tragedy: Woodrow Wilson, 1856–1924," *Military Medicine* 130, no. 2 (Feb. 1965): 134; Ross T. McIntire, *White House Physician* (New York: G. P. Putnam's Sons, 1946), 22, 67; John T. Flynn, *The Roosevelt Myth* (New York: Devin-Adair, 1948), 398–407; Hugh L'Etang, *The Pathology of Leadership*

(London: Cox & Wyman, 1969), 91–97; Joan and Clay Blair, Jr., *The Search for JFK* (New York: Berkley, 1976), 572–73; Vaughn Davis Bornet, *The Presidency of Lyndon B. Johnson* (Lawrence: Univ. of Kansas Press, 1983), 299.

4. Robert Reinhold, "A Bullet Is Removed from Reagan's Lung in Emergency Room," *NYT,* March 31, 1981, 1.

5. Jack Nelson and George Skelton, "Reagan Shot; Condition 'Good,' " *LAT,* March 31, 1981, 1.

6. Howell Raines, "Reagan Wounded in Chest by Gunman," *NYT,* March 31, 1981, 1.

7. "Excerpts from Hospital Briefing about the Victims," *NYT,* April 1, 1981, 23.

8. Reinhold, "Bullet Is Removed"; Joseph M. Giordano et al., "Delay Could Have Been Fatal," *LAT,* April 4, 1981, 1.

9. Alexander M. Haig, Jr., *Caveat* (New York: Macmillan, 1984), 159.

10. Alice M. Peck and Virginia Tritschler, "Ballistics Data and Nursing Assessment of Patients with Gunshot Wounds," in Annette Remington Harmon, ed., *Nursing Care of the Adult Trauma Patient* (New York: John Wiley & Sons, 1985), 260–66.

11. Benjamin Aaron, interview with author, Washington, D.C., Dec. 2, 1988; Giordano, "Delay."

12. Giordano, "Delay."

13. Cohn, "Bullet Lodged,", A5.

14. Pete Earley and Charles Babcock, "The Exploding Bullets," *WP,* April 4, 1981, 1; Department of the Treasury, Office of the General Counsel, *Management Review on the Performance of the U.S. Department of the Treasury in Connection with the March 30, 1981 Assassination Attempt on President Ronald Reagan* (Washington, D.C.: Department of the Treasury, Aug. 1981), 61; "FBI Confirms Malfunctioning of Explosive Bullet That Struck Reagan," *NYT,* April 4, 1980, 8.

15. John Pekkanen, interview with author, Dec. 2, 1988, Washington, D.C.

16. Aaron interview.

17. Cohn, "Bullet Lodged," A5.

18. William Knaus, interview with author, Washington, D.C., Dec. 2, 1988.

19. Mark Bloom, "All the President's Doctors," *Medical World News,* April 27, 1981, 17.

20. Lawrence K. Altman, "Physicians Move Reagan out of Intensive Care Unit," *NYT,* April 2, 1981, 22; Dennis L. Breo, "Taking Care of the Country's First Patient," *American Medical News,* May 8, 1981, 10.

21. Dr. Frank Spencer, quoted by Lawrence K. Altman, "Doctor Says President Lost More Blood Than Disclosed," *NYT*, April 3, 1981, 17.

22. Haig, *Caveat*, 152, 157; "President's Condition Was 'Grave' after '81 Shooting, Haig Says," *WP*, Oct. 4, 1987, 4; Dennis O'Leary, interview with author, Chicago, Ill., Nov. 30, 1988.

23. Larry Speakes with Robert Pack, *Speaking Out* (New York: Charles Scribner's Sons, 1988), 6; "Excerpts from Hospital Briefing."

24. Haig, *Caveat*, 161.

25. Raines, "Reagan Wounded."

26. "Reagan Seen Making Full, Swift Recovery from Gunshot Wound," *WSJ*, March 31, 1981, 1.

27. "Excerpts from Hospital Briefing."

28. "Reagan Does Business As Usual: Meese," *LAT*, April 1, 1981, 1.

29. Howell Raines, "Reagan Sees Aides and Acts on Trade; Continues to Gain; Recovery 'Amazing,' " *NYT*, April 1, 1981, 1.

30. James M. Perry, "President, in High Spirits, Signs Legislation; Bush's Role as a Substitute Is Being Expanded," *WSJ*, April 1, 1981, 2.

31. "Reagan Does Business As Usual."

32. Lou Cannon, "Reagan Staff Plan For Interim Rule: 'Business As Usual,' " *WP*, April 1, 1981, 1.

33. Speakes, *Speaking Out*, 12.

34. Donald T. Regan, *For the Record* (San Diego: Harcourt Brace Jovanovich, 1988), 169.

35. Lou Cannon, "President's Condition Continues to Improve; Brady Shows Gain," *WP*, April 2, 1981, 1.

36. David Treadwell, "Hospital Intern Says President Was in 'Acute Distress,' " *LAT*, April 2, 1981, 18.

37. Raines, "Reagan Sees Aides," 1.

38. Pekkanen, "Saving of the President," 125.

39. Susan Okie and Lee Lescaze, " 'A Little Bit of a Setback' for Reagan," *WP*, April 4, 1981, 1; Howell Raines, "Reagan Eager to Return to Work on Fiscal Plans," *NYT*, April 3, 1981, 16.

40. Tip O'Neill with William Novak, *Man of the House: The Life and Political Memoirs of Speaker Tip O'Neill* (New York: Random House, 1987), 336.

41. Okie and Lescaze, "Setback."

42. Ibid.

43. George Skelton and Rudy Abramson, "Reagan Has 'a Little Bit of a Setback,' " *LAT*, April 4, 1981, 1.

44. Don Irwin, "Jordan Gives Reagan a Tip: Follow Orders," *NYT*, April 6, 1981, 1.

45. Hugh Sidey, "That Show-Must-Go-On-Spirit," *Time,* April 27, 1981, 26.
46. Dr. Dennis O'Leary, interview with author, Chicago, Ill., Dec. 3, 1989.
47. Aaron interview.
48. Knaus interview.
49. Dr. Ben Giordano, interview with author, Washington, D.C., Dec. 2, 1988.
50. Dr. Daniel Ruge, interview with author, Denver, Colo., Dec. 15, 1988.
51. Pekkanen interview.
52. Ibid.
53. Larry Speakes quoted in "Excerpts from Hospital Briefing."
54. Edwin Meese quoted in "Reagan Does Business As Usual."
55. Nancy Reagan, public statement at George Washington University Hospital, March 28, 1991. See transcript, "MacNeil/Lehrer Newshour," March 28, 1991, 13.
56. Cohn, "Bullet Lodged."

Chapter 7: Was His Capacity
for Decision Making Unimpaired?

1. Dr. William O'Neill quoted in David Treadwell, "Hospital Intern Says President Was in 'Acute Distress,' " *LAT,* April 2, 1981, 18.
2. Diane W. Scott, "Anxiety, Critical Thinking and Information Processing during and after Breast Biopsy," *Nursing Research* 32, no. 1 (Jan. 1983): 24–28.
3. Nancy C. Andreasen, "Posttraumatic Stress Disorder," in H. I. Kaplan, A. M. Friedman, and B. J. Sadock, eds., *Comprehensive Textbook of Psychiatry,* 3d ed., vol. 2 (Baltimore: Williams & Wilkins, 1980), 1517, 1519.
4. James L. Titchener, "Management and Study of Psychological Response to Trauma," *Journal of Trauma* 10, no. 11 (1970): 974–75; Gail Pisarcik Lenehan, "Emotional Impact of Trauma," *Nursing Clinics of North America* 21, no. 4 (Dec. 1986): 732.
5. Robert C. Davis and Lucy N. Friedman, "The Emotional Aftermath of Crime and Violence," in Charles R. Figley, ed., *Trauma and Its Wake* (New York: Brunner/Mazel, 1985), 90–112; Linda Peterson, "The Psychological Impact of Trauma: Recognition and Treatment," *American Journal of Emergency Medicine* 1 (1983): 102.
6. Marek-Marsel Mesulam and Norman Geschwind, "Disordered Mental States in the Postoperative Period," *Urologic Clinics of North America* 3, no. 2 (June 1976): 201–2, 209.

7. John Pekkanen, "The Saving of the President," *Washingtonian,* Aug. 1981, 125.

8. Mesulam and Geschwind, "Disordered Mental States," 209; B. R. Simpson et al., "The Effects of Anaesthesia and Elective Surgery on Old People," *Lancet,* Oct. 21, 1961, 887–93; E. Blundell, "A Psychological Study of the Effects of Surgery on Eighty-six Elderly Patients," *British Journal of Social and Clinical Psychology* 6 (1967): 297–305; J. Riis et al., "Immediate and Long-term Mental Recovery from General versus Epidural Anesthesia in Elderly Patients," *Acta Anaesthesiologica Scandinavica* 27, no. 1 (1983): 44–49.

9. Stephen A. Green, *Mind and Body: The Psychology of Physical Illness* (Washington, D.C.: American Psychiatric Press, 1985), 1; Owen S. Surman, "The Surgical Patient," in Thomas P. Hackett and Ned H. Cassem, eds., *Massachusetts General Hospital Handbook of General Hospital Psychiatry* (St. Louis: C. V. Mosby, 1978), 65; Green, *Mind and Body,* 97; Aaron T. Beck, *Depression: Clinical, Experimental, and Theoretical Aspects* (New York: Harper & Row, 1967), 19, 23–24.

10. Rowland Evans and Robert Novak, *Lyndon B. Johnson: The Exercise of Power* (New York: New American Library, 1966), 561.

11. Ibid., 25; Eric J. Cassell, *The Healer's Art* (New York: Penguin Books, 1979), 25; A. Verwoerdt, "Psychopathological Responses to the Stress of Physical Illness," *Advances in Psychosomatic Medicine* 8 (1972): 127; Scott, "Anxiety and Critical Thinking," 27.

12. J. A. Collins, "Pathophysiology of Hemorrhagic Shock: Clinical and Therapeutic Implications," in C. Th. Sibinga, P. C. Das, and J. J. van Loghem, eds., *Bloodtransfusion and Problems of Bleeding* (Boston: Martinus Nijhoff, 1982), 105–18.

13. Pekkanen, "Saving of the President," 125.

14. Ragnar J. Vaernes, Jan O. Owe, and Ole Myking, "Central Nervous Reactions to a 6.5-Hour Altitude Exposure at 3048 Meters," *Aviation, Space, and Environmental Medicine* 55 (Oct. 1984): 921–26; G. R. Kelman and T. J. Crow, "Impairment of Mental Performance at a Simulated Altitude of 8,000 Feet," *Aerospace Medicine* 40, no. 9 (1969): 981–82; Collins, "Pathophysiology of Hemorrhagic Shock," 107.

15. J. R. Trounce, *Clinical Pharmacology for Nurses* (New York: Churchill Livingstone, 1985), 147; Fred Leavitt, *Drugs and Behavior* (New York: John Wiley & Sons, 1982), 21, 31, 369; Kari Korttila et al., "Recovery and Simulated Driving after Intravenous Anesthesia with Thiopental, Methohexital, Propanidid, or Alphadione," *Anesthesiology* 43, no. 3 (Sept. 1975): 291–99.

16. Leavitt, *Drugs and Behavior,* 20, 117; Trounce, *Clinical Phar-*

macology, 85–87; Kari Korttila and Markku Linnoila, "Psychomotor Skills Related to Driving after Intramuscular Administration of Diazepam and Meperidine," *Anesthesiology* 42, no. 6 (June 1975): 685–91;

17. Ruth R. Levine, *Pharmacology: Drug Actions and Reactions* (Boston: Little, Brown, 1983), 491; Leavitt, *Drugs and Behavior*, 4; M. M. Ghoneim and S. P. Mewaldt, "Studies on Human Memory: The Interactions of Diazepam, Scopolamine, and Physostigmine," *Psychopharmacology* 52 (1977): 1–6; Allen M. Schneider and Barry Tarshis, *An Introduction to Physiological Psychology* (New York: Random House, 1986), 171; Trounce, *Clinical Pharmacology*, 118.

18. Marlene Cimons, "Despite Fortitude, Reagan Had Fears," *LAT*, April 3, 1981, 1.

19. "Excerpts from Hospital Briefing about the Victims," *NYT*, April 1, 1981, 23.

20. Many other quips were recorded during his hospital stay. He wrote a note in the recovery room that echoed a Churchillian phrase: "There's no more exhilarating feeling than being shot at without result." Another note said, "Send me to L.A., where I can see the air I'm breathing." To an attentive nurse he wrote, "Does Nancy know about us?" To his daughter Maureen, he complained that his wound "ruined one of my best shirts." When White House aides appeared the morning after surgery, Reagan greeted them by saying, "Hi fellas. I knew it would be too much to hope that we could skip a staff meeting." See "Seriously, Folks . . . ," *Time*, April 13, 1981, 30.
    At the meeting with his aides, Reagan told Michael Deaver, the timekeeper, "I've really screwed up the schedule." See Tom Mathews, "Reagan's Close Call," *Newsweek*, April 13, 1981, 31. In another note to a nurse, Reagan wrote, "I'd like to do this scene over again—starting at the hotel." See Michael K. Deaver with Mickey Hershkowitz, *Behind the Scenes* (New York: William J. Morrow, 1987), 23. When he left the hospital to return to the White House, a reporter asked him what he would do when he got home. "Sit down," Reagan replied. See Lee Lescaze, "Feeling 'Great,' " *WP*, April 12, 1981, 1.

21. Robert Reinhold, "A Bullet Is Removed from Reagan's Lung in Emergency Surgery," *NYT*, March 31, 1981, 1.

22. "Excerpts from Hospital Briefing."

23. Deaver, *Behind the Scenes*, 24.

24. Pekkanen, "Saving of the President," 125.

25. Dr. William Knaus, interview with author, Washington, D.C., Dec. 2, 1988.

26. Tip O'Neill with William Novak, *Man of the House* (New York: Random House, 1987), 336.
27. Deaver, *Behind the Scenes,* 262; Laurence I. Barrett, *Gambling with History* (Garden City, N.Y.: Doubleday, 1983), 121–22.
28. Lee Lescaze, "Reagan Release from Hospital Delayed," *WP,* April 7, 1981, 1.
29. Lou Cannon, "Reagan Gains, Won't Rush Return to Job," *WP,* April 8, 1981, 1; Sara Fritz, "Taking Up the Slack," *U.S. News & World Report,* April 20, 1981, 23; Steven R. Weisman, "Reagan's Workload up to 2 Hours a Day," *NYT,* April 9, 1981, 1.
30. Interviews with Dr. Dennis O'Leary, Nov. 30, 1988; Drs. Joseph M. Giordano, William Knaus, and David Rockoff, Dec. 1 and 2, 1988; Dr. Daniel Ruge, Dec. 13, 1988.
31. Howell Raines, "Reagan Is Taken Off a Drug and Found in 'Good Shape,' " *NYT,* April 10, 1981, 15; Lou Cannon, "Reagan to Leave Hospital Today or Tomorrow," *WP,* April 11, 1981, 1.
32. Barrett, *Gambling with History,* 123.
33. Bob Woodward, *Veil* (New York: Simon and Schuster, 1987), 122; "President's Condition Was 'Grave' after '81 Shooting, Haig Says," *WP,* Oct. 4, 1987, 4.
34. " 'I Have Recovered,' President Declares," *NYT,* June 17, 1981, 27; Steven R. Weisman, "Reagan Steps Up His Work Schedule," *NYT,* June 4, 1981, B15.
35. "Excerpts from Hospital Briefing."
36. Woodward, *Veil,* 122.
37. "Reagan May Have Acted While Ill," *San Jose Mercury News,* Dec. 12, 1986, 1.
38. Ellen Hume, "Wary Bush Walks Fine Line between Duty, Discretion," *LAT,* April 1, 1981, 3.
39. "Reagan Does Business As Usual: Meese," *LAT,* April 1, 1981, 1.
40. Ibid.
41. "Excerpts from Hospital Briefing."
42. Lou Cannon, "Reagan Staff Plan for Interim Rule: 'Business As Usual,' " *WP,* April 1, 1981, 1.

CHAPTER 8: A Response to Presidential Disability:
The Twenty-fifth Amendment

1. Stephen E. Ambrose, *Eisenhower,* vol. 2, *The President* (New York: Harper & Row, 1986), 270–72; Elmo Richardson, *The Presidency of Dwight D. Eisenhower* (Lawrence: Regents Press of Kansas, 1979), 88.

2. Sherman Adams, *Firsthand Report: The Story of the Eisenhower Administration* (New York: Harper & Row, 1961), 191; Robert J. Donovan, *Eisenhower: The Inside Story* (New York: Harper & Brothers, 1956), 397–98; Ambrose, *Eisenhower*, 284–85.

3. Piers Brendon, *Ike: His Life and Times* (New York: Harper & Row, 1986), 321.

4. Ambrose, *Eisenhower*, 84; Dwight D. Eisenhower, *The White House Years: Waging Peace, 1956–1961* (Garden City, N.Y.: Doubleday, 1963), 65.

5. Eisenhower, speaking at a Jan. 1956 press conference, quoted in *Hearings before the House Judiciary Special Subcommittee on Study of Presidential Inability*, 84th Cong., 2d sess., April 11, 1956, 13.

6. U.S. Const., art. 1, sec. 2, cl. 1.; sec. 8, cls. 12–16; Alexander Hamilton, *The Federalist Number 69* (Cleveland: World, 1961).

7. U.S. Const., art. 2, sec. 1, cl. 5.

8. Presidential Succession Act of 1947, PL-80-199.

9. Michael A. Musmannu, judge of the Supreme Court of Pennsylvania, testimony in *Hearings before the Senate Judiciary Subcommittee on Constitutional Amendments*, 85th Cong., 2d sess., Feb. 11, 1958, 74.

10. Max Farrand, ed., *Records of the Federal Convention*, vol. 2 (New Haven: Yale Univ. Press, 1911), 427.

11. The answers to the questionnaire are published in House Committee on the Judiciary, *Presidential Inability*, 84th Cong., 2d sess., Jan. 31, 1956, 3. An analysis and summary of the replies and some of the testimony responding to the questionnaire was prepared by the Legislative Reference Service of the Library of Congress and published in House Committee on the Judiciary, *An Analysis of Replies to a Questionnaire and Testimony at a Hearing on Presidential Inability*, 85th Cong., 1st sess., March 26, 1957.

12. Brownell, in *Hearings before the House Judiciary Special Subcommittee on Study of Presidential Inability*, 85th Cong., 1st sess., April 1, 1957, 19, 29. For other instances in which the Tyler precedent is cited with regard to Wilson and Garfield, see also John H. Romani, House Committee on the Judiciary, *Presidential Inability*, 56; Peter Frelinghuysen, Jr., House Hearings, April 11, 1956, 22–23; and Lewis Powell, in *Hearings before the Senate Judiciary Subcommittee on Constitutional Amendments*, 88th Cong., 2d sess., Feb. 24, 1964, 91.

13. Strangely, this idea was not mentioned in Celler's questionnaire. It was most explicitly recognized in Eisenhower's memorandum of agreement with Vice-President Nixon, which provided for the president to declare his own inability and pass the powers and duties of

office to the vice-president. An opinion which declared the memo in accord with the Constitution was included in the congressional record as part of an analysis by Attorney General Robert F. Kennedy, in *Hearings before the Senate Judiciary Subcommittee on Constitutional Amendments,* 88th Cong., 2d sess., June 18, 1963, 87–116. The text of the memo is on p. 110.

14. For example, Joseph E. Kallenbach in House Committee on the Judiciary, *Presidential Inability,* 45–46. Although for most practical purposes the vice-president is part of the executive branch, one could argue, as President Eisenhower did, that the vice-president is really part of the legislative branch, because his only ongoing role is to preside over the Senate. See Twentieth Century Fund Task Force, *A Heartbeat Away* (New York: Priority Press, 1988), 10.

15. For example, David Fellman, in House Committee on the Judiciary, *Presidential Inability,* Jan. 31, 1956, 23, or Mark DeW. Howe, ibid., 35.

16. House Committee on the Judiciary, *Presidential Inability,* Jan. 31, 1956, 35; House, *Hearings on Presidential Inability,* April 11, 1956, 2; *Hearings before the Senate Judiciary Subcommittee on Constitutional Amendments,* 85th Cong., 2d sess., Jan. 24, 1958, 11–13.

17. For example, C. Herman Pritchett, in House Committee on the Judiciary, *Presidential Inability,* Jan. 31, 1956, 52–53.

18. For example, Senator Frederick G. Payne, in House, *Hearings on Presidential Inability,* April 11, 1956, 15–16.

19. For example, Sidney Hyman, in *Hearings before the House Judiciary Special Subcommittee on Study of Presidential Inability,* 84th Cong., 2d sess., April 12, 1956, 50–51.

20. For example, Joseph E. Kallenbach, ibid., 85.

21. James C. Kirby, Jr., "The ABA Conference Consensus," *Vanderbilt Law Review* 17 (1964): 469.

22. Sherman Adams, *Firsthand Report* (New York: Harper & Brothers, 1961), 198–201.

23. House, *Hearings on Presidential Inability,* April 1, 1957, 7–8.

24. Ibid., 27.

25. Ibid., 27–28.

26. Ibid., 29.

27. Senate Hearings, Jan. 24, 1958, 14.

28. *Hearings before the Senate Judiciary Subcommittee on Constitutional Amendments,* 85th Cong., 2d sess., Feb. 18, 1958, 155.

29. "CBS Reports, The Crisis of Presidential Succession," Jan. 8, 1964, quoted in John D. Feerick, *The Twenty-fifth Amendment* (New York: Fordham Univ. Press, 1976), 55.

30. Quoted in Robert F. Kennedy, "Opinion of the Attorney General of

the United States," Aug. 2, 1961, reprinted in *Hearings before the Senate Judiciary Subcommittee on Constitutional Amendments*, 88th Cong., 1st sess., June 18, 1963, 110.

31. Senate, *Hearings on Constitutional Amendments*, March 5, 1964, 241.
32. Kirby, "ABA Conference Consensus," 471–72.
33. Ibid., 472–73.
34. Senate, *Hearings on Constitutional Amendments*, June 18, 1963, 32–40. The text of S.J. Res. 35 is on pp. 5–6.
35. *Hearings before the Senate Judiciary Subcommittee on Constitutional Amendments*, 88th Cong., 1st sess., June 11, 1963, 12–13; Kirby, "ABA Conference Consensus," 474.
36. Senate, *Hearings on Constitutional Amendments*, Jan. 23, 1963, 67.
37. Birch Bayh, *One Heartbeat Away* (Indianapolis: Bobbs-Merrill, 1968), 53.
38. Ibid., 49–50. The text of the ABA's "Consensus on Presidential Inability and Succession, January 20 and 21, 1964," is reprinted ibid., 348–50. Panelists in the consensus conference included Herbert Brownell, Walter Craig, Paul A. Freund, and Lewis F. Powell, Jr.
39. Bayh, *One Heartbeat Away*, 28–29.
40. S.J. Res. 139, Senate Hearings, Jan. 22, 1964, 11–13.
41. Feerick, *Twenty-fifth Amendment*, 80, 206. Note that although the term "cabinet" continues to be used in this and subsequent references, the actual language of the proposal had become "the heads of the executive departments."
42. Richard P. Longaker, "Presidential Continuity: The Twenty-fifth Amendment," *UCLA Law Review* 13 (1966): 534.
43. Bayh, *One Heartbeat Away*, 275–333.
44. Ibid., 87–111.
45. Ibid., 342.
46. U.S. Constitution, Amendment XXV, secs. 1–4.

CHAPTER 9: The Failure to Invoke
the Twenty-fifth Amendment

1. White Burkett Miller Center of Public Affairs at the University of Virginia, *Report of the Miller Center Commission on Presidential Disability and the Twenty-fifth Amendment* (Lanham, Md.: Univ. Press of America, 1988), 2.
2. Lou Cannon, "The Day of the Jackal in Washington," *WP*, April 5, 1981, 1.

3. Laurence I. Barrett, *Gambling with History* (Garden City, N.Y.: Doubleday, 1983), 115.

4. Gerald M. Boyd, "Reagan Transfers Power to Bush for 8-Hour Period of Incapacity," *NYT,* July 14, 1985, 1.

5. Alexander M. Haig, Jr., *Caveat* (New York: Macmillian, 1984), 157.

6. Barrett, *Gambling with History,* 115–16; Hedrick Smith, *The Power Game: How Washington Works* (New York: Random House, 1988), 300; Larry Speakes with Robert Pack, *Speaking Out* (New York: Charles Scribner's Sons, 1988), 154.

7. Edwin Meese, interview with author, Stanford, Calif. June 2, 1989. Also, David Gergen, interview with author, Washington, D.C., June 16, 1989.

8. Haig, *Caveat,* 157.

9. Gergen interview; Smith, *Power Game,* 299–300.

10. Michael K. Deaver and Mickey Hershkowitz, *Behind the Scenes* (New York: William J. Morrow, 1987); 22; also, Meese interview.

11. "Report by Aide in White House after Shootings," *NYT,* March 31, 1981, 5

12. Gergen interview; also, Meese interview.

13. Barrett, *Gambling with History,* 114–15.

14. Dr. Joseph Giordano, interview with author, Washington, D.C., Dec. 2, 1988.

15. Dr. William Knaus, interview with author, Washington, D.C., Dec. 2, 1988; Dr. Benjamin Aaron, interview with author, Washington, D.C., Dec. 2, 1988; Dr. Daniel Ruge, interview with author, Denver, Colo. Dec. 11, 1988; Meese interview.

16. Barrett, *Gambling with History,* 114–15.

17. Ibid., 116; Meese interview; Speakes, *Speaking Out,* 9; Steven R. Weisman, "White House Aides Assert Weinberger Was Upset When Haig Took Charge," *NYT,* April 1, 1981, 20.

18. Haig, *Caveat,* 162.

19. Barrett, *Gambling with History,* 114–15.

20. Howell Raines, "A Pause, Then Government Moves Ahead," *NYT,* April 5, 1981, sec. 4, p. 2.

21. Donald T. Regan, *For the Record* (San Diego: Harcourt Brace Jovanovich, 1988), 167.

22. Miller Center, *Report on the Twenty-fifth Amendment,* 7.

23. Robert Shogan, "Attention Is Focused on Presidential Disability Law," *LAT,* March 31, 1981, 3.

24. Meese interview.

25. Ibid.

26. Speakes, *Speaking Out,* 9.

27. Meese interview.
28. Gergen interview.
29. Lou Cannon, "Reagan Staff Plan for Interim Rule: 'Business As Usual,' " *WP,* April 1, 1981, 1.
30. "Crisis Management," *WSJ,* April 1, 1981, 28.
31. Jack Nelson and George Skelton, "Reagan Shot; Condition 'Good,' " *LAT,* March 31, 1981, 1.
32. Weisman, "White House Aides," 20.
33. "Excerpts from Hospital Briefing about the Victims," *NYT,* April 1, 1981, 23.
34. "Reagan Does Business As Usual: Meese," *LAT,* April 1, 1981, 1.
35. Cannon, "Reagan Staff Plan."
36. "Reagan Does Business As Usual."
37. Cannon, "Reagan Staff Plan."
38. Hedrick Smith, "Bush Says He Sought to Avoid Acting like Surrogate President," *NYT,* April 12, 1981, 1.
39. Hedrick Smith, "Starting as an Outsider, Bush Is Now a Star among Team Players," *NYT,* April 5, 1981, sec. 4, p. 2.
40. Haig, *Caveat,* 160.
41. Speakes, *Speaking Out,* 10; Lawrence K. Altman, "President's Fever Varies over Day; His Condition Termed Satisfactory," *NYT,* April 4, 1981, 1.
42. Walter S. Mossberg, "Confusion over Who Was in Charge Arose following Reagan Shooting," *WSJ,* April 4, 1981, 31; James M. Perry, "President, in High Spirits, Signs Legislation; Bush's Role as a Substitute Is Being Expanded," *WSJ,* April 1, 1981, 2.
43. "The President's Recovery Period: Informal Exchange between the Vice-President and Reporters, March 31, 1981," in Office of the Federal Register, *Weekly Compilation of Presidential Documents* (Washington, D.C.: National Archives and Records Service, April 6, 1981), 374.
44. Ellen Hume, "Wary Bush Walks Fine Line between Duty, Discretion," *LAT,* April 1, 1981, 3.
45. Perry, "President . . . Signs Legislation."
46. Stuart W. Taylor, Jr., "Disabling of Reagan Provokes a Debate over Nuclear Authority in Such Cases," *NYT,* April 4, 1981, 9.
47. Lee Lescaze, "Bush Keeping Low Profile as Stand-in for Reagan," *WP,* April 2, 1981, 9; Edward Walsh, "Bush Assumes Ceremonial Duties, But Not Powers, of the Presidency," *WP,* April 1, 1981, 12; "A Talk with George Bush," *Newsweek,* April 20, 1981, 29.
48. Lee Lescaze, "President Exercising Regularly," *WP,* April 3, 1981, 1.

49. Weisman, "White House Aides."
50. Gergen interview.
51. Meese interview.
52. Martin Anderson, interview with author, Stanford, Calif., June 12, 1989.
53. Steven Strasser, "Who's Minding the Store," *Newsweek*, April 13, 1981, 39. "I want to do what I can, and I want to do it through you," Bush told Meese and Baker.
54. David L. Alpern, "The President's Men," *Newsweek*, April 20, 1981, 27–30.
55. Sarah Fritz, "Taking Up the Slack," *U.S. News & World Report*, April 20, 1981, 22–23.
56. Weisman, "White House Aides."
57. "Bush Statement at White House," *NYT*, March 31, 1981, 5.
58. Edwin Meese on "Nightline" (ABC Television), April 1, 1981, cited in Haig, *Caveat*, 164.
59. "Who's Minding the Store?" *NYT*, April 1, 1981, 30.
60. Dr. David Rockoff, interview with author, Washington, D.C., Dec. 2, 1988.
61. Barrett, *Gambling with History*, 94–96.
62. Tip O'Neill with William Novak, *Man of the House* (New York: Random House, 1987), 361.
63. George J. Church, "The Upstairs Presidency," *Time*, April 23, 1981, 26; Fritz, "Taking Up the Slack," 22–23; Skelton and Irwin, "Reagan's Work Style."
64. Church, "Upstairs Presidency," 25.
65. Ibid.
66. Deaver, *Behind the Scenes*, 262.
67. Aaron interview.
68. Ruge interview.
69. Ibid.
70. Dr. Dennis O'Leary, interview with author, Chicago, Ill., Nov. 30, 1988; Knaus interview.
71. Knaus interview.
72. Miller Center, *Report on the Twenty-fifth Amendment*, 2.
73. Meese interview.
74. Gergen interview.
75. Ibid.
76. Larry Speakes, response to the author's questions, Stanford Univ., Stanford, Calif., Jan. 30, 1990.
77. Ruge interview; Knaus interview; Giordano interview; Aaron interview.

CHAPTER 10: The First Use
of the Disability Provisions of
the Twenty-fifth Amendment

1. "The Perplexing, and Sometimes Perilous Polyp," *Time,* July 22, 1985, 18.
2. From Fred Fielding's Sept. 30, 1986, testimony in White Burkett Miller Center of Public Affairs at the University of Virginia, *Report of the Miller Center Commission on Presidential Disability and the Twenty-fifth Amendment* (Lanham, Md.: Univ. Press of America, 1988), 6–7.
3. "Aides Describe Reagan's Choice in Transfer of Power to Bush," *NYT,* July 15, 1985, 11.
4. "The Perplexing Polyp," 18.
5. Donald T. Regan, *For the Record* (New York: Harcourt Brace Jovanovich, 1988), 3–5
6. "Anxiety over an Ailing President," *Time,* July 22, 1985, 17; "Reagan Surgery Finds a 2D Polyp; Operation Today," *NYT,* July 13, 1985, 1; "Anxiety over an Ailing President," 17.
7. "Anxiety over an Ailing President," 17.
8. Regan, *For the Record,* 6. See also "Temporary Shift of Power Possible," *NYT,* July 13, 1985, 26.
9. Jane Mayer and Doyle McManus, *Landslide: The Unmaking of the President, 1984–1988* (Boston: Houghton Mifflin, 1988), 111; "Who's Minding the Store?" *Time,* July 22, 1985, 24.
10. Larry Speakes with Robert Pack, *Speaking Out* (New York: Charles Scribner's Sons, 1988), 190.
11. "Reagan Transfers Power to Bush for 8-Hour Period of 'Incapacity,' " *NYT,* July 14, 1985, 1; Fielding, in Miller Center, *Report on the Twenty-fifth Amendment,* 7–8; "Anxiety over an Ailing President," 20.
12. Fielding, in Miller Center, *Report on the Twenty-fifth Amendment,* 8; "Anxiety over an Ailing President," 20; "Reagan's Doctors Remove Growth from His Intestine; Say He Is 'Doing Beautifully,' " *NYT,* July 14, 1985, 1.
13. Fielding, in Miller Center, *Report on the Twenty-fifth Amendment,* 6.
14. "Reagan's Doctors Remove Growth," 1.
15. Fielding, in Miller Center, *Report on the Twenty-fifth Amendment,* 8.
16. Regan, *For the Record,* 7; "Bush Says Reagan Illness Made Him Reflect on Duty," *NYT,* July 24, 1985, 1; "A Conversation with Ronald Reagan," *Time,* Aug. 5, 1985, 17.
17. Regan, *For the Record,* 9; "Reagan Transfers Power," 1.

18. "Anxiety over an Ailing President," 20.
19. "Reagan's Doctors Remove Growth," 1; "Correction," *NYT,* July 15, 1985, Bl; "Prudent Medical Practice," *NYT,* July 14, 1985, 1.
20. "Explanations by 2 Cancer Surgeons at Bethesda News Parley," *NYT,* July 16, 1989, 10. According to Don Regan, the surgery also removed two smaller polyps (see *For the Record,* 9). A "Dukes B" lesion is one of intermediate malignancy that has penetrated the wall to involve the adjacent lymph nodes. The survival rate ranges from 50 to 80 percent.
21. "Conversation with Ronald Reagan," 16.
22. "Anxiety over an Ailing President," 23; Regan, *For the Record,* 10.
23. Fielding, in Miller Center, *Report on the Twenty-fifth Amendment,* 8.
24. Mayer and McManus, *Landslide,* 112.
25. Fielding, in Miller Center, *Report on the Twenty-fifth Amendment,* 8–10.
26. Ibid., 9; Regan, *For the Record,* 11.
27. Mayer and McManus, *Landslide,* 112; "Excerpts from Briefing by President's Medical Team," *NYT,* July 14, 1985, 20; "Reagan's Doctors Remove Growth," 1.
28. Fielding, in Miller Center, *Report on the Twenty-fifth Amendment,* 9.
29. Ibid.
30. "Reagan's Doctors Remove Growth," 1.
31. "Unusual Routine Case," *NYT,* July 15, 1985, 1.
32. Regan, *For the Record,* 11.
33. "Reagan Transfers Power," 1; "Reagan's Doctors Remove Growth," 1.
34. Fielding, in Miller Center, *Report on the Twenty-fifth Amendment,* 9.
35. "Explanations by 2 Cancer Surgeons," 10; "Reagan Reported Well; Plans Light Work," *NYT,* July 15, 1985, 1.
36. "Reagan's Doctors Find Cancer in Tumor But Report Removal Leaves His Chances Excellent," *NYT,* July 16, 1985, 1.
37. Mayer and McManus, *Landslide,* 113.
38. "President Placed on Liquid Diet after Best Night," *NYT,* July 18, 1985, 1.
39. "President Gets First Solid Food; Is Termed 'Totally Back to Normal,' " *NYT,* July 19, 1985, 1.
40. "Reagan Returns to White House; Greeted Warmly," *NYT,* July 21, 1985, 1; "Reagan Back from Camp David; Work Pressures Worry His Wife," *NYT,* July 29, 1985, 13; "Coming Along Just Fine," *Time,* Aug. 5, 1985, 14.
41. "Bush Says Reagan Illness Made Him Reflect on Duty," *NYT,* July 24, 1985, 1.

42. "Reagan's Doctors Find Cancer," 1; "Bush, after a Moment in the Sun, Slips Back into Reagan's Shadow," *NYT,* July 17, 1985, 1; "President Gets First Solid Food," 1; "Simply in Place," *Time,* July 29, 1985, 18; Mayer and McManus, *Landslide,* 115.

43. "Reagan Reported Well," 1. The speaker is unidentified here, but is identified as Regan in Mayer and McManus, *Landslide,* 113.

44. "Regan Is Key Link during Recovery," *NYT,* July 15, 1985, 1; "Reagan Reported Well," 1.

45. "Chief Operating Officer," *Time,* July 29, 1985, 20.

46. Regan, *For the Record,* 15–20.

47. Speakes, *Speaking Out,* 74.

48. "Reagan May Have Acted While Ill," *San Jose Mercury News,* Dec. 20, 1986, 1; "Meese Is Reported to Suggest Medicine Impaired Reagan," *NYT,* Dec. 21, 1986, 20.

49. "Meese Is Reported to Suggest," 20.

50. Ibid.

51. Congressional Quarterly, *The Iran-Contra Puzzle* (Washington, D.C.: Congressional Quarterly, 1987), 44.

52. Ibid., A10.

53. Senate Select Committee on Intelligence, *Preliminary Inquiry into the Sale of Arms to Iran and Possible Diversion of Funds to the Nicaraguan Resistance* (Washington, D.C.: GPO, Feb. 2, 1987), 5.

54. Mayer and McManus, *Landslide,* 127–29.

55. Ibid., 130.

56. Ibid., 112.

57. "Reagan Transfers Power," 1.

58. Birch Bayh, in Miller Center, *Report on the Twenty-fifth Amendment,* 6–8, 18, 33.

59. Fielding, in Miller Center, *Report on the Twenty-fifth Amendment,* 6.

60. Kenneth Crispell and Carlos F. Gomez, *Hidden Illness in the White House* (Durham: Duke Univ. Press, 1988), 221.

61. Mayer and McManus, *Landslide,* 113.

62. "Chief Operating Officer," *Time,* July 29, 1985, 20.

CHAPTER 11: The Next Time

1. See Senator Everett Dirksen, in *Senate Report from Committee on the Judiciary to Accompany S.J. Res. 1,* 89th Cong., 1st sess., Feb. 10, 1965, 18–19, Senator Roman Hruska, in *Senate Report from Committee on the Judiciary to Accompany S.J. Res. 139,* 88th Cong., 2d sess., Aug. 13, 1964, 15, and Senator Kenneth Keating, ibid., 16.

2. The range and depth of discussion on the question of what "inability"

means is depicted in House Committee on the Judiciary, *An Analysis of Replies to a Questionnaire and Testimony at a Hearing on Presidential Inability,* 85th Cong., 1st sess., March 26, 1957, 3–11.

3. Bayh and Robert Kennedy, Senate hearings of June 30, 1965, quoted in John D. Feerick, *The Twenty-fifth Amendment* (New York: Fordham Univ. Press, 1976), 200–202. They discuss the notion of "inability" at some length.

4. Charles Fairman, in House Committee on the Judiciary, *Presidential Inability,* 84th Cong., 2d sess., Jan. 31, 1956, 18; Emanuel Celler, in *Hearings before the House Judiciary Special Subcommittee on Study of Presidential Inability,* 84th Cong., 2d sess., April 11, 1956, 10; Frederick G. Payne, ibid., 14; Arthur E. Sutherland, in *Hearings before the House Judiciary Special Subcommittee on Study of Presidential Inability,* 84th Cong., 2d sess., April 12, 1956, 80; Michael A. Masmannu, in *Hearings before the Senate Judiciary Subcommittee on Constitutional Amendments,* 85th Cong., 2d sess., Feb. 11, 1958, 74; Frank E. Moss, in *Hearings before the Senate Judiciary Subcommittee on Constitutional Amendments,* 88th Cong., 2d sess., Jan. 23, 1964, 61.

5. Discussions with Birch Bayh in Kenneth W. Thompson, ed., *Papers on Presidential Disability and the Twenty-fifth Amendment* (Lanham, Md.: Univ. Press of America, 1988), 29.

6. *Hearings before the Senate Judiciary Subcommittee on Constitutional Amendments,* 85th Cong., 2d sess., Feb. 28, 1958, 194. See also, e.g., Thomas K. Finletter, in House Committee on the Judiciary, *Presidential Inability,* Jan. 31, 1956, 27; John H. Romani, ibid., 57; Herbert Brownell, in *Hearings before the Senate Judiciary Subcommittee on Constitutional Amendments,* 88th Cong., 2d sess., Feb. 25, 1964, 135.

7. Senator Birch Bayh, telephone interview with author, June 7, 1990.

8. John Feerick, interview with author, New York City, April 13, 1990.

9. Jane Mayer and Doyle McManus, *Landslide* (Boston: Houghton Mifflin, 1988), ix.

10. Jack Nelson, "Removal of Reagan from Office Suggested to Baker," *LAT,* Sept. 15, 1988, 20; Steven V. Roberts, "Former Aide Questions Signing of Reagan's Initials," *NYT,* Sept. 16, 1988, 16; Mayer and McManus, *Landslide,* x; Steven V. Roberts, "Book Gives Aides Conflicting Views of President," *NYT,* Sept. 15, 1988, A29; Michael K. Deaver and Mickey Hershkowitz, *Behind the Scenes* (New York: William J. Morrow, 1987), 261.

11. Mayer and McManus, *Landslide,* xi; Nelson, "Removal of Reagan";

Robert L. Jackson, "Untrue, Reagan Says of Reports of a Bid to Remove Him," *LAT,* Sept. 16, 1988, 4.

12. George E. Reedy, *The Twilight of the Presidency* (New York and Cleveland: World, 1970), 168.

13. Richard L. Madden, "When Is Top Official's Illness a Disability?" *NYT,* Nov. 26, 1980, B2.

14. See Joseph E. Kallenbach, in House, *Hearings on Presidential Inability,* 84th Cong., 2d sess., April 12, 1956, 85, and Peter Frelinghuysen, ibid., April 11, 1956, 32.

15. Herbert Brownell, in *Hearings before the House Special Subcommittee on Study of Presidential Inability,* April 1, 1957, 26, 27; Rogers endorses Brownell's view in Senate, *Hearings on Constitutional Amendments,* Feb. 18, 1958, 165; Charles S. Rhyne, in Senate, *Hearings on Constitutional Amendments,* Feb. 28, 1958, 194–95.

16. Joseph E. Kallenbach, in House Committee on the Judiciary, *Presidential Inability,* Jan. 31, 1956, 45–46.

17. White Burkett Miller Center of Public Affairs at the University of Virginia, *Report of the Miller Center Commission on Presidential Disability and the Twenty-fifth Amendment* (Lanham, Md.: Univ. Press of America, 1988), 11.

18. Kenneth Crispell and Carlos F. Gomez, *Hidden Illness in the White House* (Durham: Duke Univ. Press, 1988), 234.

19. Herbert L. Abrams, "Disabled Leaders, Cognition, and Crisis Decision Making," in *Accidental Nuclear War,* Proceedings of the Eighteenth Pugwash Workshop on Nuclear Forces (Toronto, Can.: Science for Peace and Samuel Stevens, 1990), 136–49; see also Herbert L. Abrams, "Inescapable Risk: Human Disability and 'Accidental' Nuclear War," *Current Research on Peace and Violence* 11 (1988): 48–60.

20. Howard G. Bruenn, "Clinical Notes on the Illness and Death of President Franklin D. Roosevelt," *Annals of Internal Medicine* 72 (1970): 579–91.

21. Diary of Edward House, quoted in Bert Edward Park, *The Impact of Illness on World Leaders* (Philadelphia: Univ. of Pennsylvania Press, 1986), 13.

22. Reedy, *Twilight of the Presidency,* 169.

23. Dr. Daniel Ruge, interview with author, Denver, Colo., Dec. 15, 1988.

24. Robert S. Robins and Henry Rothschild, "Ethical Dilemmas of the President's Physician," *Politics and the Life Sciences* 7, no. 1 (Aug. 1988): 4.

25. Dennis L. Breo, "Taking Care of the Country's First Patient," *American Medical News,* May 8, 1981, 10.

26. A possibility discussed in Robins and Rothschild, "Ethical Dilemmas," 4.
27. Ruge interview.
28. Park, *Impact of Illness*, 58, 59.
29. Edwin Weinstein, *Woodrow Wilson: A Medical and Psychological Biography* (Princeton: Princeton Univ. Press, 1981), 355–59.
30. Park, *Impact of Illness*, 221–94.
31. Edward B. MacMahon and Leonard Curry, *Medical Cover-ups in the White House* (Washington, D.C.: Farragut, 1987), 119–37.
32. Robert M. Veatch, *Medical Ethics* (Boston: Jones and Bartlett, 1989), 10; American Medical Association, *Opinions and Reports of the Judicial Council* (Chicago: AMA, 1977), 5.
33. Veatch, *Medical Ethics*, 11.
34. Group for the Advancement of Psychiatry, *The VIP with Psychiatric Impairment*, vol. 8, report no. 83 (Jan. 1973): 183–84.
35. Such ambivalence is widespread. A survey of over five hundred physicians during the 1980 presidential campaign found a large majority of respondents simultaneously affirming a presidential candidate's right to absolute doctor-patient confidentiality *and* the need for a physician to make public certain diagnoses against the will of his candidate patient in the name of patriotism. "Editorial: Health Status of the Candidates: A Valid Campaign Subject," *Medical World News* 21, no. 4 (1980): 4, cited in Milton Greenblatt, "Power and the Impairment of Great Leaders," *American Journal of Social Psychiatry* 4, no. 2 (Spring 1984): 17.
36. William Safire, "The Operating Room," *NYT*, Jan. 5, 1987, 17.
37. Miller Center, *Report on the Twenty-fifth Amendment*, 25; Bill McAllister, "The Precarious Role of the President's Physician," *WP*, Feb. 9, 1988, 14; Crispell and Gomez, *Hidden Illness*, 226–28.
38. Thomas C. Wiegele, "Presidential Physicians and Presidential Health Care: Some Theoretical and Operational Considerations Related to Political Decision Making," *Presidential Studies Quarterly* 20, no. 1 (Winter 1990): 78–80; John B. Moses and Wilbur Cross, *Presidential Courage* (New York: W. W. Norton, 1980), 199.
39. Ruge interview.
40. Crispell and Gomez, *Hidden Illness*, 8; Lawrence K. Altman, "Unique Problems for a Physician Who Makes (White) House Calls," *NYT*, Feb. 2, 1989, B7.
41. Miller Center, *Report on the Twenty-fifth Amendment*, 25–27; Crispell and Gomez, *Hidden Illness*, 203–41.
42. Lawrence Mohr, presentation at the George Washington University symposium entitled "Medical Care of the VIP: The Special Problems of Special Patients" (Washington, D.C., Dec. 6–9, 1990). Dr.

Mohr, in his discussion and responses to questions, and in an interview in Washington, D.C., on March 18, 1991, supplied most of the information on the current White House medical unit included in this chapter.

43. Should the president have been brought to the White House rather than to George Washington University? No. Agent Jerry Parr correctly surmised that he needed a level of expertise and experience with problem cases—with surgery nearby—that was not available in the White House. Also, no X-rays could have been obtained. The president's blood pressure could have been stabilized with intravenous fluids, but blood replacement was not feasible, because there was no blood on hand.

44. Robert Pear, "A Blunt-Speaking Doctor (Bush's Own) Leads Team Treating President," *NYT,* May 6, 1991, A10.

45. Lawrence K. Altman, "Bush Is Called Exceptionally Fit; Says He Can Now Handle Stress," *NYT,* Nov. 1, 1988, A1.

46. "Bush and Quayle Discuss Transfer of Power," *NYT,* April 28, 1989, A8; Lawrence C. Mohr, personal communication, Jan. 30, 1991.

47. Lawrence K. Altman, "New York Cancer Specialist Says Bush Has Chosen Him as Physician," *NYT,* March 9, 1989, B9.

48. Judith Havemann and David Hoffman, "Presidential Disability Discussed," *WP,* April 28, 1989, A1, A16; James Gerstenstang, "Bush, Quayle Have Agreed on Details for a Succession," *LAT,* April 29, 1989, A10.

49. In 1966, before the Twenty-fifth Amendment was ratified, Richard Longaker came to the conclusion that Sections 3 and 4 would probably not be used at all except in the clearest situations. See Longaker, "Presidential Continuity: The Twenty-fifth Amendment," *UCLA Law Review* 13 (1966): 532–61. More recently, C. Knight Aldrich reached a similar conclusion in "Memory, Information and Denial in Public Life," in Thompson, ed., *Papers on Presidential Disability,* 94–95. See also Robert S. Robins and Henry Rothschild, "Hidden Health Disabilities and the Presidency: Medical Management and Political Consideration," *Perspectives in Biology and Medicine* 24 (Winter 1981): 240.

50. Twentieth Century Fund Task Force, *A Heartbeat Away* (New York: Priority Press, 1988). The quotation is from the background paper by Michael Nelson, 23.

51. James Doyle, "A Talk with George Bush," *Newsweek,* April 20, 1981, 29.

52. Twentieth Century Fund Task Force, *Heartbeat Away,* 71.

53. MacMahon and Curry, *Medical Cover-Ups,* 136–37. A New York physician later claimed in a *NYT* article (quoted ibid., 137) that he learned of the treatments and warned Kennedy he would make it publicly known if they continued, because "no president with his finger on the red button has any business taking stuff like that."
54. Joseph J. Bookstein, "The Health of the President in the Nuclear Age" (MS, Aug. 30, 1984).
55. See Group for the Advancement of Psychiatry, *VIP with Psychiatric Impairment,* 181–87.
56. Many of these suggestions were made by Milton Greenblatt in "Power and the Impairment of Great Leaders," 17. Others who have suggested screening candidates include Martin Anderson, who recommends screening for brain tumors (interview with author), and Robins and Rothschild, "Hidden Health Disabilities," 251.
57. Bert E. Park, "Presidential Disability: Past Experiences and Future Implications," *Politics and the Life Sciences* 7 (1988): 50–66.
58. These arguments and others are also stated in Brownell's "Presidential Disability: The Need for a Constitutional Amendment," *Yale Law Journal* 68, no. 2 (Dec. 1958): 198–201.

CHAPTER 12: Looking Back
and Looking Forward

1. Daniel Ford, *The Button: The Pentagon's Strategic Command and Control System* (New York: Simon and Schuster, 1985), 144. Paul Bracken, *The Command and Control of Nuclear Forces* (New Haven: Yale Univ. Press, 1983), 196–97.
2. Testimony of Fred Fielding to the Miller Center Commission on Presidential Disability and the Twenty-fifth Amendment, in Kenneth W. Thompson, ed., *Papers on Presidential Disability and the Twenty-fifth Amendment* (Lanham, Md.: Univ. Press of America, 1988), 7.
3. Alexander M. Haig, Jr., *Caveat* (New York: Macmillan, 1984), 150.
4. Larry Speakes with Robert Pack, *Speaking Out* (New York: Charles Scribner's Sons, 1988), 4.
5. Donald T. Regan, *For the Record* (San Diego: Harcourt Brace Jovanovich, 1988), 167.
6. Ibid., 170. Fielding completed such a book after the assassination attempt. It has been passed on to the Bush administration. See Lawrence K. Altman, "Doctor Says He Erred on Presidential Power after '81 Shooting," *NYT,* Feb. 20, 1989, 7.
7. Joseph B. Treaster, "Man, 22, Is Arrested in New Haven for Threatening the President's Wife," *NYT,* April 8, 1981, 1.

8. Robert A. Freidlander, "The Origins of International Terrorism," in Y. Alexander and S. Finger, eds., *Terrorism: International Perspectives* (New York: John Jay Press, 1977), 31.

9. Department of the Treasury, Office of the General Counsel, *Management Review on the Performance of the U.S. Department of the Treasury in Connection with the March 30, 1981 Assassination Attempt on President Ronald Reagan* (Washington, D.C.: Department of the Treasury, Aug. 1981), 33.

10. "Reagan Undergoes Minor Surgery to Remove Fluid from His Brain," *NYT,* Sept. 9, 1989, 1; "Earlier Blood Clot on Brain Disclosed by Reagan Doctor," *NYT,* Sept. 11, 1989, 10.

11. Martin Anderson, personal communication, June 20, 1989.

12. Ed Meese, interview with author, Stanford, Calif., June 2, 1989.

13. David Gergen, interview with author, Washington, D.C., June 16, 1989.

14. Martin Anderson, interview with author, Stanford, Calif., June 12, 1989.

15. Lawrence I. Barrett, *Gambling with History* (Garden City, N.Y.: Doubleday, 1983), 115–16.

16. "Power and the President" (editorial), *LAT,* April 1, 1981, pt. 5, p. 6.

17. The importance of planning early in the administration for emergencies, formulating procedures for specific contingencies, and preparing emergency guidelines is discussed by the Miller Commission in Thompson, ed., *Papers on Presidential Disability,* 169–70, and in Crispell and Gomez, *Hidden Illness,* 239.

18. See Haig, *Caveat,* 152–53; Regan, *For the Record,* 165.

19. Lieutenant Colonel Paul Lebras, personal communication, April 10, 1989.

20. The need for more routine planning, public discussion, and use of the amendment has been pointed out by, among others, the Miller Commission, Birch Bayh, the Twentieth Century Fund Task Force (*Heartbeat Away,* 100–101), and in interviews with the author with the Reagan administration members Edwin Meese and David Gergen.

21. Birch Bayh, telephone interview with author, June 7, 1990.

22. "Bush Suffers Shortness of Breath during a Jog and Is Hospitalized," *NYT,* May 5, 1991, 1; Peter Gosselin and Michael Kranish, "Racing Heart Sends Bush to Hospital," *San Francisco Examiner,* May 5, 1991, A1, A15; Andrew Rosenthal, "President Is Given 2nd Drug to

Treat Balky Heart Beat," *NYT,* May 6, 1991, A1, A10; Elizabeth Rosenthal, "Effort Grows to Restore Normal Beating," *NYT,* May 6, 1991, A11.

23. Charles Green, "Bush Back to Regular Routine," *San Jose Mercury News,* May 7, 1991, 8A.

24. Maureen Dowd, "Political Worries, Quiet and Outspoken, on Quayle," *NYT,* May 6, 1991, A10; William E. Schmidt, "Europeans Are Jittery with Quayle an Irregular Heart Beat Away," *NYT,* May 9, 1991, A13; James Reston, " 'A Lot of Hoopla about Nothing?' No Way," *NYT,* May 6, 1991, A17; Robin Toner, "Worry on Quayle Continues with News of Bush's Health," *NYT,* May 10, 1991, A10.

25. Andrew Rosenthal, "Heart Controlled, Bush Returns to Work," *NYT,* May 7, 1991, A1, A16; "Excerpts from Medical Assessments on Bush", *NYT,* May 7, 1991, A16.

26. "Fibrillations Can Increase Stroke Risk," *San Francisco Examiner,* May 5, 1991, A15; Elizabeth Rosenthal, "Prognosis for President Concerns Some Doctors," *NYT,* May 7, 1991, A16; Lawrence K. Altman, "Bush Begins Tests to Treat Thyroid That Disrupted Heart Rhythm," *NYT,* May 9, 1991, A13.

APPENDIX 2:
The National Command Authority

1. Steven R. Weisman, "Bush Flies back from Texas Set to Take Charge in Crisis," *NYT,* March 31, 1981, 1; "Questions Raised: Who Was in Charge?" *Congressional Quarterly Weekly,* April 4, 1981, 580; Stuart W. Taylor, "Disabling of Reagan Provokes a Debate over Nuclear Authority in Such Cases," *NYT,* April 4, 1981, 9.

2. Steven R. Weisman, "White House Aides Assert Weinberger Was Upset When Haig Took Charge," *NYT,* April 1, 1981; "Questions Raised."

3. Ibid.

4. Caspar Weinberger, *Fighting for Peace* (New York: Warner Books, 1990), 85.

5. Walter S. Mossberg, "Confusion over Who Was in Charge Arose following Reagan Shooting," *WSJ,* April 1, 1981, 31.

6. According to Weinberger, he was told on the phone by Meese, "Under these circumstances, it is my understanding the National Command Authority devolves on you." See Weinberger, *Fighting for Peace,* 85.

7. Peter Pringle and William Arkin, *SIOP: The Secret U.S. Plan for Nuclear War* (New York: W. W. Norton, 1983), 209.

8. Mossberg, "Confusion over Who Was in Charge." Similar descriptions of an emergency succession to military command appear in Alexander M. Haig, Jr., *Caveat* (New York: Macmillan, 1984), 160–61; Weinberger, *Fighting for Peace,* 85; and Laurence I. Barrett, *Gambling with History* (Garden City, N.Y.: Doubleday, 1983), 120.

9. Forrest Holmes, Office of the General Counsel to the Office of the Secretary of Defense, personal communication, Aug. 27, 1990.

10. Joint Chiefs of Staff, *Official Dictionary of Military Terms,* 239.

11. Weinberger, *Fighting for Peace,* 85.

12. Alfred Goldberg, historian for the Office of the Secretary of Defense, personal communication, Aug. 20, 1990.

13. Pringle and Arkin, *SIOP,* 128, 135.

14. Paul Bracken, *The Command and Control of Nuclear Forces* (New Haven: Yale Univ. Press, 1983), 123.

15. Sheikh R. Ali, *The Peace and Nuclear War Dictionary* (Santa Barbara: ABC-CLIO, 1989), 159.

16. C. Kenneth Allard, *Command, Control, and the Common Defense* (New Haven: Yale Univ. Press, 1990), 196; "Authority to Order the Use of Nuclear Weapons", *Report of the House Subcommittee on International Security and Scientific Affairs of the Committee on International Relations,* Dec. 1, 1975, 1.; Frank Klotz, Jr., "The President and the Control of Nuclear Weapons," in *The American Presidency,* ed. David A. Kozak and Kenneth N. Ciboski (Chicago: Nelson-Hall, 1985), 47.

17. Eric Semler, James Benjamin, and Adam Gross, *The Language of Nuclear War* (New York: Harper & Row, 1987), 179.

18. Willard Webb, historian of Joint Chiefs of Staff, personal communication, Aug. 20, 1990.

19. Department of Defense, "Concept of Operations of the World-Wide Military Command and Control System," Directive S-5100.30, Oct. 16, 1962.

20. Ibid., 2.

21. Ibid.

22. Department of Defense, "Continuity of Operations Policies and Planning," Directive 3020.26, Aug. 25, 1967, A-1.

23. Nick Fleischman, personal communication, Aug. 27, 1990. According to the Joint Chiefs of Staff historian, the definition first appeared in its current form in the Aug. 25, 1967, version of Department of Defense Directive 3020.26.

24. Department of Defense Directive 5100.30, Dec. 2, 1971, 2.

25. Ibid.
26. Department of Defense, "Continuity of Operations Policies and Planning," Directive 3020.26, Oct. 24, 1985, 2.
27. U.S.C. 10, Sec. 142.
28. John N. Moore and Robert F. Turner, *The Legal Structure of Defense Organization Prepared for the President's Blue Ribbon Commission on Defense Management*, President's Commission on Defense Management (Washington, D.C.: GPO, Jan. 15, 1986), 75.
29. Bruce Blair, personal communication, Sept. 6, 1990.
30. NSC-30, Sept. 10, 1948, "United States Policy on Atomic Warfare," reproduced in the Department of State, *Foreign Relations of the United States, 1948*, vol. 1 (Washington, D.C.: GPO, 1976), 624–28.
31. Public Law 99-433, Oct. 1, 1986, Sec. 211, pt. 162.
32. See Bracken, *Command and Control*, 202.
33. Patrick E. Tyler and Bob Woodward, "Reagan N-Code Taken by FBI in Hospital," *Boston Globe*, Dec. 13, 1981, 26.
34. Taylor, "Disabling of Reagan."
35. Bruce Blair, personal communication, Sept. 5, 1990.
36. Paul Bracken, personal communication, Sept. 5, 1990.
37. George Church, "Business as Usual—Almost," *Time*, April 13, 1981, 22–23; Bill Gulley with Mary Ellen Reese, *Breaking Cover* (New York: Simon and Schuster, 1980), 190.

APPENDIX 3:
The Situation Room

1. Richard V. Allen, letter to author, April 7, 1989; Paul LeBras, personal communication, April 10, 1989.
2. Paul LeBras, personal communication with author, April 10, 1989.
3. Bradley H. Patterson, *The Ring of Power* (New York: Basic Books, 1988), 121, 122.
4. Allen, letter to author, April 7, 1989.
5. Martin C. Anderson, interview with author, Stanford, Calif., June 12, 1989.
6. Patterson, *Ring of Power*, 120.
7. Anderson interview.
8. Ibid.
9. Richard V. Allen, personal communication, June 27, 1989.
10. Bradley H. Patterson, personal communication, May 31, 1989.
11. David Gergen, interview with author, Washington, D.C., June 16, 1989.

12. National Security Act of 1947, Section 202(a).
13. Bromley K. Smith, *Organizational History of the National Security Council during the Kennedy and Johnson Administrations* (n.p., 1988), 5.
14. Steven R. Weisman, "White House Aides Assert Weinberger Was Upset When Haig Took Charge," *NYT,* April 1, 1981, 20.

APPENDIX 4: The Interregnum
—Election Day to Inauguration

1. James P. Pfiffner, *The Presidency in Transition* (New York: Center for the Study of the Presidency, 1989), 76, 92–95.
2. Dwight D. Eisenhower, *The White House Years: Waging Peace, 1956–1961* (Garden City, N.Y.: Doubleday, 1965), 617–18.
3. Carl M. Brauer, *Presidential Transitions, Eisenhower through Reagan* (New York: Oxford Univ. Press, 1986), xiv; Frederick C. Mosher et al., *Presidential Transitions and Foreign Affairs* (Baton Rouge: Louisiana State Univ. Press, 1987), 7, 20.
4. Mosher, *Presidential Transitions.*
5. Paul T. David and David H. Everson, *The Presidential Election and Transition, 1980–1981* (Carbondale: Southern Illinois Univ. Press, 1983), 198, 199.
6. Ibid., 197–98.
7. Thomas C. Hayes, "The Reagan Team's Chief Recruiter," *NYT,* Nov. 7, 1980, D1.
8. David and Everson, *Presidential Election, 198, 199.*
9. Ibid., 199.
10. Dick Kirschten, "The Reagan Team Comes to Washington, Ready to Get Off to a Running Start," *National Journal* 12 (Nov. 15, 1980): 1926.
11. Wallace Earl Walker and Michael R. Reopel, "Strategies for Governance: Transition and Domestic Policymaking in the Reagan Administration," *Presidential Studies Quarterly* 16, no. 4 (1986): 740.
12. Brauer, *Presidential Transitions,* 236, 261; Douglas E. Kneeland, "Triumphant Reagan Starting Transition to the White House," *NYT,* Nov. 7, 1981, 1, 14; Walker, "Strategies for Governance," 740; Pfiffner, "The Carter–Reagan Transition: Hitting the Ground Running," *Presidential Studies Quarterly* 13, no. 4 (1983): 639; "So Far, So Good—So Far," *New Republic,* Dec. 6, 1980, 8.
13. David and Everson, *Presidential Election,* 202; Brauer, *Presidential Transitions,* 262.
14. George Church, "How to Charm a City," *Time,* Dec. 1, 1980, 15.

15. Bob Shieffer and Gary Paul Gates, *The Acting President* (New York: E. P. Dutton, 1989), 22, 23.
16. "Choosing for the Chairman," *Time*, Dec. 8, 1980, 22.
17. David and Everson, *Presidential Election*, 205; Brauer, *Presidential Transitions*, 227.
18. Pfiffner, "Carter–Reagan Transition," 633–34; Brauer, *Presidential Transitions*, 237.
19. David and Everson, *Presidential Election*, 203; Mosher, *Presidential Transitions*, 59.
20. Tom Morganthau, "A Bloated Transition," *Newsweek*, Dec. 29, 1980, 18; David and Everson, *Presidential Election*, 203.
21. Hugh Sidey, "Reading the Portents," *Time*, Dec. 22, 1980, 14.
22. David and Everson, *Presidential Election*, 208.
23. Walker, "Strategies for Governance," 741, 746; Pfiffner, "Carter–Reagan Transition," 629; David and Everson, *Presidential Election*, 209, 210.
24. Brauer, *Presidential Transitions*, 230; Mosher, *Presidential Transitions*, 124, 226–27.
25. Mosher, *Presidential Transitions*, 124.
26. David and Everson, *Presidential Election*, 206.
27. Brauer, *Presidential Transitions*, 230; Pfiffner, "Carter–Reagan Transition," 635.
28. Walker, "Strategies for Governance," 741; Pfiffner, "Carter–Reagan Transition," 627, 629.
29. Sara Fritz, "Setting the Stage," *U.S. News & World Report*, Jan. 12, 1981, 18; Joseph J. Sisco, "Selective Engagement," *Foreign Policy*, no. 42 (Spring 1981): 29–36; Mosher, *Presidential Transitions*, 228.
30. Mosher, *Presidential Transitions*, 94; Peter Goldman, "The Making of the Cabinet," *Newsweek*, Dec. 15, 1980, 28.
31. Brauer, *Presidential Transitions*, 225.
32. Hedrick Smith, "Reagan Seeks to Emphasize Role of Cabinet Members as Advisers," *NYT*, Nov. 8, 1980, 1, 8; Brauer, *Presidential Transitions*, 240; Walker, "Strategies for Governance," 753, 754.
33. Allen Mayer, "Changing of the Guard," *Newsweek*, Nov. 24, 1980, 41.
34. Tom Bonafede, "The Other Side of the Transition—Leaving Office Isn't As Much Fun," *National Journal* 12 (Dec. 20, 1980): 2160.
35. Brauer, *Presidential Transitions*, 234.
36. David and Everson, *Presidential Election*, 215–16.
37. David Gergen, interview with author, Washington, D.C., June 16, 1989.
38. Birch Bayh, telephone interview with author, June 7, 1990.

Acknowledgments

Many contributed to making this book a reality; I have tried to give credit where credit is due. Any omissions are purely inadvertent and reflect on my memory rather than on my intent.

I am deeply indebted to the Carnegie Corporation, which provided major support for this project. David Hamburg, president of the Carnegie Corporation, and Fritz Mosher, program officer, have been continually interested and helpful in facilitating this study of disabled leadership and continuity. The W. Alton Jones Foundation also encouraged and supported my work over a period of six years and made possible the funding of research assistants essential to the project. I owe a particular debt to my good friends Frances Lehman, president of the New Prospect Foundation, and Elliot Lehman, a member of the board, for their faith not only in this project on the Twenty-fifth Amendment but also in a series of projects on human reliability in the handling of nuclear weapons and on the subject of accidental or inadvertent nuclear war. The Ruth Mott Fund also endorsed and assisted the larger project on the theme "Human Effects and Prevention" for which I have been responsible during this period.

John Lewis, professor of political science and director of the Center for International Security and Arms Control, at Stanford, together with Sidney Drell, professor of physics and codirector of the Center, invited me to become a member of the Center in 1980, during a sabbatical year at Stanford, and encouraged my more active participation when I returned in 1985 as a professor at Stanford once more. In effect, they gave me access to an extraordinarily stimulating and provocative environment, one in which I could both pursue my research interests and be certain of a critical evaluation by others in different disciplines. William Perry, when he replaced Sidney Drell as the Center's codirector, was equally hospitable and warm in his support for my research. David Bernstein, assistant director of the Center during my period as a member, has been unfailingly helpful and interested. Gerry Bowman, administrator of the Center, provided the answers to a series of vexing questions and did much to make my work at the Center productive and effective, as did Nancy Okimoto during her period as associate director. All of the staff have been immensely helpful, and the faculty associated with the Center have been a constant source of intellectual stimulation and ideas.

Alexander George, professor of political science at Stanford, provided a high level of sustained encouragement from the moment I initiated this project. He accompanied it by a personal investment: he took the time and trouble to read important parts of the manuscript, both at an early stage and toward the end. His critical suggestions were pointed, constructive, and targeted at improving the quality of the enterprise.

Barton Bernstein, professor of history at Stanford, Phil Farley, senior research associate at the Center for International Security and Arms Control, and Mike Levitas, an old and valued friend, were kind enough to review the manuscript critically and to make many valuable suggestions.

Over the last seven years I have been fortunate in having a group of superb research assistants, including Elizabeth Poliner, Annette Makino, Margaret Sullivan, Chon Noriega, Glen Brand, Kenneth Fried, Jennifer Cumming, Christine Mergen, and Dan Pollack. Among these, the work of Annette Makino, Chon Noriega, Kenneth Fried, Jennifer Cumming, and Dan Pollack was particularly oriented to the issues that are central to this volume. Their contributions were of great importance.

Mrs. Jeffery Stoia, editor for the Department of Radiology at the Brigham and Women's Hospital, used her sharp editorial mind, eye, and pen on the manuscript as it developed and was immensely helpful in tightening some of the more wordy areas and in pruning the repetitive sections.

In the process of bringing together the information on the assassination attempt, I interviewed many individuals. All of them were gracious and open in their response to questions that were sometimes probing and controversial. John Feerick, dean of Fordham University Law School and an authority whose book on the Twenty-fifth Amendment is not only profoundly informative but also spellbinding, was gracious enough to be interviewed and later to read some of the chapters critically and respond in detailed fashion. Senator Birch Bayh also consented to be interviewed and provided illuminating observations on a number of knotty issues. Edwin Meese III, counselor to the president and later attorney general, David Gergen, director of communications, and Martin Anderson, chief of domestic policy planning in the first Reagan administration, all graciously responded to my questions on many of the issues and facts relevant to the event as they perceived them. Richard Allen, national security adviser at the time of the attack, provided a number of detailed answers to questions about the Situation Room.

The physicians at George Washington University were uniformly helpful. Among those who consented to be interviewed were Drs. Ben Aaron, David Davis, Joseph Giordano, William Knaus, and David Rockoff. Dr. Dennis O'Leary, now the head of the Joint Commission on Hospital Accreditation and spokesman for the George Washington University Hospital at the time of the attack, also answered my questions with directness and candor.

John Pekkanen, a Washington writer who pieced together much of the medical information and published a compelling article on the attack on Reagan, was a wonderful source of information and opinion about many aspects of the event and its implications.

The physician to the president, Dr. Daniel Ruge, was gracious enough to afford me the necessary hours at his home in Denver not only to answer many of my questions but also to furnish me with a fund of important information about the event, the people involved, and his own role both at the time of the attack and as White House physician before and after. Dr. Ruge also took the trouble to read some of the relevant chapters and to suggest a number of important changes that rendered them more accurate and precise.

Dr. Lawrence Mohr, the executive physician to the White House in the Bush administration, was kind enough to respond to many of my questions, as well as to take me on a personally conducted tour of the medical facilities at the White House and the Executive Office Building.

Dr. Joseph J. Bookstein, of the University of California at San Diego, shared with me many of his concerns and his thoughts on the health of the president in the nuclear era.

My secretary, Ann McGrath, put in an enormous amount of work with skill and good humor, never complaining at the frequent revisions and the numerous drafts through which each chapter evolved. I owe her a special vote of thanks.

Mary Cunnane, my editor at W. W. Norton, not only made many valuable suggestions but also carried the publication process forward with an insistent attention both to quality and to the need for expeditious handling. Donald Lamm, the president of W. W. Norton, was kind enough to suggest that the book be published by Norton in the first place, at a time when I was still persuaded that its proper home might be the university press.

Finally, last on the list but by no means least in her help and contributions, my wife, Marilyn, read each and every chapter many times, offering a stream of helpful suggestions that were essential to clarifying obscure sentences, processes, and events. Beyond that, she suffered my commitment to the painstaking process of completing this study with grace and supportiveness and with the conviction that there was a story to be told and important lessons to be learned.

Herbert L. Abrams

Index